Spring 73

CINEMA & PSYCHE

A JOURNAL OF ARCHETYPE AND CULTURE

Spring, 2005

SPRING JOURNAL
New Orleans, Louisiana

CONTENTS

BOOK REVIEWS

ARCHETYPAL PERSPECTIVE

AND

AMERICAN FILM

GLEN SLATER

"Ladies and gentlemen, we are about to begin our descent into Los Angeles."
—*The Graduate*

Film is a thoroughly psychological medium. Despite the superficiality and fabricated emotion that often surrounds American film, filmmakers cannot ultimately avoid the medium's need to tap the deepest layers of the psyche. Sensationalism and spectacle carried by formularized narrative may provide light entertainment and distraction, but the experience is quickly forgotten. There's a slew of these "movies," but it is a stretch to call them "films." We recognize their failure to fulfill an intrinsic requirement: Film demands that its visual presentation serves hidden *depth*—shaded, secreted, semi-conscious or unconscious elements, the presence of which is first felt or intuited but may enter our awareness more fully only upon reflection. Depth makes meaning and brings poignancy. It results

Glen Slater is a core faculty member in the Mythological Studies program at Pacifica Graduate Institute where he teaches various courses that include Jungian and archetypal approaches to film. He was until recently the regular film reviewer for *Zion's Herald*, a national magazine.

from patterned complexity and backward gazes into cultural history, ancestry, and personal pasts. Depth also occurs in the basic movement of our mind from the simple to the nuanced and subtle. If the cinematic arts have any fundamental characteristic, it is the call to create depth. This call makes film and psyche natural kin.

Seeing a film of any significance is not a passive activity; it requires from the beginning a kind of descent. As the theater darkens so does our daylight consciousness. We enter a realm closer to the dream than to waking life, a place where the raw, subversive, and sublime can come to light, where the "sympathy of all things" is more manifest. The screen may capture images but those images release the imagination, involving us in a series of interiorizing moves that submits on-screen events to timeless, universal stories running in the background of life. All depth experience ultimately points us in the direction of these universals. These factors make film-going a form of ritual. And when we cross over into this ritual space we start salivating for archetypal food.

When graduate Benjamin Braddock (Dustin Hoffman) gets off his plane and moves into the terminal at Los Angeles airport, he steps onto a moving walkway and stares hypnotically ahead. Opening credits roll. Simon and Garfunkel's "The Sound of Silence" begins: "Hello darkness my old friend . . ." Benjamin is carried along, framed against a blank wall. In the next scene, sitting in his bedroom, head against the bottom of a fish tank, he tells us he's worried about his future and "wants it to be different." Downstairs his parents have a sea of thick L.A. personas waiting to welcome him into their fold. Young Ben doesn't know where he's headed, but he knows for sure he'll drown in the world of his parents and their friends. A different kind of submersion awaits him.

The elements that allow these scenes to convey such an essence of story and character may not be immediately apparent, but we feel them as they come together like the select ingredients of a perfect dish. The first moments of *The Graduate* are both familiar and fresh— familiar enough to convey self-discovery and confusion on the cusp of adulthood, fresh enough to engage our curiosity and need to find out who this person is and what will happen to him. Like the opening of a juicy dream, these first minutes suggest an archetypal terrain with distinct animal tracks. Add a satirical tone and we realize there's also a larger mirror of reflection being held up here. This rich confluence of factors draws us in. We follow Benjamin through erotic misadventure and dogged pursuit of the woman he loves, avoiding a possible "future in plastics" and discovering the complications of a fully engaged life. In the process we glimpse the underbelly of an era's ideals. As it turns out, darkness *is* a friend to this young American everyman—it helps him find out who he is.

Whereas a film's depth may be more apparent in dramas with weighty content, even summer blockbusters or whimsical romantic comedies need layers beneath their lush surfaces to make any impact. There's a mantra in film: If the scene is about what the scene is about, the scene isn't working. Audiences need to *discover* something when watching a film. This experience requires both an engaging surface and an emotionally resonant background, the combination of which allows us to dart back and forth, knitting together the surface and what's beneath the surface. When superficiality and cliché reign on the surface, a film falls flat. When underlying grand themes and sweeping universal patterns are too transparent, each scene lands with thud. It is the combination of the familiar and the fresh, the universal and the unique, together with a finely tuned veil between them that generates strength in a film, irrespective of genre. This layered quality folds past and future into the immediate present, revealing at each turn the way particular on-screen moments are also horizons for lives already lived and things yet to come. Films don't show entire life stories; they show intense episodic distillations of life's major patterns, leaving us to feel our way into everything unseen and inviting the possibility that events in our own lives might carry the same rich dimensionality. The best actors only show a thin slice of who their characters are and leave the rest for us to imagine into; the best scenes are portals to what is underground. The essence of film is not about what appears on the screen, it's about the way the screen becomes a window, a window through which, ultimately, come the movements of the archetypal psyche. Peel off the tinsel and you find out we go to the movies to engage the gods.

A significant amount of Jungian exploration of film has taken place. Most of this work utilizes classical concepts and the kind of analytical understanding evident in the interpretation of dreams, myths, and fairytales. What I wish to do here is to show how a Jungian engagement with film might alter its focus when the specific insights of James Hillman and archetypal psychology are given more emphasis. Whereas this necessarily involves use of certain psychological notions, my primary intention is to describe the experience of depth that binds film and psyche, paying particular attention to how depth is created by the filmmaker. Aside from discussing several examples of American cinema from an archetypal perspective, I have two specific aims: First, I want to show that film gains its archetypal quality primarily through *the way a story is told*. This shifts our usual locating of psychological gravity in plot and character to finding psyche in the multiple aspects of cinematic vision, which both bring the story to the screen and determine how we as audience engage it. Here we learn that the depth quality of film does not necessarily stem from the narrative being tied to motifs of the collective unconscious. Arguing that archetypal qualities in film come from the *way* a story is told/shown reinforces Hillman's assertion that "the demonstration of archetypal images is . . . as much in the act of seeing as in the object seen."[1] Second, I will argue that the most compelling and significant American films reflect a sustained descent into the underworld. Contrary to what we might assume, celebrated American films are often counter-cultural, showing both a protagonist's downward movement and the shadow side of typical American values. These films exemplify the archetypal axiom taken from Keats that sees the world as "the *vale* of soul-making." They also reflect the classical Jungian notion that shadow material forms a gateway to the deeper reaches of the psyche.

Part One: Archetypal Resonance

Film relies on metaphor and subtext to create its sense of depth. Jung wrote that "archetypal content expresses itself first and foremost in metaphors."[2] Hillman suggests metaphor to be soul's own language.[3] He also speaks of the process of "seeing through" as "the soul's root and native activity,"[4] an activity that "justifies itself."[5] At its most elemental, seeing through describes a movement from the visible "to the less visible"[6] or invisible, a process that occurs throughout film whenever we perceive the subtext of an action or dialogue. The thoroughly metaphorical nature of film, in which visual images become psychic images, combined with the multilayered quality of character and plot become key points of entry for archetypal perspective.

Sunset Boulevard begins with a shot of the famous street name, not high on a sign, but down in the gutter where street names are sometimes stenciled. The choice is not arbitrary. While this street already conjures an arterial sense of Hollywood high and low life, "sunset" points to the theme of death that pervades the film. Seeing this name in the gutter builds these associations into a potent metaphor for a story of failure, desperation, and faded stardom. When an out-of-work screenwriter (William Holden) escapes from debt collectors by pulling into the Sunset Boulevard driveway of forgotten silent screen star Norma Desmond (Gloria Swanson), he enters a decrepit world. Desmond mistakes the writer for an undertaker who is bringing a coffin for her recently diseased chimpanzee. The writer uses the situation, hatching a scheme to keep his career afloat. Ironically, this ends up working to expedite his own demise. All becomes omen. It was the wrong driveway to pull into. The writer doesn't see it, but we do. When he finally recognizes the old star, he says, "You used to be big." She retorts, "I *am* big. It's the pictures that got small." We see through her character in this one instant, perceiving the cavernous emptiness and desperation behind her defensive and garish façade. The subtext opens a door to a story behind the story, a story that courses back and forth through the gutters of Sunset Boulevard.

If the subtext has gravity, if it is concerned with elemental emotional drives and conflicts, then one line, look, gesture, or action appearing on screen can become a perfect opening to soul. This is why we remember great lines. For instance, when cyborg Arnold Schwarzenegger stares through dark sunglasses at a desk cop in *The Terminator* and says, "I'll be back," he is voicing an utterly ordinary phrase. However, as we know he is a relentless killing machine, an archetypal monster that never dies, the polite statement conveys something of the terminator's essential archetypal character. The desk cop has no idea what he is dealing with, which only underscores the experience of subtext. Similarly, when in *Silence of the Lambs* serial killer Dr. Hannibal Lector (Anthony Hopkins) strokes Agent Clarice Starling's (Jodie Foster) finger in a stolen second of physical contact, the simple gesture conveys an entire world. At once, we see that the cannibal-psychopath has a gentle side, that he means Clarice no harm, that he is a consummate seducer, that there is an erotic aspect to their relationship, perhaps even that he might care for her. It is a multivalent moment and we delight in all that is in back of it. Moreover, when Dr. Lector and Agent Starling touch, it entwines their worlds, initiating a psychic infection that intensifies the entanglement of light and dark forces that drive this story.

When subtext and metaphor gather force and aggregate in thematic patterns, a process occurs that we might call "archetypal resonance." We start to track what is going on beneath the surface and sense when that which is underneath appears on the surface. The strength of a film depends entirely on its capacity to create moments where the immediate on-screen action reveals a universally significant subtext which is consistently amplified by visual metaphors. This implies that film depends far more on its capacity to create this process than it does on the raw content of its stories. For this reason a one hundred million dollar production of the Trojan War (*Troy*) can bore us, while a simple low budget film that follows a midget watching trains in a small town (*The Station Agent*) can engross us. Pointedly, this also implies that the archetypal quality of film has little to do with its content being full of recognized archetypes. Both the devil and the divine sparks are in the details. So is the depth.

One way into the psychology of film is to see events and secondary characters as aspects of the main character's psyche, as if what occurs is a kind of dream with the protagonist as the dreamer. This move can open the soul terrain of any story. In most films we see a convergence of the protagonist's inner and outer lives. We should, however, resist the temptation to *reduce* the surrounding world to a mere projection of the protagonist's psyche. This simply gathers everything psychic and puts it back into literal persons. In film the basis of this link between character and setting stems from the nature of visual art: Just as a dream portrays complexes as events and persons, film has little choice but to animate inner life in an outer way. It can't use introspective reflection and recounting of thoughts and feelings in the same way as a novel. This restriction of the medium fosters its enchanted quality, revealing the taproot of psychological life that pulls for the meaningful confluence of all things. Obsession becomes alphabetized soup cans, fear becomes layers of heavy clothing, passion becomes a preponderance of red objects, inspiration becomes a bird flying through an open window. In *Sunset Boulevard* Norma Desmond's empty, rat-infested swimming pool and tangled garden *are* Norma Desmond. Yet when we perceive her home, we cannot separate our perception of it from who she is. A soulful eye sees psyche in all things and this is the eye the camera lens endeavors to open. Rather than having to overcome the distance between inner and outer through synchronicity, projection, and narrow symbolic links, film pushes us to consider everything participating in a psychic field. Hard facts and ego separations dissolve into a dream fabric woven with archetypal thread.

Film thus forces us to deliteralize inner and outer. Each setting, each event becomes a psychic presence. In more precise terms, this enchanted quality comes through the movement Hillman calls "personifying,"[7] which follows the imagination's innate need to be *addressed* by the world around us. Personifying reminds us that psychic persons can't be confined to literal characters and that intelligence and agency can appear outside actual people. This can be seen in overt ways like Charles Foster Kane's childhood sled, "Rosebud," which carried his deeply unconscious longing for Eden-like pleasure and simplicity (*Citizen Kane*), or the red plastic bag dancing with numinous intensity in the wind for *American Beauty*'s boy-next-door, Ricky. The plastic bag portrays an animation of utterly simple things, a sensibility sorely absent from the lives of most everyone else in this film. Personifying can also be as subtle as sensing intentionality in an out of control locomotive (*Runaway Train*) or fatefulness in a musical instrument (*The Red Violin*). Needless to say, I'm not talking about actual animation of inanimate objects—for example *Herbie Rides Again*. Personifying requires an *imagining into*, not an overt personification.

What is overlooked in many psychological readings of film is that the metaphorical dimension has more to do with creative choices made in the filmmaking process than with basic elements of the story: Where a conversation takes place, what's on the walls, how the camera tracks the faces, what appears in close-up, what kind of shirts are worn. Of course the story guides these choices, but the sense of meaning and poignancy is governed by the crafting. In a film with any depth of vision, houses lived in, cars driven, drinks ordered, papers read, cereal eaten speak to the underlying narrative—sometimes whispered, sometimes shouted. The layered effect of these choices largely determines the psychic depth of the visual images. Whether or not a runaway train seems to have malicious intent will depend on what the camera shows us.

In *Ferris Bueller's Day Off*, an enduring classic of the teen flick genre, we feel our way into a pitch perfect channeling of the god Hermes. Ferris (Matthew Broderick) lies his way out of another day at high school, managing the ruse through hoodwinking communications, craftiness, theft, fleet-footedness, and an uncanny knack of "disappearing" or disguising himself at crucial moments. Though his methods are deceiving, his purpose is inspiring. He wants to put some spark back in his somber best friend Cameron, whose bedroom has the feel of a mortuary and whose beaten up SAAB won't start. Yet the Hermes presence in Ferris's character does not just appear in his own actions and dialogue. It is felt mainly through juxtaposing Ferris's exploits with masterfully rendered images of deadly apollonic high school instruction — "Anyone? Anyone?" Too, Ferris is pitted against the ruinously saturnine Dean of Students, Mr. Rooney. The hermetic quality also lies in a string of happy and challenging coincidences that pepper the story. Ferris may be the focal point of this energy, but it comes from the entire context. In considering this film, it is much more accurate to describe an archetypal *field* wherein each scene is tuned to resonate with the deeper narrative: salvation through a kind of intelligent play and circumventing of repressive authority. The impact of this resonance depends upon multiple elements, not simply character traits. Spirited editing reflects the field just as much as dialogue and action; Mr. Rooney's obsessively clean desk conveys the drive to banish Hermes as much his demeanor does. The archetypal narrative of this film comes to a climax when the pristine, never driven red Ferrari belonging to Cameron's father, having been "borrowed" for the day, takes an unexpected plunge, by itself, into a woody ravine. It's a close encounter of the trickster kind and the event serves as a symbolic vehicle for finally cracking open Cameron's father complex. Ferris just prepared the ground. Once the field was constellated the gods stepped in.

Even though archetypal psychology contemplates the mythic background of life, its concern tends to be with the phenomenal foreground. It wants to build archetypal figures and motifs into perceptual acuity rather than excavating foundations in order to expose recognizable substructures. If a mythic, religious, or classic literary figure is named, it tends to begin the discussion not be embraced as a goal in itself. The naming orients our vision, so that we view more keenly what is before us, prioritizing certain aspects of what we see over others. In many ways films follow this same process, directing our eye, most overtly by the choices of what comes into frame and what stays out, but more subtly in composing all the elements of a given scene. The screenwriter provides many details. The production and costume designers fill out the ideas. The actors interpret each line. The cinematographer and director together decide what ends up on film, moving our vision in, pulling it back, making it linger, snapping it away. The editor puts the pieces together. And so on. Archetypal resonance results from the sum of these choices, choices as subtle as whether a face comes into frame with a sweaty brow, a nervous tick, or a mouth full of food. What becomes metaphor in film depends on all these contributions. And if, as Vico said, metaphor is "myth in brief,"[8] then we must assign much of the mythic quality of film to those who craft each aspect.

To see the anima, the mentor, the magician, or the crone in a film character is to name an archetypal presence. Likewise, to perceive a dragon fight, a wrestle with an angel, or the longing for paradise as the driving pattern behind a scene or plot is to locate an archetypal process. In both instances we are doing something akin to understanding a building through its blueprint, looking for elemental structural lines. Yet even classical Jungian theory recognizes actual archetypal experience comes with the immediate image—the texture and shape of the character or event presenting the universal in the here and now. Archetypal perspective emphasizes this immediacy of the image, deepening awareness of its apparent qualities rather than moving too quickly—and sometimes abstractly—to historical and symbolic amplification. For the archetypalist a snake is not first a symbol of instinctual wisdom; a snake is an image of "snakeness," and the kind of snakeness is given by the kind of snake, its setting, and what it is doing. The affect that comes with something of archetypal significance comes with the specific, not the general.

In film, particular things take on significance through consideration of the surrounding context. One of the most memorable scenes in American film history appears in *Apocalypse Now* when Robert Duval's Colonel Kilgore, morning cup of coffee in hand, leads his chopper mounted air cavalry into an attack on a Vietnamese village with musical accompaniment from Wagner's "Ride of the Valkyries." Kilgore's cup of coffee doesn't "symbolize" very much, but in the context of going into battle, carefully sipped while the soldiers in back sit on their helmets so they "don't get their balls blown off," it is a potent image. It invokes the discordant feel of someone driving through the suburbs to pick up the morning paper; it smacks of routine; it points, anachronistically, to being at home; it is part of who Kilgore is. The cup of coffee combined with a few other precise images creates an archetypal resonance—a scene that captures war's craziness and Vietnam's particular brand of it. On the ground, battle raging about him, Kilgore concerns himself with the surfing break at the edge of the action—he wants to see his soldiers surf. He struts through exploding mortar rounds with an omnipotent nonchalance before announcing: "I love the smell of napalm in the morning." Placing "love" and "napalm" together in the same sentence gives us Kilgore's particular mix of Patton-like passion and transcendent immunity.

Coffee cup, surfing, a way of walking, and a few choice words convey something quite deep, but we would be hard pressed to fruitfully amplify Kilgore's character with reference to mythology. He is his own animal. But he embodies something archetypal, growing out of the whole scene with an astounding aptness. We just feel it. His madness hovers above death like the helicopter he rides in on and this mirrors the madness of the entire war. His love of the surf is a religious homage to life back in California. We end up sensing on some level that Kilgore *is* the war; he *is* America in Vietnam. Up river, Brando's Colonel Kurtz may be in a psychosis tending the heart of darkness but Kilgore hits closer to home. *Apocalypse Now* shows Vietnam as the American underworld, all by placing certain characters in certain settings. No more mythologizing necessary.

Sometimes a film's depth cannot be placed behind or underneath as much as seen in the connective tissue holding the elements of a narrative together. In *Alien*, Sigourney Weaver's Ripley does battle with a creature whose nature is both organic and mechanistic (designed by the artist H.R. Giger). Although this creature is indeed most alien, it is imagistically related to the dark, predatory technology that surrounds the human side of this story. Their spaceship is the "Nostromo," an interplanetary mining vessel whose character echoes exploitative themes from the Conrad novel of the same name. In many scenes the predator alien is hardly distinguishable from the industrialized innards of the ship—a good hiding strategy but also suggestive of their thematic kinship. Whereas those around Ripley seem preoccupied with their financial wellbeing and the interests of the mining corporation, her governing concern is human welfare. Although thrust into a warrior role, she carries a feminine presence that preserves life, a principle that is ironically contrasted by the ship's computer, called "mother," which prioritizes the interests of the corporation and announces that the crew is "expendable." As the alien picks off her fellow space travelers, Ripley's survival seems like poetic justice. In the intelligently crafted sequel, *Aliens*, the heroine's mothering instinct comes full circle as she once again takes center stage in a battle with the creatures, culminating in a confrontation with the alien queen, supreme mother, which must be destroyed to save a child's life. The mix of reptile and machine in these aliens presents an unmitigated titanic urge that is also detectable in the soulless images of certain techno-futures. This film, like many others, presents outer space as the new locale for the return of the repressed. Ripley's instinctive and human bearing provides the opposing force. Alien, setting, characters, and heroine are perfectly matched—the depth is in the relationships.

Discussion of arche*types* in film is now a part of the mainstream. In-depth treatments of archetypal patterns may remain within the realm of Jungian studies, but the notion that a film's strength is largely dependent upon its expression of archetypes has become a fixture in Hollywood consciousness. Particularly over the last thirty years, the explicit discussion of archetype and myth in film can be found in many publications dedicated to the craft. Joseph Campbell's influence on George Lucas and the *Star Wars* saga probably represents the threshold moment in the development of this awareness. It has been argued that Campbell's work, especially *The Hero with a Thousand Faces*,[9] is reflected in the films of Steven Spielberg and Francis Coppola (*The Godfather, Apocalypse Now*), among others.[10] Consider, for example, how screenwriting guru Robert McKee introduces his subject in the very first pages of his book, *Story*:[11]

> No matter where a film is made—Hollywood, Paris, Hong Kong—if it's of archetypal quality, it triggers a global and perpetual chain reaction of pleasure that carries it from cinema to cinema, generation to generation.

> Story *is about archetypes, not stereotypes.*
> The archetypal story unearths a universally human experience, then wraps itself inside a unique, culture-specific expression. A stereotypical story reverses this pattern: It suffers a poverty of both content and form. It confines itself to a narrow, culture-specific experience and dresses in stale, nonspecific generalities. (Emphasis in original).[12]

The problem is that Hollywood is just as likely to use its recent insights to produce stereotypes as archetypes. As it turns out, making films with archetypal characteristics is not that easy and has in no way become so with Hollywood's newfound fascination with depth psychology. Even the close Campbell disciple George Lucas seems to have lost the path (or maybe The Force!). Commercial and cultural forces work to turn even the freshest visions into packaged products for easy digestion. To the extent an awareness of archetypes is employed in the filmmaking process, the problem may be in part due to the concept itself. For although Jung insisted that the archetype *per se* can only ever be approximated and never fully grasped, certain mythic figures and psychological formulae have come to stand in for archetypes on a regular basis. As David Miller has pointed out, even in Jungian psychology archetypes devolve into stereotypes.[13]

In sum, there may be a parallel between the challenge McKee poses to the screenwriter and that posed to the psychologist or film student utilizing Jungian concepts: How to avoid the stereotype. Here I believe work with images and depth experience may be applied to filmmaking and film studies in a way that mitigates formulaic offerings. Filmmakers can become enamored with grand themes and mythic patterns, but a film's depth depends far more on small things: a gesture here, a line there, the look of a room, the right light at the right time, eye contact between two characters. Enough of these elements and you have a memorable scene; enough memorable scenes and you have a fine film. And as the director David Lean reportedly said, a couple of great scenes and you have a great film. In psychological terms, the impact of these elements can be termed "archetypal," meaning they have the power to reach into the psyche and invoke an emotional response with timeless and universal undertones—undertones that don't necessarily need *The Odyssey* or *Gilgamesh* for back up.

Part Two: Underworld Characteristics

Beyond "good guy" versus "bad guy" plots and moralistic tales about overcoming inner demons, there's a whole category of films that show a more complex interaction between light and dark aspects of the psyche. Many films mentioned so far find a good part of their depth dimension through courting dark themes. Shadow is compelling, and we are fascinated by characters who struggle against it as well as by those who succumb to it. Most importantly for this discussion, dark things provide a perfect basis for processes of seeing through and discovering subtext. Intuiting the presence of hidden greed or hatred in an otherwise agreeable character creates more complex motivations, often dividing a character's inner world in a way that ultimately reveals the character's essence.

The dark is not, of course, necessarily evil. However, evil seems to be a special category of darkness, growing when dark things are not engaged and having a special liking for environments where righteousness has scrubbed clean all traces of shadow. Evil comes from the neglect of the dark—in Jungian terms from the repressed shadow taking control. Thus battles between good and evil not only create tension and drama, these battles can also indicate the intrinsic link between the persona world with its social niceties and the shadow world with its baser motivations. Alfred Hitchcock understood this dance between psychic layers, achieving iconic status with masterful films that track raw impulses and play on unconscious fears. His major works were made in America between 1940 and the early 1960's, and they vividly contrast the heroic idealism and domestic bliss often portrayed during that time. Filmmakers like David Lynch (*Blue Velvet, Twin Peaks, Mulholland Drive*) and the Coen brothers (*Blood Simple, Fargo*) specialize in showing subterranean worlds beneath American purity and naiveté, which make a particularly good landscape for the appearance of evil.

In *Fargo*, a car salesman with a feeble conscience (William H. Macy), seduced by his desire for money and feeling of powerlessness, cannot close the shadowy door he opens and a deeper darkness pours in. The folksy surrounds of Minnesota and North Dakota make the perfect setting for kidnapping plots and bodies being pushed into woodchippers. On one side of Macy's character is pregnant police

chief Marge Gunderson (Frances McDormand), on the other a loser
thug (Steve Buscemi) and his cohort. With black comedic brilliance,
McDormand's Chief Gunderson maintains a quirky goodness as she
moves through the criminal world with pragmatic dispatch. The "luv
ya hon" world of the Chief and her stamp illustrator husband "Norm"
provides vivid contrast for the surrounding murk. *Fargo* shows the
archetypal relation between an overabundance of light and a gathering
dark. It also shows how an individual's failure to wrestle with the dark
can invite a deeper evil.

The theme of light over dark is most evident in the *villain*, an
omnipresent figure in American film. Whereas some villains are
undisguised devils, a characteristic of the best villains is that they
don't wear their darkness on their sleeves. The best villains seduce and
lure and sometimes charm us before their traps become more apparent.
Think again of Hannibal Lector, whose cannibal style killings are simply
planted in our imaginations and linger there as we behold a gentleman-
scholar with an uncanny grasp of human psychology. It is far more
compelling to intuit a horror that remains partially obscured than it is
to meet it head on; it's what we don't see that generates the most fear.
In this instance, Lector's unnerving mix of high culture and ease with
the darkest of impulses draws protagonist Clarice Starling's lesser
darkness into the light, deepening her resolve and filling out her
character. Drawing out a protagonist's wounds and complexes is a
common function of the villain. Michael Douglas's ruthless Gordon
Gekko does the same thing for Charlie Sheen's Bud Fox in *Wall Street*.
Possession by the dark has destructive consequences, but the darkened
eye sees more deeply, less naively.

The role of darkness in the creation of depth and the revealing of
soul cannot be assigned to the box full of heroes who need a night in
the belly of the whale to put a dent in their hubris. Nor can we assign
the motifs of descent and decline to a particular point in character
development—like Jesus going into the wilderness—seeing these
merely as natural forerunners of redemption and ascent. Heroes can
have their moments of undoing and still remain stale cardboard cutouts
of social ideals. These patterns may work for stories that propel
underdogs through accomplishments against the odds (a Hollywood
favorite) or stories that track personal transformations with fairytale
endings. But beyond these types of films there exists a whole other

category of drama with a dark weave that colors the whole fabric. In these works, whether it's running from then turning towards trauma (*Ordinary People*), being consumed by pathological envy (*Amadeus*), incest and corruption (*Chinatown*), or repressed desires (*The Remains of the Day*), what lives in the dark or is kept in the dark provides the central *gravitas*. Films of this ilk explore a kind of depth experience where character is revealed through a pervasive downward pull, showing how pathos cannot be detached from soul's nature. These films have a special relation to archetypal perspective.

Hillman has argued that the psyche has an affinity with the underworld and says, "more bluntly: underworld is psyche."[14] Reflecting this notion, he suggests that soul is located more in the "vales" and is damaged when we turn too exclusively to spiritual goals and abstract principles found at the "peaks."[15] While he acknowledges that psychological life ultimately requires a meeting of soul and spirit, he argues passionately that our habitual western style of consciousness strives with heroic abandon for order and control (a spiritual drive), leaving behind the complications and vitalities of psychic depth. Combating this one-sidedness, depth psychology's primary task becomes a resuscitation of soul and its underworld associations. Certain films seem to follow the same course, expressing themes and sensibilities that cultivate soul by following the underworld pull to the bottom of the vale, where our vision adjusts to the dark.

No American film of recent years reflects these understandings better than *American Beauty*, a work that shows both the shadow of the American dream as well as a somewhat clumsy process of soul recovery. Lester and Caroline Burnham live middle class lives behind a white picket fence. Lester (Kevin Spacey) enters the picture disillusioned and resigned. His enthusiasm has come down to "watching the James Bond marathon on TNT." When Carolyn (Annette Bening) is not tending her perfect red roses, she is selling tacky real estate, pursuing the next level of material wellbeing. Their marriage is dead in the water. Then things start to unravel. Lester has an epiphany watching his teenage daughter's best friend in a cheerleading routine. Carolyn breaks down when her manic efforts to sell a house fail, then, literally pulling herself together, exemplifies the kind of aversion to deeper reality that Jung called "the regressive restoration of the persona."[16] The divide between the two opens even further: Lester, entranced by

his newfound anima woman, confronts his malaise, quits his job, and
begins to follow his bliss. Lost parts of him now return, including a
revitalized masculinity and fathering instinct, as well as a youthful
indulgence with music, drugs, and fast cars. Caroline reacts and resists.

The soul's "underworld affiliation"[17] is apparent in the inextricable
ties between Lester's obsession, anger, adolescent pursuits, and the
reenchantment of his life. Lester drops into unwieldy passions and
regressive behavior, but it activates the search for something richer.
Carolyn's exploits put the underworld in a different light. Unable to
digest any darkness, she merely reinforces her particularly narrow idea
of success, jumping into bed with the "the king of real estate," Buddy
Kane. With his unnaturally white grin, Kane oozes sleazy dealmaker
with Teflon personality. Here a stereotype is purposefully drawn (rather
than accidentally created). Screenwriter Allan Ball uses the character
of Buddy Kane to show the condition of Carolyn's psyche, including a
bedroom scene that has Carolyn, legs apart, screaming "Bang me your
majesty, Bang me," revealing with comedic affect the degree to which
Carolyn is merging with her ideal as a defense against her underlying
feelings of failure. Buddy Kane then turns Carolyn on to guns, which
further amplifies her desperate reach for power and control. The
associational subtext of "Kane," "bang-me" sex and guns also provides
a crude image of phallic potency that has disappeared from her
marriage. The stereotypical Kane ends up amplifying Carolyn's
dissociation from anything of substance, setting her up for an
enantiodromic fall at the end of the film.

I noted the dreamlike quality of film at the beginning. When
underworld forces are at work in a film, its dreamlikeness is even more
accented, for in dreams we become the subject of everything going on
around us, losing the sense of self containment that goes with normal
waking consciousness. The protagonist caught in some underworld
darkness becomes, as we do in dreams, the subject of overwhelming
forces and experiences a psychic dissolution into these forces. Since
arguing in *The Myth of Analysis* that depth psychology's real goal is to
produce a more "imaginal ego"[18] (which would reflect the experiences
of the dream-ego), Hillman's project has been to make psychological
perspective more representative of the kinds of circular and dissolving
energies experienced in dreams. These ideas culminate in *The Dream
and the Underworld*[19] where he challenges us to see what dreams, Hades,

and psychological ideas supporting soulfulness have in common: Mostly its the derailing of the everyday ego. He furthers the argument by pointing out that the hero—from which both the everyday ego and most protagonists in film seem to take their cue—has become severed from its psychic and mythic roots: Originally the hero had underworld ties too and was associated with burial mounds, sacrifice, and earthiness. When we see films that show a pull from below overcoming the characters, leading not to transcendence but to a deeper, on-going familiarity with the depths, visions of a hero that reflects an earlier archetypal background may be drawing us in. Along these lines Joanna Dovalis has argued that many independent and art films now portray the "postmodern hero," whose character arc is more nebulous and whose process shows a greater integration of unconscious factors.[20]

American Beauty ends with a dead Lester Burnham revisiting the most salient moments of his life. In profound contrast with the incessant drive for success and material wellbeing that had surrounded him, his departing memories are of simple events—watching stars, his grandmother's hands, his cousin's new car, an amusement park ride, the face of his daughter. He seemed to have recovered his soul sense only moments before his death, taking in the glow he had rediscovered in his daughter's cheerleader friend, "Angela." The poetic twinning of death and soul is matched only by the bitter irony that his newfound vision can't be lived.

American films of note very often show flawed protagonists whose wounds resonate with the shadows of the culture and whose characters are more colored than merely transformed by their underworld experiences. In *Chinatown* we see this in private eye Jake Gittes (Jack Nicholson) who cannot finally extract himself from the incestuous relations of corrupt L.A. businessmen and city officials. Similarly, in *Thelma and Louise*, we see two women (Geena Davis and Susan Sarandon) who cannot find their way through a misogynistic world. In *Fight Club* an initially listless Edward Norton is initiated by his alter ego, Brad Pitt, into a brutal shadow realm. To varying degrees some other examples include Robert De Niro in *The Deer Hunter*, Jon Voight in *Midnight Cowboy*, Timothy Hutton and Donald Sutherland in *Ordinary People*, Meryl Streep in *Out of Africa*, Charlie Sheen in *Wall Street*, Harrison Ford in *Bladerunner*, Ian McKellen in *Gods and Monsters*, Ralph Fiennes in *The English Patient*, Julianne Moore in *Far*

From Heaven, Clint Eastwood in *Million Dollar Baby* and, most recently, the ensemble cast of *Crash*. The travails of these characters bring pathos and pathology into view and keep it there. Though Hollywood spends most of its time on triumphant and uplifting heroics, it more often achieves critical acclaim with films showing a depth that comes from characters learning to live with the dark.

To summarize: Film reflects soul's hunger for depth. A primary source of that depth is found in the layering effect of metaphor and subtext through which a story is conveyed, suggesting much of a film's archetypal quality stems from the multiple elements of its crafting. Acclaimed American films show a process of soul-making that moves from the light into the dark or locates small flames in forgotten places, reminding us of the necessary relationship between soul and pathos. These films have all the elements of what I described in terms of archetypal resonance and in addition explore the basements of life. Uplifting works aren't under any threat, but we live in a culture with an unrelenting optimism that provides few containers for what's rumbling below. Films that reveal what societies neglect strike deeper cords, which reinforce the medium's dreamlike vision and ritual significance. With these films we are not just engaging the gods but allowing them to transport us into their realm.

NOTES

1. James Hillman, *Archetypal Psychology: A Brief Account* (Dallas: Spring Publications, 1983), 12.

2. C.G. Jung, *The Collected Works of C.G. Jung*, tr. R.F.C. Hull (Princeton: Princeton University Press, 1953), Vol. 9, i § 267.

3. James Hillman, *Archetypal Psychology*, 20.

4. James Hillman, *Revisioning Psychology* (San Francisco: Harper Collins, 1975), 115.

5. Hillman, *Revisioning*, 140.

6. Hillman, *Revisioning*, 140.

7. Hillman, *Revisioning*, 1ff.

8. Quoted in Hillman, *Archetypal Psychology*, 19.

9. Joseph Campbell, *The Hero with a Thousand Faces* (Princeton: Princeton University Press/Bollingen Series, 1973).

10. Christopher Vogler, *The Writer's Journey* (Los Angeles: Michael Wiese Productions, 1992), 13.

11. Robert McKee, *Story: Substance, Structure, Style and the Principles of Screenwriting* (New York: Harper Collins, 1997).

12. McKee, *Story*, 3-4.

13. David L. Miller, "An Other Jung and an Other . . .", in *C.G. Jung and the Humanities: Towards a Hermeneutics of Culture* (Princeton: Princeton University Press, 1990), 325-340.

14. James Hillman, *The Dream and the Underworld* (New York: Harper and Row, 1979), 46.

15. James Hillman, "Peaks and Vales: The Soul/Spirit Distinction as Basis for the Differences between Psychotherapy and Spiritual Disciplines," in *Puer Papers* (Dallas: Spring Publications, 1979), 54-74.

16. C.G. Jung, *Collected Works*, 7 § 254ff.

17. Hillman's phrase.

18. James Hillman, *The Myth of Analysis* (Evanston: Northwestern University Press, 1998), 183ff.

19. Hillman, *Dream*.

20. Joanna Dovalis, *Cinema and Psyche: Individuation and the Postmodern Hero's Journey*, unpublished dissertation, Pacifica Graduate Institute, 2003.

THE EYE AT THE HEART OF THE WORLD

JOHN BEEBE

"Film is the art of seeing," a projector repairman is told by the owner of a movie theater in Wim Wenders' 1976 film *Kings of the Road.*[1] The Jungian critic is in a position to complicate this observation by noting that what is seen is not merely physical, not just a picture of "outer" reality, but also a perception of the reality of the psyche.

It is not hard to demonstrate that film is a medium for the recognition of the psyche. As I have discovered in a quarter century of writing and lecturing on movies from a Jungian standpoint, a satisfying movie regularly displays the complexes, archetypes, and types of consciousness that make up the phenomenological manifestations of psychological life. It lets us "see" them.[2] That is the art a film *auteur* practices. But what is the attitude that emerges through the practice of this art? The *auteur* directors—from Ford down to Wenders—have for the most part remained silent on this point, or changed the subject when an interviewer tried to bring it up.

It was the rise of the *auteur* theory that not only canonized the forebears of Wenders but also grounded his generation of filmmakers

John Beebe, M.D., is a psychiatrist and Jungian analyst who lectures and writes frequently about film. His movie reviews appear in *The San Francisco Jung Institute Library Journal*, and his essay "The Anima in Film" can be found in *Jung & Film*, edited by Christopher Hauke and Ian Alister.

in what their own work might be about. The recognition of film as the objectified expression of a director's subjective psychology coincided with the development of the academic discipline of film studies (including those studies that have preferred to see film as the expression of a culture's, rather than just a director's, complexes). But an appreciation of how very psychological film can be does not, in itself, get us very far in understanding how the medium of film, a scientific breakthrough in the history of photography and (more generally) of the mechanical archiving of lived experience, came to take up the psychological standpoint that is so characteristic of it today.

Most contemporary Jungian critics—Berry, for instance—have approached this question through the synchronism of film's appearance on the cultural scene with the emergence of depth psychology.[3] Freud and the Lumière brothers made at the same time their demonstrations of what their new technologies could do, and we can say that the apparatus of psychoanalysis and the mechanics of filmmaking occupy a common position in history. Both emerged, it would seem, as a way to solve the same problem, that of reflecting about the experience of modernity. Without too much of a stretch, a psychological historian can say that both psychoanalysis and cinema offered modernity a way to see its own shadow.

But how do filmmakers themselves see their turn to psychology? What is cinema's myth of its own origin as a medium for psyche? An unusual film by the contemporary Canadian director Guy Maddin provides an interesting answer to these questions, advancing the understanding of the medium for his own generation to the same degree that Wenders was able to do thirty years ago.[4]

The Heart of the World (2000), originally made by Maddin to serve as one of the short film "Preludes" to the Toronto International Film Festival in honor of its 25th anniversary year, has a running time of just five minutes, and may be the only film of its length and limited first release to appear on the annual ten-best lists of the *New York Times* and the *Village Voice*. It is currently available from Zeitgeist Video on a DVD that also includes two full-length features in Maddin's seemingly-throwback expressionist style that I have described elsewhere as Canadian Surrealism, to convey the flat-footed quality of his melodramatic forays into the fantastic, and the emotional integrity of his uncanny evocations of silent and early sound cinema.[5]

Victoria Nelson, a knowing cultural critic of the art movements that can be seen to intersect in Maddin's work, has described the sensibility in which he participates, in common with other contemporary film directors with whom he can be said to share a "family resemblance" — Joel and Ethan Coen, Tim Burton, and Lars von Trier — as "New Expressionist." In her book, *The Secret Life of Puppets*, which is about the strange ways the Neo-Platonic transcendent has managed to survive in offbeat twentieth century literature, theater, art, and film, she lists the following as defining features of the New Expressionism that had emerged by century's end: (1) the inner is made visible in the outer; (2) a metaphysical dimension is present; (3) in contrast to the Old Expressionism found in German silent films like *Caligari*, *The Golem*, *Nosferatu*, and *Metropolis*, the supernatural is no longer only the grotesque, i.e., it dares to be not of the Devil; (4) a high-art edifice is constructed on a low-art foundation; (5) extreme melodrama does not alienate us; extreme action is essential for deep identification with the main character; and (6) cliché is likewise deliberate, nonironic, and serves a high purpose as allegory.[6]

All of these qualities are richly evident in *The Heart of the World* and made easily palatable by the energy and humor that Maddin brings to his work. As the first titles appear, the manic, propulsive soundtrack ("Time, forward!" — the climactic movement of Georgy Sviridov's score for a 1967 Soviet film of the same name, itself an echo of a famous Soviet realist novel that celebrated workers' attempts, under the first Soviet Five-Year Plan, to construct a huge steel plant in record time) has already started us on our wide-eyed ride through Maddin's agitprop scenario: chaos and misery will prevail unless a new world order is found. The immediate impression, heightened by the calligraphic style of the titles, exact replicas of the futurist fonts of the first decade of the Soviet Union, is a send-up of Russian silent propaganda film. Maddin's tricksterism in pre-empting (and thus getting us to distance ourselves from) our own disbelief is calculated to make us attend to the seriousness of his message, which is conveyed by the passionate face of his central character, "State Scientist" Anna, played by Lesley Bais, who as made up by Maddin somewhat resembles the young Gloria Swanson, though she is even more beautiful. She is the anima figure of the film who makes clear with the anguished sincerity of her eyes, the lids heavily outlined with *kohl*, that the matter that concerns her is urgent: the world is dying because it is losing its heart, and only the right kind of attention can save it. Anna's job, as an astronomer, is literally to keep her eye on things of cosmic proportions, and initially a female eye, presumably hers because it is widely flared as if peering into a telescope, is made to occupy a large part of each frame while the film proceeds to expose what is troubling Anna.[7]

As this is a silent film, except for the overheated soundtrack, much of the exposition is done through titles in juxtaposition with the telling, and almost ridiculously intense images that nevertheless (as in actual silent cinema) have enormous emotional force. They are melodramatic in their own right, however, and they tell us that there are "TWO BROTHERS...who love the Same.....WOMAN," and she is revealed to be Anna, who "loves <u>both</u> brothers!" Already, Anna has assumed an anima role as co-conspirator in the brothers' competitive narcissism because she is the obscure object of their shared desire. We are drawn into wondering who she is, even as the film, hurtling forward in synch with the galloping soundtrack begins to take as its theme what she is going to do next, in the decision she has to make between the brothers. (The suffering they share is symbolized by "a wildly scrambled cardiogram" that appears "over the heart of each ... brother.")[8] But, as ever in melodrama, our curiosity about her is interrupted by a more urgent crisis to which she must turn her—and our—attention. Instead of looking into her own heart to resolve the problem of which brother she really wants to marry, she has, with the logic of the new expressionism, in which the inner is met as the outer, directed her telescope toward the earth's interior, where indeed a heart is beating fitfully. It is there that she finds, as the next titles tell us, that the heart of the world is dying!

This heart is one of Maddin's slyest visual achievements. It is, so to speak, an agitated prop, like something lifeless jiggled by a stage hand on the set of a Buck Rogers film. With its excess of tubes and ventricles resembling more a rubber-toy octopus or spider than a human heart, it is a vile thing, aesthetically, that we want to be rid of as soon as possible and that's obscene to think of as the source of the vital pulse of our world. The comedy of its abject ugliness is that it is so *literal* an image, divorced from any possibilities beyond itself.

We cannot, however, shake the authority of the insistent titles: this is the heart of the world, and there is "NO" doubt that it is dying. Here the pathetic fallacy, the ascription of human traits or feelings to the entities of nature, with the hint of the hidden sympathy of all things, takes on a comic force in our conviction that this dilapidated organ of the world's plumbing is incapable of caring. The electrocardiogram we saw earlier has now become a signifier neither of the brothers' lovesickness nor of Anna's feeling confusion but rather of the moribund state of the world's eros. In his published script for *The Heart of the World*, Maddin says "the Heart has a rip in it," and this reference to a frank inner split is a clue to what he conveys cinematically in the finished film, that the world is becoming more hysterical because its real condition is schizoid.[9]

Anna takes up the role of oracle:

> Now ANNA addresses a crowd of people gathered at her observatory, not just people, but proles, bowed and beaten from long years of punishing toil, meaningless grinding years going nowhere until this surprise culmination in crushing news. From the aerie of her perch by the eye-piece, ANNA, the great scientist orates and gesticulates to the stricken people. Overcome with emotion, she announces in super-imposed titles:
>
> Title: Cataclysm!
>
> The End of the World!
>
> Little Time Remains![10]

Crazily, the film goes back from this world crisis to the love problem of which brother to choose. As Anna turns her attention back to the brothers, Osip and Nicolai, the two try to win her with feats. Osip, the elder, has been playing Christ in a passion play, and as the more "spiritual" brother he now enacts the part of the Messiah with missionary zeal, exhorting sinners to change their ways, and healing the sick. Nicolai, a youth who is already a mortician, is the more "practical" of the brothers, but he is no less manic than Osip in the way he dresses the dead and places them on an assembly line into coffins, which he himself nails shut so as to better direct them into hastily dug graves. The film forces us into an allegorical reading in which Anna, the scientist with her telescope, stands as symbol for the new technology of seeing that is the science of cinema, and the brothers as choices with regard to the way that technology may end up being deployed. The clichés surrounding the brothers' displays of spiritual and practical prowess, however kitsch their presentation, are entirely serious at the level of signification. We come to recognize that they are used by Maddin (in accord with Victoria Nelson's criteria for a New Expressionist filmmaker) as allegory to point to an ambivalence at the core of filmmaking itself: whether this new technology will be used idealistically, to exhort and to heal; or realistically, to encapsulate lived experience into so many cinematic coffins, the documents of a now dead reality. Anna must decide which of these goals to ally herself with. Does she want the science of observation to nail reality or to revive it?

Maddin has set up the brothers as a pair of opposites that lead nowhere: archetypally, one can spot in Osip's messiah complex the heavy-handedness of a developing *senex* (though still a young man, he looks a lot more like Rasputin than Christ) and in Nicolai's grandiose craftsmanship the narcissism of the *puer*, and it is not hard to see why Anna cannot decide between them. In an inspired turn to the style of Fritz Lang's Dr. Mabuse, Maddin dips unexpectedly into the shadow to provide a third alternative for Anna's affections, one that shocks us not only stylistically, but ethically. This is the industrialist Akmatov — a stage-villain plutocrat that Maddin initially imagined as resembling "Mr. Monopoly from the Parker Bros. Game."[11] His excessive, rotund torso encased like sausage in a tuxedo, Akmatov exudes an unmistakably German air, with his straight-across-the-lip brush moustache and his open, Weimar-Republic lechery. As soon as she sees his money, Anna falls for him (surely, in the allegory, a demonstration of the seductive power of filmmaking for profit.) We are appropriately grossed out when they wed and an obscenely phallic cannon, previously constructed by Osip, ejects gold coins in celebration.

At just this point, the heart of the earth gives out. People panic, buildings lurch, and the dead that Nikolai has buried tear open their coffins. Anna awakens from her trance and finally realizes "the right course of action." She

> strangles the industrialist AKMATOV right in the middle of some apocalyptic love-making. Then she dashes to the top of her great inverted telescope, hefts open the glass manhole lid which is its eye-piece, climbs head-first into the cylindrical instrument as a girl entering some kind of Constructivist water

slide, then hurls herself downward through the telescope and into the centre of the world, thus becoming its new heart. A human, a loving human, a naked human radiating great thermal and political and comradely warmth, is now the new Heart of the World.

And a warm beam of light shoots from the glass eye-piece of the telescope! The telescope is now a movie projector! ANNA is its lamp! . . . ANNA pulses from the centre of her nimbus, limbs spread apart, her head supplying the fifth point to a great, powerful subterranean star.[12]

At this point, projected images begin to appear all over the world—first of Anna, and then, most significantly, of a dancing man who somewhat resembles Nijinsky. We recognize that the dance is in celebration of the birth of the new art form, cinema, with KINO, the word for cinema taken up by the early Soviet filmmakers, appearing in repeated exuberant titles.

This is a thrilling denouement, in which Anna's identity and romantic choice are resolved: she has become the anima of cinema itself, transforming the science of observation into a creative medium. At the same time, she consummates the melodrama of the unknown woman by emerging from a marriage that would have been a false identity to reveal her own expressive power.[13] To amplify Anna's final gesture in taking her position at the center of things, it is helpful, as a Jungian critic, to be informed by James Hillman's book *The Thought of the Heart & The Soul of the World*, which successfully pairs two lectures this mentor of archetypal psychology gave in different parts of Europe between 1979 and 1982, years in which aesthetic theory was striving to consolidate a postmodern standpoint. In the first of these lectures, Hillman discusses Henri Corbin's seminal work, *Creative Imagination in the Sufism of Ibn 'Arabi*.

Corbin[14] states quite clearly that the heart's characteristic action is not feeling, but sight...The heart is not so much the place of personal feeling as it is the place of true imagining, the *vera imaginatio* that reflects the imaginal world in the microcosmic world of the heart. Feelings stir as images move.[15]

This passage seems to me to clarify the ethic of the New Expressionist filmmaker who seeks to create emotion through the movement of images. Corbin (via Hillman) advances the discussion of "pure" cinema that began with Vertov, was revived by Hitchcock after his contact with the French New Wave, was thoughtfully probed in Germany and America by Wenders, and is so excitingly reprised in *The Heart of the World*. It was always the *vera imaginatio* that such filmmakers sought to project through their films. In the cinema, emotion that is authentic can only be created by filmmakers who have the integrity that comes from seeing from the heart, and we should look with a similar empathy when we try to understand their films psychologically. We have therefore to emend Wenders' landmark formulation: Film is not just the "art of seeing," but *the art of seeing from the heart*. The science of cinema becomes the art of film when it takes residence in the place of the heart—and we can only really see what it intends when we recognize from where the vision springs.

But we cannot stop with "the thought of the heart." We have as well to understand "the soul of the world," or we will miss something sacred about cinema. Anna's courageous, unexpected journey to the center of the earth has many echoes in contemporary Jungian thought: the descent of the goddess (Perera[16] and Meador[17] interpreting Inanna), the World Soul establishing the ego-Self axis (Edinger interpreting Robert Fludd[18]), and the "integrity in depth" that I have written about (interpreting Jung).[19] The essence of this journey is the taking up of the psychological attitude itself.[20] As Anna assumes her new position, she becomes a star, and the new attitude is constellated for others, in an alchemical realization of heaven on earth — the heaven of captivating projected images, the language of cinema. Can there be any doubt, at the end of Maddin's creation myth of cinema, that what we are looking at is the birth of depth psychology's own medium, and that film's way of looking is the way to read experience with the heart so that the *anima mundi* can do her healing work?

Hillman, in the other essay in his indispensable little book, provides the rationale for the sane slowing of pace that follows on Anna's apotheosis as an *aesthetic* anima mundi, that is, her personification of a cinematic way of poesis. His argument helps us to understand why as her vision becomes more aesthetic, it also becomes more psychological:

> Cultivation of the aesthetic response will affect issues of
> civilization that most concern us today and which have remained

largely intractable to psychological resolution. First, an aesthetic response to particulars would radically slow us down. To notice each event would limit our appetite for events, and this very slowing down of consumption would affect inflation, hyper-growth, the manic defenses and expansionism of the civilization.

...Attention to the qualities of things resurrects the old idea of *notitia* as a primary activity of the soul. *Notitia* refers to that capacity to form true notions of things from attentive noticing.[21]

This returns us with a different understanding to Wenders definition of film as the "art of seeing." Cinema, the aesthetic wing of the depth psychological edifice, is the *notitia* of our time, and we should read Maddin psychologically as serving notice that this is so. And notice that he returns us to the noticer, the kino-eye he borrowed from Vertov and gave to his central character, Anna. Maddin makes us see that the eye belongs to the anima and not to the modern filmmaker's ego for making movies. It is not the manic eye of the man with the movie camera, but the conscientious eye of the *anima mundi*, which through her present incarnation as cinema has managed to give the world, exhausted to the point of catastrophe by literal perspectives,[22] a new lease on heart.

NOTES

1. Robert Craig, "The Art of Seeing Rescues the Existence of Things: Notes on the Wenders Road Films and Henri Bergson's Creative Evolution," (online: *http://www.horschamp.qc.ca/new_offscreen/artofseeing.html* [2002]).

2. John Beebe, "Jungian Illumination of Film," *Psychoanalytic Review* 83.4 (1996): 579-587.

3. Patricia Berry, "Image in Motion," in Christopher Hauke and Ian Alister (eds.), *Jung & Film: Post-Jungian Takes on the Moving Image* (Hove, England: Brunner-Routledge, 2001), 70.

4. Guy Maddin (writer, editor, photographer, and director), *The Heart of the World*, black and white 16mm film (Toronto International Film Festival, 2000 [available on DVD from Zeitgeist Video, 2002]).

5. John Beebe, "Canadian Surrealism," *San Francisco Jung Institute Library Journal* 23.3 (2004), 85–89.

6. Victoria Nelson, *The Secret Life of Puppets* (Cambridge, MA: Harvard University Press, 2001), 215-217.

7. This image is appropriated from Dziga Vertov's *The Man with the Movie Camera* (1929), in which the eye of the filmmaker is seen fleetingly peering through the camera and thus made to symbolize the mechanical cinema eye itself. The 'kino-eye,' according to Vertov, is "more perfect than a human eye for purposes of research into the chaos of visual phenomena filling the universe" (Dziga Vertov, "The Writings of Dziga Vertov," in *Film Culture Reader*, P. Adams Sitney (ed.), [New York and Washington: Praeger, 1923/1970], 356.)

8. Guy Maddin, Script for *The Heart of the World*, in Caelum Vatnsdal, *Kino Delirium: The Films of Guy Maddin* (Winnipeg, Manitoba: Arbeiter Ring Publishing, 2000), 149.

9. *Ibid.,* 149. We recognize the schizoid "core" in the fantasy of world catastrophe, which we must understand not only clinically, but culturally. James Hillman has noticed how frequently people everywhere now fear a catastrophic end to the world, an end that he deliteralizes, prophetically, to mean the impending demise of the modern fantasy that the world is soulless. This imagined mechanical world—introduced to us in the 17th century, with William Harvey's discovery that the heart's function in circulating blood is mechanistic—would have to be, like any machine, at risk of running down. (*The Thought of the Heart and the Soul of the World* [Woodstock, CT: Spring Publications, 1995], 125; 18-25).

10. Maddin, in Vatnsdal, 150.

11. *Ibid.,* 151.

12. *Ibid.,* 152. The sequence accords with Jung's notion of the anima as "the projection-making factor" (*Aion, Collected Works*, 9,ii § 26).

13. Stanley Cavell, *Contesting Tears: The Hollywood Melodrama of the Unknown Woman* (Chicago: The University of Chicago Press, 1996), 20.

14. Henry Corbin, *Creative Imagination in the Sufism of Ibn 'Arabi* (Princeton: Princeton University Press, 1969), 221 & n (cited in Hillman).

15. Hillman, "The Thought of the Heart," in *The Thought of the Heart and the Soul of the World*, 28.

16. Sylvia Brinton Perera, *Descent to the Goddess: A Way of Initiation for Women* (Toronto: Inner City Books, 1981).

17. Betty De Shong Meador, *Uncursing the Dark: Treasures from the Underworld* (Wilmette, IL: Chiron Publications, 1992).

18. Edward F. Edinger, *Ego and Archetype* (Baltimore: Penguin Books, 1973), Frontispiece.

19. John Beebe, *Integrity in Depth* (College Station: Texas A & M University Press, 1992).

20. Joseph Henderson, *Cultural Attitudes in Psychological Perspective* (Toronto: Inner City Books, 1984), 79-86.

21. Hillman, "*Anima Mundi*: The Return of the Soul to the World," in *The Thought of the Heart and the Soul of the World*, 115.

22. *Ibid.*, 201.

WHY SHOULD WE TAKE JUNGIAN FILM STUDIES SERIOUSLY?

DON FREDERICKSEN

I.

The question posed in the title to this article is too big, of course, and I will not attempt to answer it fully in this small essay. Instead, I will touch upon several crucial aspects of any larger answer, and refer the reader to other parts of the answer in the endnotes.

A proper starting point is the question of attitude; it is smaller that the initial question, but is itself foundational. A Jungian attitude works within a governing sense of the *reality of the psyche*, and toward a restoration of our acknowledgement of the reality of this *third* realm. Residing between matter and spirit, partaking of both, but epiphenomenal to neither one, it is to be taken *sui generis*, on its own terms. It is neither the subject of physics or biochemistry, nor of theology or spiritual disciplines, but has its own field of reflection and insight: psychology, which is to say, the study of the logos of the psyche. In film studies, it is an attitude not yet solidly articulated.

Further, a Jungian attitude acknowledges for deep and compelling reasons the reality of *symbolic* expressions alongside *semiotic* and

Don Fredericksen is director of undergraduate studies in film, Department of Theatre, Film, and Dance, Cornell University, and a Jungian psychotherapist in private practice in Ithaca, New York.

allegorical ones. It does so in contradistinction to the utter dominance of the latter two in both film and the study of film. This domination carries profound cultural ramifications, insofar as semiotic films and semiotic and allegoric interpretative attitudes are self-perpetuating systems of self-confirming defense against mystery, the great embarrassment to twentieth-century persons, as noted many years ago by the American writer Flannery O'Connor.

Jung differentiates *signs* from *symbols* according to the presence or absence of unknown or unknowable referents. When an expression stands for something known, it is a *sign,* appropriately addressed by equally semiotic methods of interpretation. When an expression stands for something unknown or unknowable, it is a *symbol.* Such expressions are only inappropriately addressed by semiotic interpretations—or by allegoric ones. The latter take symbolic expressions to be paraphrases of semiotic ones, which is to say, to present a situation where the known feigns the unknown, a feigning that can be reduced to the known according to some allegoric code known to the initiated.[1]

The squeezed quality of the box in which we find ourselves when all possible meanings circulate within the putatively known or knowable is suggested by two recent comments: one advertising the merits of a subscription to the *Channel Guide,* an American weekly guide to television programming, the other, part of an attack upon semiotic theories and interpretative methods by an erstwhile prominent practitioner. In the first, a woman is heard to say: "With the *Channel Guide* I know exactly what the film is all about before I ever turn on the television set." This speaks volumes about the redundant quality of the time spent with the television on. In the second, Frank Lentriccia, a Duke University literature professor and major Marxist theorist, notoriously turned against the hegemony of semiotic literary theories, *including his own,* commenting: "tell me your theory and I will tell you in advance what you will say about any work of literature, especially those you have not read."[2]

Both comments point to the operation of large, cultural, semiotic meaning-assigning machines in which the distance between what one assumes beforehand and what one finds produces circles of the smallest circumference, leaving us the task of re-imagining a more spacious geometry—one that can honor the reality of the mysteries that come from the depths of our lives and our world, and from the open system we call the future.

For this purpose, a Jungian attitude calls forth a distinct method, a *hermeneutic of amplification*, in contrast to the *hermeneutic of suspicion* that pervades film studies and the humanities at large. The latter is summarized, perhaps, by Nietzsche's claim that "every word is a masking," expanded to encompass the audio-visual registers of film and video by the scholarly legacy of Nietzsche, Marx, and Freud, our masters of suspicion.[3]

In its several forms the hermeneutic of suspicion is a powerful and necessary hermeneutic, especially as it functions at various levels to unmask the cultural semiotic machine which produces the vast majority of films. *But this hermeneutic is itself semiotic in character and function; the meaning it unmasks is not unknown or unknowable.* Rather, it has been hidden through self-deception, false consciousness, or repression, or through a decision to deceive others, or it has slipped its moorings through a "free play of signifiers." The hermeneutic of suspicion is itself blind, on one hand, to the frequently indexical quality of symbolic expressions, their causal linkage with the deeper, transpersonal unconscious (as, in another level, the sailor's gait is to life at sea). And blind, on the other hand, to the sometimes acausal, albeit meaningful, synchronistic linkage between this same deep unconscious and outer reality. Both the symbol's indexical quality and synchronistic events are instances of the fundamental mystery about which Jung speaks when he says "everything in the unconscious seeks outward manifestation."[4] Call this outward seeking the eros of the psyche—indeed its auto-eroticism—as psyche seeks its own outward manifestation within the lives of individuals and the culture at large, including the medium of film.

This is the erotic mystery of symbolic art about which Fellini, Bergman, Buñuel, Herzog, and Tarkovsky have spoken, about which Basil Wright spoke in describing the genesis of his 1930s documentary *Song of Ceylon*, about which the American personal filmmakers James Broughton, Jordan Belson, Stan Brakhage, Bruce Baillie, Larry Jordan, and Jerome Hill have spoken—and the matrix out of which they have all brought forth films. Their work is not well served by some hermeneutic of suspicion which ignores, downplays, or explains away the symbolic register.[5]

A hermeneutic of amplification, by contrast, signals our conscious nurturing of the search for outward manifestation by the unconscious. It is a form of midwifery, a *co-creative* activity yielding dignity, aiming not to unmask, but at psychological animation and revelation. It seeks a wisdom through a kind of on-going conversation with images whose roots in the depths of the psyche we intuit. It was for this reason that Jung, understanding that we mistakenly "imagine [we] are only what [we] know about ourselves," states that "*it is important and salutary to speak also of incomprehensible things.*"[6] The American poet Charles Olson, in "These days," makes the point this way:

> whatever you have to say, leave
> the roots on, let them
> dangle
>
> And the dirt
>
> just to make clear
> where they come from

A hermeneutic of amplification speaks of "incomprehensible things" by seeking their *functional parallels*. Jung cautions:

> It does not . . . suffice simply to connect a dream about a snake with the mythological occurrences of snakes, for who can guarantee that the functional meaning of the snake in the dream is the same as in the mythological setting? In order to draw a valid parallel it is necessary to know the functional meaning of the individual symbol, and then to find out whether the parallel mythological symbol has a similar context and therefore the same functional meaning....As the symbols must not be torn out of their context, one has to launch into exhaustive descriptions, personal as well as symbological.[7]

This kind of work, applied to film analysis, and undertaken over an extended period of time, necessarily calls upon intuition, the perceptive capacity that does not rest on our five senses, but, as it were, looks around the corner of things. Of course, intuition can be wrong, or wrongheaded, and one develops ways to ascertain this; but, lacking intuition's help, reason, or feeling, or sensation alone find their capacity to see hampered by a kind of literalism.

In this work, one finds oneself worked *upon*, just as one does attending over a period of time to one's dreamlife. This signals that the logos and the eros of the psyche are likely two sides of one coin, an awareness more likely evoked when one approaches symbolic expressions with a symbolic attitude, like to like, rather than "against the grain."

Unfortunately, for too many Jungians the reality of the psyche implies a facile dualism of inner and outer worlds, with the latter essentially devoid of psyche and psychological significance. The psyche has its undeniably introverted register, manifest in film, for example, in the American personal filmmaker Maya Deren's call for "*vertical structuring*," whereby a film "drops a plumbline" into the emotional experience of an event rather than placing this event in a causal chain between antecedent and subsequent events.[8] But the psyche's depths show up vividly in documentaries as well, a fact to which films by Basil Wright in England, George Rouquier in France, and Robert Gardner in the United States, among others, give testimony.[9]

Among Jungian authors James Hillman has argued most persuasively for this openness to the depths of the outer world, thus augmenting Jung's own observation that:

> the psyche is not always and everywhere to be found on the
> inner side. It is to be found on the outside in whole races or
> periods of history which take no account of psychic life as such.[10]

Hillman's observations go farther, and are not compelling to many Jungians, because his sense of psyche's boundaries escapes the limits of individual psychology. To Hillman's eye psyche inheres in nature as such, displaying itself at nature's very surface in myriad forms that approach exhibitionistic splendor. Thus, he reanimates our sense of nature's self-display, including its *beauty*.[11] This is part of the spectrum of human-life-in-this-world that contemporary film studies have displayed little interest in studying for its own sake, but which some filmmakers return to again and again with loving attention. An introverted attitude is no guarantee of depth, nor is an extraverted attitude the nemesis of depth. The symbolic attitude is possible in both.

II.

So far, I have made some remarks about attitude, and some remarks
about the method of treating "like with like" that this attitude
entails. Now, some remarks about just one area of application: Several
years ago, reading canonical anthropological literature on rites of passage
by Arnold van Gennep and Victor Turner, and Jungian clinical literature
on the midlife passage, I came upon a conceptual scheme that threw
bright light upon the nature and function of the creative process in
many of the filmmakers to which a symbolic attitude had attracted
me.[12]

Van Gennep, researching at roughly the same time Freud published
The Interpretation of Dreams, discerned in traditional rites of passage
three distinct steps or stages. In the first, the person who is to undergo
the rite of passage is separated out from the community, effectively
ending the social identity or persona held by the person up to this
point. In the second, the person is *between* the discarded former identity
and the new one, which the rite will eventually bestow. The person is,
as we say, betwixt and between. For this reason this second stage is
called *liminal*, from the Latin word *limen,* meaning threshold. The
person is in liminality. Here, without fixed social identity, the person
is psychologically open to the depth dimension of collective life—to
the community's defining stories, its secrets, its deepest sense of itself.
These latter stories and secrets are given to the liminal person by others
who have previously passed through the same passage. This liminal
experience yields the knowledge of the person's new identity, and in
the third stage, the person re-enters the community with it.

The Jungian literature on the midlife passage gives this
anthropological scheme a psychological inflection, by working within
the common knowledge that communal rites of passage have mostly
lost their presence or power in the contemporary culture of modernity.
*This observation was sufficient to allow me to see that many filmmakers
amenable to a symbolic attitude are, in the absence of communal rites of
passage, using filmmaking as their self-chosen medium for self-initiation
into the psychological depths once accessible through those now absent or
powerless communal rites.* By various means these filmmakers place
themselves in liminality, intuiting that in the liminal state the depth
dimension of life is most vivid—a fact embodied in the films they give

us. I call this kind of filmmaking the *liminal cinema*. It is a distinct pattern in the history of film seen from a psychological and anthropological perspective. The sounds, images, and stories contained in this liminal cinema are frequently symbolic, and more appropriately interpreted by the hermeneutic of amplification than the hermeneutic of suspicion.[13]

One of the more sobering lessons about psychological life contained in the liminal cinema is the function of what James Hillman calls *"pathologizing,"* described as "the psyche's autonomous ability to create illness, morbidity, disorder, abnormality, and suffering in any aspect of its behavior and to experience and imagine life through this deformed and afflicted perspective."[14] Hillman suggests that pathologizing is an ontological fundament of the psyche, "valid, authentic, and necessary," and that "the psyche uses complaints to speak in a magnified and misshapen language about its depths." *"The soul,"* he says, *"sees by means of affliction...the wound and the eye are one and the same."*[15] Viewed through this particular Jungian lens, liminal films such as Stan Brakhage's *Anticipation of the Night*, Bruce Baillie's *Quick Billy*, and Bergman's *Persona* can be seen to embody something fundamental about the logos of the psyche—its pathos-psyche-logos, or "psychopathology."

Some crucial registers of liminality are less personally centered; in these situations Jungians can collaborate in a complementary manner with others working from different premises. In passing I would mention the American studio-produced rites of passage pictured in so-called *teenpixs*. These are more accurately described as substitutions for traditional rites of passage, but perhaps are no less real in their effects for being *ersatz*. In 1998 at the Krakow Short Film Festival a significant number of Polish, Estonian, and Russian documentaries attended to the liminality of Eastern European cultures no longer structured by communism, but not yet wholly structured by Western economic and cultural ideas. *Krok*, a Polish television documentary, even produced an extremely witty metaphor for the liminal cultural condition Eastern Europe is now passing through. It posed the problem as a search by the Polish military for a march-step that would meet the approval of NATO's commanders in Brussels, whom, it was rumored by Polish military intelligence officers, found Poland "out of step." A related register of liminal cinema has been created in those countries passing out of colonial domination into post-colonial conditions. The films of Senegal's Sembène can stand as an example, but there are many others.[16]

I want to return, in conclusion, to the more personally-centered register of liminal cinema, and to the wounding that occurs in it. Psychologically, to be in liminality is to be bereft of previously efficacious ego-structures, and without any promise that others will replace them. Liminality is a tomb for the ego. Whether or not this deadly wound to the ego will transform into a womb depends on how one reacts to being entombed. The lesson liminal filmmakers teach us is that the way through is to put the ego's wound in the service of the psyche's wound—to understand the latter wound as the psyche's seemingly unquenchable thirst for depth. When this happens, the ego's eye sees what it cannot see when it is in a defensive posture towards those depths and their mysteries. It sees, perhaps only dimly, but sometimes with uncanny vividness, what the American poet Denise Levertov means when she says: "the cosmos is not made of atoms; it is made of stories." Here we come very close to Jung's insight that psychic reality is not essentially chaotic, but animated by fields and vectors of energy he called *archetypal*. Liminality is not a call into chaos, but into the deeper stories, about which Jung and others have much to tell us. These stories do not form closed systems; how they unfold is in part a function of how we engage with them. The cosmos of stories is an open system. At its best, Jungian film studies understand this co-creative situation, and the responsibility it places upon both the artist and critic.

NOTES

1. C.G. Jung, *Psychological Types, Collected Works of C.G.Jung* (Princeton: Princeton University Press), Vol. 6, 473-481 (pages, not paragraphs).

2. Frank Lentriccia, "Last Will and Testament of an Ex-literary Critic," *Lingua Franca* (Sept.-Oct. 1996), 59-67.

3. C.G. Jung, *Two Essay in Analytical Psychology, 2nd ed., Collected Works,* Vol. 7 (Princeton: Princeton University Press, 1953 and 1966), 81. For an introduction to the hermeneutics of suspicion, see Noel Carroll, "Anglo-American Aesthetics and Contemporary Criticism:

Intention and the Hermeneutics of Suspicion," *Journal of Aesthetics and Art Criticism* 51:2 (1993).

4. C.G. Jung, *Memories, Dreams, Reflections* (New York: Vintage, 1965), 3.

5. For a fuller discussion, see Don Fredericksen, "Jung/Sign/Symbol/Film," in *Jung and Film*, ed. Chris Hauke and Ian Alister (Philadelphia: Brunner-Routledge, 2001), 17-55.

6. C.G. Jung, *Memories, Dreams, Reflections*, 300.

7. C.G. Jung, *Archetypes and the Collective Unconscious*, 2nd ed., *Collected Works*, Vol. 9,i (Princeton: Princeton University Press, 1959 and 1969), 50.

8. "Poetry and the Film: A Symposium with Maya Deren, Arthur Miller, Dylan Thomas and Parker Tyler," in *Film Culture Reader*, ed. Adams Sitney (New York: Preager, 1970), 173-174.

9. See Don Fredericksen, "Jung/Sign/Symbol/Film" for a long amplification of bird imagery in Basil Wright's *Song of Ceylon*.

10. C.G. Jung, *Civilization in Transition*, 2nd ed., *Collected Works*, Vol. 10 (Princeton: Princeton University Press, 1964 and 1970), 78.

11. James Hillman, "Anima Mundi: Return of the Soul to the World" in *City and Soul*, Vol. 2, *Uniform Edition of the Writings of James Hillman* (Putnam, CT: Spring Publications, forthcoming 2005).

12. The seminal literature includes the following: Arnold van Gennep, *Rites of Passage* (Chicago: University of Chicago Press, 1960), Victor Turner, *The Ritual Process* (Chicago: University of Chicago Press, 1969), and Murray Stein, *In Midlife* (Dallas: Spring Publications, 1983).

13. My writing on the liminal cinema includes the following: *Bergman's Persona* (Poznan: Adam Michiewicz University Press, 2005); "The Condition of Being 'In Between' in Anthropology, Jungian Depth Psychology, and Film," *Studia Filmoznawcze* 25 (2005); "*8 1/2* Felliniego a Jung: Narcyzm I Kreaywnosc Wieku Sredniego" [Fellini's *8 1/2* and Jung: Narcissism and Creativity at Midlife] in *Mysl Carla Hustava w Analizach Teoretycznych, w Praktyce I Badaniach Empirycznych*, ed. Krystyna Weglowska-Rzepa (Wroclaw: Institute of Psychology, Wroclaw University, forthcoming); "Liminalnosscnarodowa I jednostkowa w ujciu Andrzeja Wajdy" [Wadja's Treatment of National and Personal Liminalities], in *Filmowy Swait Andrzeja Wajdy*, ed. Ewwelina Nurczynska-Fidelska and Piotr Sitarski (Krakow: Univeritas, 2003); and "Individuation as Artistic Vocation: Jerome Hill's *Film Portrait*,"

Millennium Film Journal, 35/36 (Fall 2000). (This last essay is available on-line at the Millennium Film Journal website.)

14. James Hillman, *Re-Visioning Psychology* (New York: Harper Colophon, 1975), 57.

15. *Ibid.*, 82 and 107.

16. For a full discussion, see Don Fredericksen, "Polskie Liminalne Filmy Dokumentalne Epoki Postkommunistycznej" [Polish Liminal Documentary of the 1990s], *Studia Filmoznawcze* 23 (2003).

CINEMA AS ILLUSION AND REALITY

LUKE HOCKLEY

A t best Jung had a somewhat ambivalent attitude to the cinema and the media in general. There are only a handful of references to films in his writing, and most of these are made in interviews with journalists or found in records of group seminars. The main body of the *Collected Works* is virtually devoid of references to movies. However, when Jung did mention cinema he seemed to appreciate the creative potential of the medium. He was particularly impressed by its ability to unlock the unconscious and to represent on-screen what are normally internal psychological processes.

> The movies are far more efficient than the theatre: they are less
> restricted, they are able to produce amazing symbols to show the
> collective unconscious, since their methods of presentation are
> so unlimited.[1]

Jung made this remark sometime between 1928 and 1930. Almost thirty years later, he seems to have changed his mind as the cinema

Luke Hockley, Ph.D., is Associate Dean - Media at the University of Sunderland, UK, and the author of *Cinematic Projections* (University of Luton Press, 2001). His forthcoming book is provisionally entitled *Frames of Mind* and will be published in 2006. Luke has lectured widely on Jung and cinema in the USA, UK, and Europe (including the C. G. Jung Institute in Zürich).

now seems to have fallen out of favor with him. In an interview with the foreign correspondent for the *Daily Mail* in 1955, Jung comments:

> The strains and stresses of twentieth-century living have so affected the modern mind that in many countries children are no longer able to concentrate. Here in Zürich the schoolteachers of the upper part of the lake asked me why it is that they are no longer able to carry out the full curriculum. The children, they said, seemed unable to concentrate. I told them that the fault lay with the cinema, the radio, television, the continual swish of motor-cars and the drone of planes overhead. For these are all distractions…Worst of all is television.[2]

I suspect that what Jung was anxious about was the pervasive nature of media, and the manner in which they were, and are, consumed. For example, elsewhere in the same interview Jung comments that he has nothing against music, but that he cannot stand background music, particularly if the music is good. He adds that while he can tolerate jazz in the background, Bach deserves to be listened to properly, as it is, in his view, music which nurtures the soul. Perhaps the same might also apply to the movies. As such, Jung was not expressing a view about the intrinsic worth of the medium *per se,* but rather commenting on the psychological attitude adopted towards it. This is typical of Jung, who tried to stay away from making aesthetic judgements about the artistic merit of a piece of art or literature. This approach is congruent with the clinical practice he established in which patients were encouraged to paint images from their dreams, not as an aesthetic exercise, but as a way of opening up psychological dialogue with the unconscious.

While Jung might not have had much to say about the cinema, he certainly seemed to know what he liked. He comments, "The best movie I ever saw was *The Student of Prague* [1926]. It shows the separation of the conscious man and his shadow, so that the shadow moves by itself."[3] Elsewhere he remarks:

> The great asset of the movies is the amazing effects they can produce. One sees the man and his reflection of the student in the mirror, and the devil stands behind and beckons to the reflection of the student in the glass, and the reflection comes out in a quite extraordinary way and follows the devil. The

student stares into the mirror and can no longer see himself, he
is a man without a shadow. And the devil walks away.[4]

Interestingly, Jung made these observations at a time when the
movies were striving to achieve greater degrees of realism in the way in
which they structured their narratives. At that time cinema was still
in its infancy. The *Jazz Singer* (1927), the first feature-length film to
use synchronized sound, only had a limited number of sequences of
dialogue and singing — mostly the sound was courtesy of a Vitaphone
Orchestra score. The rules of continuity editing and the conventional
processes of film production had yet to be fully embodied within the
Hollywood studio system. But what intrigues Jung is not the realist
quality of the movies rather it is the capacity of the cinema to create an
illusory, or magical, world — a world where shadows can move by
themselves, where reflections take on a life of their own.

I suspect there are at least two factors at work here which need to
be kept in mind as we reflect on Jung's comments. One is Jung's
longstanding and pervasive interest in the metaphorical, and the other
his passion for the symbolic. While this is just conjecture on my part,
it may well be that the type of realist cinema which was to become the
norm as the Hollywood studio system came to dominate film
production was not as likely to appeal to Jung as the more intense and
visually expressive world of early cinema.

Another factor that we need to bear in mind is that much early
cinema was based upon mythological and psychological themes —
The Student of Prague is one such film, being a reworking of Faust. It is
also in the tradition of German Expressionist film. This film movement
is generally taken to refer to films produced between 1919 and 1923,
and it encompasses numerous genres, including romances, thrillers,
and fantasy. Visually the films are characterized by dramatic lighting
design, with large shadows, stereotypical characters, and acting that
draws on the stagecraft of the German theatre to create a stylized
décor. The result is an almost poetic film language which was ideally
suited to the creation of an atmospheric setting.

Jung's interest in the cinema, such as it was, seems to be with its
ability develop what was at the time a new visual and symbolic language
which he believed could breath new life into ancient myths and
revitalize them for contemporary times. I suspect that what also
intrigued Jung were the magical and phantasmagorical elements of

the cinema as he was captivated by illusions which appeared to be real, as is well-documented in his interests in spiritualism and mediumistic activities. Indeed, Jung often suggests that the distinction between reality and fantasy is much less clear-cut than we generally assume it to be in our everyday lives:

> What is "illusion"? By what criterion do we judge something to be an illusion? Does anything exist for the psyche that we are entitled to call illusion? What we are pleased to call illusion may be for the psyche an extremely important life-factor, something as indispensable as oxygen for the body — a psychic actuality of overwhelming significance.[5]

In the preceding passage from *The Aims of Psychotherapy* Jung is exploring the nature of the images produced by his patients and, in so doing, he implicitly places the image center stage as a means by which to understand unconscious processes. He goes on in the article to make the distinction between psychological reality and conscious reality, with the *proviso* that both realities are equally full of illusion. Following this lead, there are two interwoven themes to follow. The first explores the central role that the visual image has in analytical psychology. The second develops these observations in relation to the cinematic experience. In so doing I hope to suggest why it is that analytical psychology is a particularly useful approach in coming to an understanding of how images, and in particular films, convey meaning. Analytical psychology gives an insightful framework through which to explore the shared and individual meaning of films. It also gives a language through which to articulate the shifting psychological nature of cinematic images, which, on the one hand, are illusory and collective, but which also have the capacity to speak to us in a relevant and meaningful manner. In fact, the way in which we engage with the on-screen fictional worlds of film is unlike any other art form in the way that it blurs the boundaries between the conscious and unconscious aspects of the psyche.

It is a fundamental tenet of analytical psychology that the unconscious and its images are real. This central principle points us towards one of Jung's most profound insights, namely that in order to understand the fantasies of patients, their dreams, neuroses, psychoses, auditory and visual hallucinations, and such like, the 'delusions' must be accepted as real. For Jung, the realms of imagination and fantasy were part of the fabric of the material world. This will prove important as we come to consider the psychological relationship that we have with movies and the cinematic experience more generally. The blurring of the divisions between real and not real, between conscious and unconscious, between personal and collective will be of central concern, since images facilitate the merging of what typically are regarded as separate realms.

For Jung, the image exists somewhere in the space between the unconscious and consciousness. It serves as a mediator between unconscious contents and outer reality. He describes it as follows:

> When I speak of "image" in this book, I do not mean the psychic reflection of an external object, but a concept derived from poetic usage, namely, a figure of fancy or *fantasy-image*, which is related only indirectly to the perception of an external object. This image depends much more on unconscious fantasy activity, and as the product of such activity it appears more or less abruptly in consciousness, somewhat in the manner of a vision or hallucination, but without possessing the morbid traits that are found in a clinical picture. The image has the psychological character of a fantasy idea and never the quasi-real character of an hallucination, i. e., it never takes the place of reality, and can always be distinguished from sensuous reality by the fact that it is an "inner" image.[6]

It therefore follows that such images need not be pictorial; rather they are metaphorical, like the image 'heard' in a piece of music. A psychological film theory needs to be concerned with both types of images. More explicitly, our interest rests on the interplay between the overtly audio-visual experience of films and their capacity to both awaken and to be part of our inner lives. The image exists not just on the screen but also somewhere in the space between the viewer and the screen. Interestingly, this view is consistent with the observation of Roland Barthes in his article *Death of the Author*[7] in which he outlined his view that meanings come not just from the text, but also from what the reader brings to the text. In the case of the cinema, this may be an unconscious fantasy-oriented process in which the individual plays a role in creating an image — a unique psychosomatic relationship of conscious and unconscious processes activated by the progression of images and sounds on the screen. From this perspective the image captures the psychological reality of a given situation and encapsulates the complex dynamics that arise from the interplay of archetypal forces and their relationship with consciousness as it tries to come to an informed understanding of what is at hand.

> The inner image is a complex structure made up of the most varied material from the most varied sources. It is no conglomerate, however, but a homogenous product with a meaning of its own. The image is a *condensed expression of the psychic situation as a whole*, and not merely, nor even predominately, of unconscious contents pure and simple...Accordingly the image is an expression of the unconscious as well as the conscious situation of the moment. The interpretation of its meaning, therefore, can start neither from the conscious alone nor from the unconscious alone, but only from their reciprocal relationship.[8]

This is, as Jung puts it, a 'vital activity' as the drive towards individuation requires us to understand the complexities of the contradictions that are housed within each one of us. In his book *Re-Visioning Psychology*, James Hillman develops this theme:

> Since we can know only fantasy-images directly and immediately, and from these images create our worlds and call them realities, we live in a world that is neither "inner" nor "outer." Rather the psychic world is an imaginal world, just as image is psyche. Paradoxically, at the same time these images are in us and we live in the midst of them. The psychic world is experienced empirically as inside us and yet it encompasses us with images.[9]

The important points that I want to focus on are firstly that the psyche is imagistic and secondly that these images are both inner and outer, *at the same time*. Jung suggests that these fantasies occur independently of consciousness but in relation to it. It follows from this that unconscious fantasies may incorporate real people, real events, and actual memories. However, since conscious experiences are not directly related to the fantasy, it becomes important to distinguish between the projection of the fantasy onto real people and events and the fantasy itself. As Jung puts it:

> The psyche creates reality every day. The only expression I can use for this activity is *fantasy*. Fantasy is just as much feeling as thinking, as much intuition as sensation. There is no psychic function that, through fantasy, is not inextricably bound up with the other psychic functions. Sometimes it appears in primordial form, sometimes it is the ultimate and boldest product of all our faculties combined. Fantasy, therefore, seems to me the clearest expression of the specific activity of the psyche. It is, preeminently, the creative activity from which the answers to all answerable questions come; it is the mother of all possibilities, where, like all psychological opposites, the inner and outer worlds are joined together in living union.[10]

It is therefore clear that fantasy is not in and of itself pathological. In fact quite the opposite is true, as fantasy is integral to living life in a creative and fulfilling manner. But in order for this to happen, consciousness must be able to discriminate between what belongs to the unconscious and what has been, and can be, integrated into consciousness. Thus, the fantasy manifests itself in the form of images that contain both unconscious and conscious elements, and, in so doing, forms a bridge between inner and outer worlds. However, to derive benefit from the image any projections must be withdrawn so that consciousness (some might say ego-consciousness) gains a better understanding of the reality of a given situation.

Jung terms this ability to hold together opposing views of a situation the transcendent function, and it enables the psyche to move from one psychological approach, or attitude, to another. Such an approach can be regarded as transcendent in as much as it enables the individual to 'see', or be aware of, the competing 'push' of the unconscious and 'pull' of consciousness. The result is the ability to contain these differing perspectives and, in so doing, to 'transcend' what would otherwise be a purely instinctual response to a situation. The transcendent function is the mechanism by which the psyche gains fuller insight into how our unconscious selves influence our engagement with the outer world in symbolic form.

Here we have a clear difference in terminology between psychoanalytic language and that used by analytical psychology. For Freud, the symbol was a sign or symptom of a repressed idea or wish, normally sexual in origin. By contrast, Jung sees the symbol as something that depicts the psychological reality of a situation as it is, or will be.

As such, the symbol has a quasi-allegorical role in depicting and mediating between conscious and unconscious elements — it is expressive of the tensions that are inherent aspects of the transcendent function.

As mentioned earlier, underpinning all these activities the psyche has a propensity towards growth. As such, there is a teleological imperative behind its activities, which constitutes what Jung refers to as the process of individuation. This means each individual becoming who they are, fully aware of themselves and their interactions with others.

The following quote from Jung neatly summarizes much of the preceding discussion and highlights the natural and creative role that fantasy plays for the psyche in resolving neuroses and in ensuring that the psyche is regulated and healthy.

> If, as in this book, fantasy is taken for what it is — a natural expression of life which we can at most seek to understand but cannot correct — it will yield possibilities of psychic development that are of utmost importance for the cure of psychogenic neuroses and of the milder psychotic disturbances. Fantasies should not be negatively valued by subjecting them to rationalistic prejudices; they also have a positive aspect as creative compensations of the conscious attitude, which is always in danger of incompleteness and one-sidedness. Fantasy is a self-justifying biological function, and the question of its practical use arises only when it has to be channelled into so-called concrete reality…Fantasy is the natural life of the psyche, which at the same time harbours in itself the irrational creative factor.[11]

*   *   *   *   *

Cinema has the capacity to draw us into fictional worlds that become momentarily almost real. These worlds are collective (in both the social and psychological senses of the term) and personal. What we experience in the cinema is an awakening of personal and collective psychological material, which mirrors the way in which images behave in the psyche. It therefore follows that we can derive psychological benefit from many different types of films and not just good, high-art, worthy films. In *The Dream and the Underworld* (1979), Hillman refers to, "the polymorphous and pornographic desires of the psyche" and "to the underworld of images."[12] Making a similar point, Jung uses an alchemical image to show that what might appear to be without meaning may, actually, turn out to be important.

> Like this [alchemist's] apprentice, the modern man begins with an unseemly *prima materia* which presents itself in unexpected form — a contemptible fantasy which, like the stone that the builders rejected, is 'flung into the street' and is so 'cheap' that people do not even look at it. He will observe it from day to day and note its alternations until his eyes are opened...The light that gradually dawns on him consists in his understanding that fantasy is a real psychic process which is happening to him personally.[13]

It may well be that the most unlikely of movies, the most contemptible fantasies, the least palatable to our aesthetic and conscious-focused senses, actually capture some of the desires of the unconscious. Zombie movies, where the dead come back to life but only as destructive soulless bodies; vampire movies, where the dark sexual stranger kills or incarcerates you in a body that needs fresh human blood to stay alive; the paranoia of the guilty secret coming to light; overt eroticism; enjoying the spectacle of death, all are regularly experienced in the cinema. Indeed, much of this is bound up with genre expectations, leading us to express strong preferences one way or the other not just about individual films, but a whole genre. Significantly, these are not just aesthetic judgements but also psychological ones.

While he was not writing about films *per se*, Hillman in *Re-Visioning Psychology* (1977) suggests that it is in such pathologized images that we find the most potential for transformation.

> Thus the most distressing images in dreams and fantasies, those we shy from for their disgusting distortion and perversion, are precisely the ones that break the allegorical frame of what we think we know about this person or that, this trait of ourselves or that. The "worst" images are thus the best, for they are the ones that restore a figure to its pristine power as a numinous person at work in the soul.[14]

As images unfold in front of us, watching them can require us to undertake a "heroic" activity, while inner and outer, collective and personal, light and dark, the real and the illusory, temporarily coexist and have to be contained within our own experience of the moment. The psychological insight which analytical psychological offers is that when the term image is used to describe the cinematic experience, it actually encompasses the image on screen, our physical reactions, and our conscious and unconscious engagement in the process. As the images and sound on the screen pass frame by frame, so too do these other psychological and metaphorical images.

The mythological analogue to this cinematic experience can be expressed in numerous images. The alchemic vessel within which the *prima materia* is transformed; alternatively, there is the bright rectangle of moving light, which is differentiated from the still darkness of the auditorium. At risk of an overly inflated image, each screening of film embodies a little moment of creation, as something comes into being which requires us as viewers to engage with its contents — to come to terms with what we find in the darkness.

> The hero's main feat is to overcome the monster of darkness: it is the long-hoped-for and expected triumph of consciousness over the unconscious. The coming of consciousness was probably the most tremendous experience of primeval times, for with it a world came into being whose existence no one had suspected before. "And God said, 'Let there be light'" is the projection of the immemorial experience of the separation of consciousness from the unconscious.[15]

I suspect that there is a benefit in just being exposed to movies and that there is something satisfying in the physical and psychological aspects of watching a film—identifying with the characters on-screen as we encounter the embodiment of fragmented parts of our selves and recognize aspects that are like us and elements that are different. Experiencing opposites is one way of noticing similarities, and in part we use the movies as a type of imagistic transitional object, as a transformative space in which to experience aspects of our psyche. Put differently, Hillman writes about the importance of adopting an underworld perspective that, "...takes the image as all there is."[16] The suggestion is that immersion in the unconscious act and state of image making is enough, since the psyche needs to experience itself as image, as metaphor, and to comprehend its own interior image-based relationships. Later in the same piece he adds, "It is better to keep the dream's black dog [image] before your senses all day than to "know" its meaning…Interpretation arises when we have lost touch with the images…"[17] But this immersion, the loss of discrimination and conscious engagement, is worrying. Perhaps there is more.

> "Reflection" should be understood not simply as an act of thought, but rather as an attitude. It is a privilege born of human freedom in contradistinction to the compulsion of natural law. As the word itself testifies ("reflection" means literally "bending back"), reflection is a spiritual act that runs counter to the natural process; an act whereby we stop, call something to mind, form a picture, and take up a relation to and come to terms with what we have seen. It should, therefore, be understood as an act of *becoming conscious.*[18]

To this extent, to derive maximum psychological benefit from a film, we as viewers need to question. Mirroring what physically happens as light is shone on the screen, this process is one that involves both projection and reflection — it is one that involves an on-going process of seeing and recognizing. Using language that is reminiscent of the viewer's relationship to the cinema screen, Jung puts it like this:

> This recognition is absolutely necessary and marks an important advance. So long as he simple looks at the pictures he is like the foolish Parsifal, who forgot to ask the vital question because he was not aware of his participation in the action. Then, if the flow of images ceases, next to nothing has happened even though the process is repeated a thousand times. But if you recognize your own involvement, you yourself must enter into the process with your personal reactions, just as if you were one of the fantasy figures, or rather, as if the drama being enacted before your eyes were real. It is a psychic fact that this fantasy is happening, and it as real as you — as a psychic entity —are real.[19]

It therefore follows that the therapeutic aspect (the viewer-as-therapist, if you will) really comes into play when we start to ask, why? Why do I find this film boring? Why am I repelled by its explicit sexual imagery? Is it due to my politics, or my psyche, or is it more likely the interplay between the two? Why do I feel this? What does it tell me about myself, and what I am going to do? Films can activate 'complex' material. Adopting a psychological approach to film, we work with our experiences of them. We can pay attention not just to our psychological reactions to what we see but also to our bodily responses. We cry, cringe, hold our partner's hand for comfort, we may even be unable to stay in the cinema. Crucially, we take these reactions with us when we leave the cinema. Then we test our personal reactions to the film with those of our friends or partners as we reflect on what we have seen.

NOTES

1. Seminar Papers, Vol. 1, *Dream Analysis: Notes of the Seminar given in 1928-1930*, ed. W. McGuire (London: Routledge, 1984), 12.

2. C.G. Jung, *C.G. Jung Speaking: Interviews and Encounters*, ed. W. McGuire and R.F.C. Hull (London: Picador, 1980), 240-1. (Edited version of interview given to Frederick Sands, foreign correspondent for the *London Daily Mail*, 25-29 April, 1955.)

3. Seminar Papers, Vol. 1, *Dream Analysis: Notes of the Seminar given in 1928-1930*, ed. W. McGuire (London: Routledge, 1984), 259.

4. *Ibid.*, pp. 49-50.

5. *Collected Works*, 16 § 111.

6. *Collected Works*, 6 § 743.

7. Roland Barthes, *Image, Music, Text*, trans. S. Heath (London: Fontana, 1977).

8. *Collected Works*, 6 § 745.

9. James Hillman, *Re-Visioning Psychology* (New York: Harper and Row, 1977), 23.

10. *Collected Works*, 6 § 78.

11. *Collected Works*, 18 § 1249. From the foreword to Wickes, *Von Der Inneren Welt Des Menschen*.

12. James Hillman, *The Dream and the Underworld* (New York: Harper and Row, 1979), 45.

13. *Collected Works*, 14 § 752. Jung may be referring to the passage which occurs in all the synoptic gospels where Jesus asks: "Have you not read this scripture: 'The stone that the builders rejected has become the cornerstone [or keystone]; this was the Lord's doing, and it is amazing in our eyes'?" Mark 12:10-11, also Matt 21:42 and Luke 20:17-18. The passage of scripture that Jesus is referring to is Psalms 118: 22-23. He does so in order to suggest that in fact he is the overlooked keystone (the son of God), a claim which does not sit well with the

scribes and chief priest who realize that this parable is being told against them.

14. James Hillman, *Re-Visioning Psychology* (New York: Harper and Row, 1977), 8.

15. *Collected Works*, 9i § 284.

16. James Hillman, *The Dream and the Underworld* (New York: Harper and Row, 1979), 80.

17. *Ibid.*, 122-123.

18. *Collected Works*, 11 § 235n.

19. *Collected Works*, 14 § 753. According to the version of the story by Chrétien de Troyes, Perceval (Parsifal) is told by his cousin Signe that on seeing a "a lance whose tip bleeds without there being any flesh or vein there" he should have asked "why it bled?" On seeing the grail and its attendants he should have enquired, "where they were going like this?" (Lines 3543-3586) Failing to ask these questions, she renames him, "Perceval the wretched!" For asking the questions "would have brought such benefit to the good king who is crippled that he would have completely regained the use of his limbs and governed his land; and from that you would have reaped such profit! But now you may be sure that many misfortunes will befall you and others."

ARCHETYPES, COHERENCE,

AND

THE CINEMA

T he reality of the psyche and soul are all too quickly being eclipsed
in modern times. Today dreams, symptoms, images, and
fantasies, while belonging to the domain of the deep
unconscious, tend to be understood from the perspective of personal
consciousness. The sense of wonder about the profundity, depth, and
vastness of the objective psyche found in the work of Jung and the first
generation of Jungians is less seen in the modern literature. This material
generated a great sense of excitement and discovery. Even as third and
fourth generation Jungians, we can still feel the richness and depth
which comes when we acknowledge the vastness of the psyche. While
we continue to describe our work as soulful, I think it has shifted away
from psyche and its images to mining the world of the ego. Fortunately
the road to psyche is still open and if we are to reverse a number of ill-
fated personal and collective tendencies, we need to find our way back
to the psyche and soul.

Michael Conforti, Ph.D., is a Jungian analyst and the Founder and Director of The
Assisi Conferences. He maintains an active lecture schedule, presenting in the United
States and in Italy, Venezuela, Denmark, Canada, and the Jung Institute in Zürich. He
also provides consultation and mentoring to organizations, and works with screenwriters
and members of the film industry on archetypal coherence.

Early cultures understood the centrality of spirit in their lives. Their rituals, myths, and traditions were vehicles to allow spirit and psyche to infuse their world with innate and perennial wisdom. This need is still alive, but the riverbeds where psyche once flowed freely have been diverted to commercialism, pragmatism, and for all too many of us, a sense of meaninglessness. Fortunately, the world of psyche is still alive and brought to life in the cinema. Watching a movie, we are free to enter domains which seem to exist otherwise only in our imagination. Theatre is imagination, is psyche, and a world where the gods of our ancient myths live on. These archetypal kings and queens, heroes and heroines, tricksters and lovers, may look different from those in our high school mythology books, but their mission and path are the same.

Virtually everyone loves movies. We love to be entertained, to be transported from everyday life into another world, which may be more glamorous, more adventurous, and often more tragic. Luke Skywalker and Rocky follow the path of ancient heroes, David and Goliath are battling again in the hit film *Miracles*, and love and grief are the creative daimons driving the drama in *Madame Butterfly*. On and on we can delve into past and present themes, and the point is that cinema allows us to do so—it provides a safe arena to be with our ancient heroes and gods, at least for the span of a two-hour movie. In this article, I will discuss the role of archetypes in film, and examine what I call *cinematic archetypal coherence,* which is a capacity to accurately and creatively capture the underling archetypal structure inherent in a story.

Cinema is a telling of ancient truths, which provide access to the world of archetypes and the reality generated by them. Each archetypal drama is lived in accordance with the dynamics and dominants of that field. These fields carry with them mandates, behaviors, proclivities, and tendencies, all specific to that field. Consciousness is what allows the individual to both establish a relationship to the archetypal and create a more personal response to an archetypal event. It was this appreciation and awareness of archetypal wisdom which prompted George Lucas to ask Joseph Campbell to work with him on the original *Star War* series. Campbell's job was to insure that the characters maintained an alignment, integrity, and coherence with their archetypal roots. Both Lucas and Campbell realized that if the presentation of Luke Skywalker as hero was to be convincing, this role had to be consistent with that of heroes throughout history. While there are variations in the expression of the hero myth, there are nevertheless certain well-worn heroic patterns that each and every hero has to take in life. This is the domain within which Campbell excels. His many books on mythology, especially *The Hero with a Thousand Faces,* chronicle heroic journeys throughout history. Much of *Star Wars'* success lay in its fidelity to archetypal dominants, and the consistency of the movie's story line with the underlying archetypal theme it sought to represent.

Generally we find a familiar refrain in stories and music. Even with the most avant-garde jazz musicians, such as Ornette Coleman and John Coltrane, we can recognize a melodic theme both before and after it plays "out." For instance, the jazz artist may begin a well-known piece by playing it in the traditional manner, and then, once the original chord progressions and refrain are solidly established, move to the improvisational "playing out" mode, and end by a return to the familiar. If we look closely at a story line, we also notice a richly textured and patterned progression of action and activity. There are certain things—familiar refrains—a hero will complete in the course of assuming a heroic identity. Tragedy, as we see in *Sophie's Choice,* also follows a relatively stable trajectory. Stories, both contemporary and ancient, match up surprisingly well with eternal, archetypal themes. Part of the magic of movies is their ability to make us care about the characters of a story. And, like children, we too listen to and watch the same stories time and time again, and laugh and cry over endless renditions of them. There are tales of heroes, of fathers and sons (The *Star Wars* Series), fathers and daughters (*Million Dollar Baby*), mothers and sons (Lina Wertmuller's *Seven Beauties*), the mid-life struggle (*American Beauty*), aging (*On Golden Pond*), premature death (*Terms of Endearment*), and on and on. We watch these because we need to, because their deeply embedded motifs satisfy a primal psychological and spiritual need in us.

A film's ability to accurately and creatively convey its archetypal roots is what I refer to here as cinematic, archetypal coherence. We could simply say that movies work when they capture these eternal stories, and fail when they do not. Coherence, like a skilled weaver, takes all the disparate threads and parts and combines them into a richly textured, coherent tapestry. The importance and workings of coherence are now a central theme in the new sciences. Perhaps one of the most original researchers in the field is Mae-Wan Ho, a biophysicist from Hong Kong, and now Director of the Institute for Science in Society. Ho suggests that coherence "means correlation, a sticking together, or connectedness; also a consistency…Thus, coherence always refers to wholeness."[1]

Every creative act is an expression of this coherent flow pattern. The person is temporarily lifted from the confines of individual experience and transported into a world of collective wisdom, a world where things make sense, where story line, character, and action all work so well together they create a seamless whole. In dance, music, and sports, we also witness moments where each participant moves in such a natural and highly choreographed manner that it gives the appearance of a single movement. At such times, each player or dancer responds to the anticipated gesture of a partner, and their interactions create a beautifully coherent whole.

Archetypal consistency is compelling, while archetypal estrangement repels. *Sophie's Choice* serves as an excellent illustration of the presence of archetypes in film, and the workings of what I have termed "cinematic archetypal coherence." In *Sophie's Choice*, tragedy begins when she and her children are taken into the concentration camps. Then, as if internment were not devastating enough, Sophie is forced to choose which of her two children should live and which should die. To select one child over the other is an unimaginable situation, and we soon realize this act will seal her fate. There is virtually no way Sophie can ever resume a life of meaning, pleasure, or joy after this horrendous "choice." Watching this scene, we too are brought to a place of despair. Sophie eventually chooses, and yet we know what must ultimately follow. In choosing the life of one child over the other, she has chosen death, not only for the child but also for herself. From the moment this choice is made, we sense that there is really only one fitting ending to this story.

I have worked with a number of patients who had to make very difficult decisions about the fate of an unborn and the care of their young children. In every case, the ravages of the "choice" continued to take their toll. Unable to bear the conscious responsibility for these decisions, the individuals unconsciously identify with the dead or abandoned child. Coupled with deep unconscious guilt and their subsequent existence and immersion within an archetypal field of death, they too die emotionally, and their self-punishing behavior reflects these realities.

Just as in Sartre's *No Exit,* when one is in the throes of this drama, there seems to be no way out. Unconscious guilt refers to our inability to consciously acknowledge the *effects* of our more troubling behavior. While the individual may feel free of any remorse, the self-punishing behavior reflects the underlying guilt.

The character Sophie is pushed farther than any patient I have ever treated. In a strange and almost convoluted way, her choice brings her into the world of spiritual sacrifice. As Abraham willingly offered up his son to prove his love for God, Sophie's decision must have involved a degree of faith as well. Her faith must have suggested that this decision, this giving over, would insure the life of her surviving child. Abraham's actions were ultimately *self-serving* in that he sought his own redemption, and his son was simply a vehicle towards that goal. Sophie instead offered up her child with the hope that her other child would be allowed to live. Though perhaps like Abraham, she had her own personal reasons for not resisting, and it is for both these reasons that she suffers.

And so her future is lost through the horrors of her past. However, as we see in this movie and similar life situations, memory is not a remembrance of the past, but a reminder that we live in multiple worlds, multiple realities simultaneously. How else can we explain the hold the past has on our future? As we find in the stories of many concentration camp survivors, their lives as "free" men and women are really not very different from the lives they had in the camps. In many cases, they remain tortured souls. How could Sophie find pleasure in the world against the backdrop of having given her child over to the death squad? I believe that a re-emergence into life would necessitate a deep soul-searching, and that pleasure and meaning would ultimately go against the brutal truth of her past actions. She too was internally dead, like her dead child. Stepping out of this world of death, horror, and constant deprivation would be akin to leaving her child alone in the tomb.

On the other hand, entry into life would represent a leave-taking, a severing of her unconscious bond with her child. The contrast between her tortured experience and the prospect of a good life were too much for Sophie, and too much for many camp survivors. In *And the Sea Is Never Full*, Eli Wiesel speaks about the suicide of his good friend Primo Levi. Outsiders suggested that if only Levi could have found help for his psychological problems, for his suffering, and his horror, then the suicide could have been averted. Taking umbrage at this facile approach to the effects of unbearable suffering, Wiesel calls out in chilling resentment that there are experiences beyond the range of integration. "Here we have existential evil, the lifelong incandescent wound of a soul, reduced to a nervous breakdown common among writers whose inspiration becomes blocked..."[2] Essentially there is no way to metabolize, sanitize, or cauterize oneself from such experiences.

Movies present us with a drama, a situation, which the main character either resolves or does not. *Sophie's Choice* is an excellent example of the latter. The world of hell she enters is one she may never escape, though it is the choice which seals her fate.

There is perhaps no greater spokesperson for the atrocities and effects of the Holocaust on the human psyche than Eli Wiesel. In what I believe is his greatest novel, *The Accident*, he tells the story of a survivor who attempts to make a life in New York:

> With us—those who have known the time of death—it's different. There, we said we would never forget. It still holds true. We cannot forget. The images are there in front of our eyes. Even if our eyes were no longer there, the images would remain. I think if I were able to forget I would hate myself. Our stay there planted time bombs within us. From time to time one of them explodes. And then we are nothing but suffering, shame, and guilt. We feel ashamed and guilty to be alive, to eat as much bread as we want, to wear good, warm socks in winter. One of these bombs...will undoubtedly bring about madness.[3]

And in the following, Wiesel captures what I believe is the inner state of Sophie's heart and soul:

> It's too late. To change, we would have to change the past. But the past is beyond our power. Its structure is solid immutable...You speak of happiness...as if it were possible. It isn't even a dream. It too is dead. It too is up above. Everything has taken refuge above. And what emptiness here below!...Here, we have nothing. Nothing...Here an arid desert. A desert without even a mirage. It's a station where the child left on the

platform sees his parents carried off by the train. And there is
only smoke where they stood. They are the smoke. Happiness?
Happiness for the child would be for the train to move backward.
But you know how trains are, they always go forward.[4]

Sophie's world is one of internal despair and perhaps the deepest
sorrow anyone could imagine. The story's progression perfectly captures
the archetypal field within which she resides. The ending, while tragic,
is anticipated throughout the story.

Sophie desperately needed a deep reckoning with her conscience
if she was to survive. To live, she would have to accept the devastating
reality and consequences of her "choice." In all honesty, I really do not
know how anyone could survive such a situation. From the perspective
of archetypal coherence, we can see that in "choosing" she had entered
a domain where both hope and unbearable guilt would reside. I imagine
that in choosing, she had hoped to insure the survival of one child.
And yet the cost to the psyche of this hope was tantamount to choosing
death for an innocent child. The choice placed her on a life path that
was virtually fixed and determined by conditions. We can look at the
choice and the events in the movie as the behaviors, tendencies, and
influences residing in a field where such a choice was made. In this
regard, her choice, the death of her child, and her own eventual suicide
were all coherent features of this drama. However, this would have
been a totally different movie had she not made the choice. While she
would have had to live with the atrocities of the camps and the reality
that she was virtually helpless to secure her children's survival, in not
making the choice, the story and perhaps Sophie's life would have
been very different. In particular, the guilt and horror of her own
actions would probably not have been a major factor.

Sophie's choice and the remainder of her life represent the expression
of the field she entered once she made her "choice." I applaud the
integrity of the filmmakers to clearly and accurately represent the
archetypal world of horror and decay with such gritty honesty and
pain. I am sure they were tempted to alter the ending to find some
version of a happy ending. But they did not. This film provides a gift
to all of us, in that it allows us to enter with Sophie a tragic world and
see its consequences.

An essential theme to consider here is the issue of redemption.
Freed from its religious connotations, redemption involves a freedom

from a curse and spell, a breaking of an unconscious, archetypal constellation and possession. Like many camp survivors, Sophie never found redemption. However, the question remains open on what could have provided her with redemption and a liberation from this death field. In studying the literature on redemption motifs, we find that "hitting bottom" is a prerequisite for redemption. We sometimes find ourselves in a situation where we just can't go on, our heart is broken, or we have faced a mortal threat to our own life. At such moments, at such breaking points, one either goes deeper into the previous field, or breaks free. In the leave-taking of the field, a tremendous amount of self-reflection is necessary prior to the emergence into a new field. A deep act of reflection, of contrition, and acknowledgment of the results of our actions are all needed to initiate this change. I believe that Sophie's suicide was an indication that she had not left this death field, and perhaps had avoided this deeper level of work. However, while only a survivor could understand the depths of concentration camp life, there may still have been a way for Sofie to break the spell of this death field. If she had allowed herself to live and perhaps even to prosper, then by way of contrast, she would have more honestly faced the realities of life and death. Only in more fully living would she have been able to accept the reality of her "choice." Here guilt may be allowed to be transformed into remorse, and the tenacious hold of the unconscious guilt may be lifted. While Sophie would always live with the reality of her "choice," there would then be no distortion, no denial, no merging with death in her own life. To remain unconsciously and archetypally identified with this death field suggests the degree to which she had not developed a conscious relationship to these events. From my clinical experience, this appears to be one of the only ways to integrate such horrors. However, we have to also consider the possibility that with an event as devastating as Sophie's choice, integration and redemption may not be possible. Only further work exploring the nature of unbearable suffering, terror, and trauma will help us more fully understand the effects of such events on the psyche. The movie is a rare gem, and captures much of what I consider to be archetypal coherence.

We can further illustrate this concept of archetypal coherence through the opera and film, *Madame Butterfly*. While Butterfly is in love with the American sailor, his more carnal and lighthearted affections are obvious from the beginning of the story. When she announces her pregnancy, we sense that this story can only end in tragedy. She loves a man who just wants her as a playmate, a mere distraction. When in the final scene she agrees to give her child to her former lover and his new American wife, we arrive at an ending which we sensed all along. Her suicide, the story's climax, was already suggested by the beginning, and the narrative moved within an archetypally patterned and constrained manner, towards its inevitable finale. This was to remain within the archetypal death field, within this possession, the lysis being determined by the field. In this scenario, Butterfly was to die, because even by giving her child over to what might be a better life, she nevertheless gave away what she most loved.

On the other hand, other movies may make us feel good and suggest unlimited potential, but are flawed from an archetypal perspective. Several Ron Howard films, for instance *Splash* and *Cocoon,* have this feel-good quality with an archetypally discordant ending. In *Splash*, Tom Hanks falls in love with the mermaid Daryl Hannah, and then has to decide whether to let her go back to sea and lose her, or join her forever in the ocean. She tells him that if he decides to be with her, he can never return to his previous life. Looking back at his friends and family, he joins his love and forever trades his human life for one in the sea. A similar whimsical ending is found in *Cocoon*, where a group of elderly men and women find a fountain of youth and discover that the source of this "gift" are pods from outer space. They resolve to go off and live in this other world for the rest of their lives, hoping to transcend the limitations and fragility of old age.

Both films provide a whimsical, cute, and happy ending to a story. However in each there are intrinsic archetypal challenges that are presented, yet avoided. In *Splash*, the main character needs to wrestle with the dual aspect of his life—his existence in the world of the ego and his earlier childhood existence in what Neumann describes as the oceanic state of existence found in the uroboric stage. As we go through life, we need to remain in relationship with both parts of our nature. We have a number of biblical and mythological references and reminders of this issue. One is the motif of the dual birth, where the hero comes from another planet like Superman, and is later adopted by mortal parents. In the story of Moses and in the story of Jesus, we find this same motif of original birth from a divine source, and our subsequent second birth by human parents. This theme is also found in the tradition of a child having godparents. Standing side by side with the birth parents, the godparents represent the child's spiritual nature, and remind us that we are born of both mortal and divine parents, meaning we must live in both the worlds of spirit and matter.

When Tom Hanks looks back at his friends and then at his mermaid lover, he is faced with a deep, existential, archetypal challenge. How can he continue with the love and awareness for that part of his nature that can live in the deep unconscious—like a mermaid, while also living in the world of matter? The movie frames this as a duality, where a choice has to be made. To keep it an either/or situation suggests the adolescent attitude of both the director and the nature of the choice itself. We have to find a viable way to live in both worlds simualteously, and to realize that these are two dimensions of a unified world. His choice allows him to escape the real work needed to build this integration of the matter-spirit world into his daily life. From this perspective, the film is archetypally discordant, and while its fun-loving lysis is attractive, it remains nevertheless inadequate from the perspective of working with archetypal material.

The same is true for *Cocoon*, where the challenges of integrating both the hope for everlasting life and youthful vitality must be matched with the reality of the aging process. From the perspective of archetypally coherent stories, both films fail to capture the depth of the life process and proffer the audience a simplistic, ego-driven solution to a profound, archetypal, and self-driven situation.

Disney's film rendition of the Hercules myth is perhaps one of the more disturbing illustrations of the corruption of archetypal material in service of the profit motive. This film sought great commercial and merchandising success by playing off a terribly loose adaptation of the mythic tale. While Hercules represents an important component in the canon of hero mythologies, Disney's hope to utilize the film as a merchandising enterprise compromised the archetypal integrity inherent in the story. Except for a few glimpses of the original tale, this marketing device was more of a ploy to Americanize the image of Hercules than it was to remind children of the importance of the underlying myth.

The most pronounced example of distortion and misuse of archetypal material is the film's depiction of Hercules' relationship with his mentor. Several recent films, such as the original *Star Wars* trilogy and Clint Eastwood's *Million Dollar Baby*, have succeeded in presenting the tender, disciplined, and transformative nature of the mentoring process. Through this and the learning of specific skills, we come to understand that the hero is actually being initiated into a truly spiritual and transcendent process. However, Disney's presentation of this apprentice-mentor relationship is a travesty when viewed in relationship to its archetypal backdrop. For instance, we find Phil, the jubilant, sagacious mentor, so pleased to have found a new apprentice that he breaks into song. In the song "One Last Hope" we hear the following from this sage mentor:

> But you need an advisor
> A satyr, but wiser
> A good merchandiser...

And later we hear the muses singing the praises of Hercules with the following:

> He was a no one
> A zero, zero
> Now he's a honcho
> He's a hero...

And later:

> From appearance fees and royalties
> Our Herc had cash to burn
> Now nouveau riche and famous
> He could tell you
> What's a Grecian urn?

Continuing on:

> Who put the glad in gladiator?
> Hercules!
> Whose daring deeds are great theater?
> Hercules
> Is he bold?
> No one braver
> Is he sweet?
> Our fav'rite flavor
> Hercules, Hercules...

This distortion and misrepresentation of the hero myth continues as Hercules faces his first major heroic challenge. Learning that two children are trapped in a cave, Hercules' initial response is in effect: "Wow, this is great! Now I can save someone and really become a hero."

As the film progresses, we find the Disney merchandising machine in high gear, as images of the accoutrements of Hercules' world are proffered to an audience willing to pay the price for such "worthy" souvenirs. "Authentic" Hercules sandals, drinking mugs, and a credit card are quickly flashed across the screen to entice a hero-hungry audience to purchase these items from theater concessions at the movie's conclusion.

Everything about this movie speaks to the perversion of a mythic tale for ungainly profit. From an archetypal perspective, the entire presentation of the hero's journey is distorted. While the archetypal hero traditionally brings cultural and psychological advances to his world, Hercules and his mentor seek personal aggrandizement. The authentic hero is driven by a spiritual motivation not personal advance. Mentors pass on their wisdom for a greater goal, not as a way of winning favors from women.

This movie is not only a cinematic disappointment, but also a blatant abuse, misuse, and disregard for the innate wisdom contained in archetypes and within the psyche. Anytime we seek to commodify archetypal wisdom, we enter dangerous territory. Perhaps this is akin to Arachne challenging Athena, and of Agamemnon's hope for world dominance. The entire world of psychopathy, originally termed moral insanity, is replete with deception and smoke and mirrors. Individuals are asked to believe in the seductive yet corrupt actions of others. To quote P.T. Barnum: "A fool is born every day," and this tawdry truth is ever so present in this movie's attempts to sell the public on yet another false hero.

Psyche and nature will never be tamed or subdued; rather their autonomy must be recognized and respected to ensure a successful integration of archetypal material into the human experience. Heroes and gods, mentors and students are all expressions of a deep archetypal world. To de-spiritualize archetypal reality for the purpose of ego gratification in either personal life or in the cinema is a foolhardy process. Not only is it bad business, it does an injustice to a reality which transcends the world of ego consciousness. The *Hercules* movie was a disappointment not only for its audience, but for its financial backers as well.

The obvious question is why the movie failed to captivate its audience. While we can talk about the problematic issues of production, writing, characterization, etc., I suggest that the more compelling reason was its estrangement from its mythic, archetypal roots. The *Hercules* movie was *primarily* a product of commercial intent. The original *Star Wars* film, on the other hand, owed its success in large part to its relationship with underlying archetypal patterns. Joseph Campbell's involvement as creative consultant insured the films fidelity to an archetypal reality which transcends human intent and desire, and his collaboration with Lucas's *Star Wars* proved that archetypal, cinematic coherence could translate well into box office sales.

For all its lush visuals and intriguing twists, the movie *Under the Tuscan Sun* provides another example of what a lack of coherence looks like in a film. Drawing on the true-life experiences of California-based writer Frances Mayes, Diane Lane stars in this picturesque jaunt into the Tuscan countryside. The film takes us through the author's breakup with her lecherous husband, into the near communal dwelling of other divorcees, and later on a trip to Italy, courtesy of her good friends. While there are many delightful moments here, I want to discuss its ultimate fate among just 'good enough' films—those we pull off the shelf when we need visual stimulation and a sense of happy endings.

Certainly you want to keep your eyes on Diane Lane throughout this film. She is beautiful, earnest, genuinely seeking a better life, and like many of us, finds Italy and Italians irresistible and, at times, impossible. We all want to join Frances as she begins the work of rejuvenating the century-old estate named Bramsole, which loosely translates to 'something that yearns for the sun.' She puts her heart, soul, and virtually every dollar into this home, and after what may have been years of work, finally sees the fruits of her labor. Bramsole once again displays its majestic presence. This home will house all her hopes, especially her dreams of having a family.

Unfortunately though, she falls into an ill-fated relationship with a man whose depth of emotion is as shallow as his feigned Neapolitan accent. His adolescent charm affects us like chewing on aluminum foil—we want to scream out to our heroine to just get away from him.

But he is dark, alluring, and extremely cute. Cute is not handsome, of course; cute is boyish attractiveness, replete with great potential for a frolicking roll in the hay, but nothing more. His real intentions are apparent to all but our heroine. Perhaps she is continuing in a field of betrayal—she was betrayed by her husband, and will be betrayed again by this new lover.

We all sense from the start that this relationship will have to end. While von Franz speaks of the psyche's innate tendency to respond to archetypal themes, I think we are also primed to find the simplistic and overly sentimental nauseating. It is boring to know exactly where a story is going. Even in great films, where we may realize that the hero will find his beloved and live happily ever after, or instead will die, the beauty and artistry of the film is that it *still* pulls us into its magic and allows us—no, encourages us—to temporarily suspend belief and feel the characters' emotions, to live the film's highs and lows. In *Million Dollar Baby*, for instance, even though we should not have been surprised by the fate of our heroine, we were, and we cried with her and Clint Eastwood as they said their final goodbye.

But let's turn once more back to Tuscany. With yet another 'failed' love relationship under her belt, Frances buries herself in the work of making a home. The three Polish workers she employs are a bit like mythical elves, who under the cover of darkness turn threads into gold. This mismatched trio consists of a former university professor who relaxes by reading Milosz's poetry, a young man perhaps in his late teens or early 20's, and a hard-working *terrone*, Italian for 'man of the earth,' who harbors a growing infatuation for Frances.

Frances too develops a deep bond with these men, and slowly we see the daily encounters, shared meals, and poetry readings weave them all into a makeshift yet tender family unit. She soon discovers that the young man has fallen in love with the Italian girl living next door. Hoping to ease the young lovers' pain and to facilitate their hopes to be together, Frances sets out to persuade the girl's parents to accept this young man as their son-in-law. This leads to a particular scene which illustrates the importance of coherence in films.

Frances urges the young couple to ask the father for his blessing. But once at the parents' house, she herself launches into a sappy, sentimental diatribe on the virtues of love and the need for this young couple to be married. They "love each other," she declares, and should be together. But perhaps the writers got tired here and just borrowed from a Harlequin romance, because this monologue lacks any kind of fire or credibility. Even Diane Lane, whom I otherwise loved watching, was painfully blasé in this uninspired scene.

The film dives even deeper into banality as the parents respond to Frances's plea on the couple's behalf. This scene evidences a blatant misunderstanding and misrepresentation of Italian emotions. The writers let us down, neglecting to draw from our collective understanding of Italians and how the authentic nature of the Italian life, values, and soul has been captured in the cinema. Through Fellini's *Satyricon*, *Amarcord*, and *Juliet of the Spirits*, as well as Lena Wertmuller's *Swept Away*, and the now classic *Seven Beauties*, we experience traits and behaviors much more characteristic of the Italian soul.

Nevertheless, when the time comes for the parents' response, the father calmly quiets his just slightly emotional wife—her upheaval conveyed merely by a half-hearted rise from her chair. Likewise, the all-knowing father explains blandly that love is just not enough to guarantee happiness, adding that the boy has nothing, so what kind of life could he provide the daughter? I must say that I have routinely seen more emotion in a Brooklyn barber shop, when customers rage on about the virtues of the Yanks vs. the Mets.

Because the writers here failed to capture anything realistic about the Italian psyche or cultural norms, the audience leaves this scene feeling empty. In fact, we are more affected by the film's inconsistency, and herein lies its failure. Sure, I can be accused of stereotyping Italians, but the truth is that most Italians do tend to react in a very lively and passionate manner, even about the smaller details of life.

In order to bring about a greater sense of archetypal coherence to this scene, the writers would have to consider the characters' actions from the perspective of the Italian psyche. Portraying these roles in ways that are inconsistent with the Italian culture is equivalent to changing a timeless fairytale to fit our own wishes and thoughts about the nature of the story.

These ideas on archetypal coherence parallel Jung's work on the ontology, or dominant, of an image. For Jung, the task of translating images and symbols into psychological language involved a search for the essence of an image. (See Yoram Kaufmann's *Way of the Image* for an excellent discussion on this theme.) Jung lamented that too often we work to create meaning for an image. However, a deeper understanding of Jung's work teaches us that images have their own unique meaning and identity and do not need to be created by human consciousness. The same is true for movies and the stories they tell. Our job is to climb into the skin of the plot and work with its intrinsic story line. In this way, we create a meaningful alignment with the archetypal core of the story.

Personal and creative variation is needed, but within certain limits. The story and image still need to be seen as an expression of a pre-figured field, with certain dominant features and traditions of its own. In many regards, this approach of allowing the image to express its own story, freed of personal editorializing, is the work of spiritual traditions. They teach us to quiet the mind and to free ourselves from all the ego's clanging around, so as to allow for a deeper relationship with the transcendent. All too often though, our conscious ambitions run contrary to the psyche's intent for us. In so many ways, Jung's insights into the wisdom of the psyche and the natural rhythm inherent in psychic life, can make a meaningful contribution to our understanding of the archetypal current guiding the development of a movie.

Conclusion

The primacy of the archetype is now recognized in many divergent fields, from psychology to the sciences and the arts. Perhaps the unifying force is the realization that a life lived in accordance with archetypal principles brings us into alignment with a world far more vast than human cognition. These deep-seated principles are now finding their way into the movie industry, and not simply because good archetypal coherence makes for better box office sales. Anything can be manipulated for ill-gotten gains. If the Hollywood machine realizes the financial gain in abiding by archetypal truths, so be it. If in the process more people are exposed to the workings of archetypes and ultimately learn something essential about life, then everyone wins.

Fortunately, there is growing appreciation of the importance of archetypes in the movie industry. George Lucas and Joseph Campbell opened the door to this arena, and modern producers and directors have followed this lead.

While it may be a bit trite to quote Shakespeare and say "all the world's a stage," we can say that all the world's a screen, upon which these eternal dramas play to a full house. In learning about the workings of archetypes, we find that the temporal events in our life are expressions of a non-temporal domain. Daily life is replete with chores, challenges, and activities which, upon reflection, are the tasks of an individual striving for a relationship with the Self. So the world and our relationships are the screen upon which the archetypes make their presence and ask us for understanding and integration. Films too encourage us to engage with them, to enter into their world, and in the traditions of the world's greatest storytellers, provide a door through which we can enter this other world. This world of eternal truths has the capacity to change us, if we are open to its influence. So from this perspective, filmmakers have a great responsibility.

Perhaps the yardstick for assessing cinematic success may change to include the degree to which a film has creatively and accurately captured the archetypal dimensions of the story. One day, we may even find Ebert and Roeper giving thumbs up or down, describing films which have succeeded in this task.

* * * I want to thank Shari Smith for her thoughtful and creative editing of this text, and to Diane Antczak for her final reading of this article.

NOTES

1. Mae-Wan Ho, *The Rainbow and the Worm* (New Jersey: World Scientific, 1998), 199.

2. Elie Wiesel, *And the Sea Is Never Full* : *Memoirs 1969-*, (New York: Random House, 1999), 346.

3. Elie Wiesel, *The Accident* (New York: Bantam Books, 1999), 105.

4. *Ibid.*, 106.

CIN-IMAGO DEI: JUNGIAN PSYCHOLOGY AND IMAGES OF THE SOUL IN CONTEMPORARY CINEMA

TERRILL L. GIBSON

> The artist reveals his [sic] world to us, and forces us either to
> believe in it or reject it as something irrelevant and unconvincing.
> In creating an image he subordinates his own thought, which
> becomes insignificant in the face of that emotionally perceived
> image of the world that has appeared to him like a revelation. For
> thought is brief, whereas the image is absolute. In the case of
> someone who is spiritually receptive, it is therefore possible to
> talk of an analogy between the impact made by a work of art and
> that of a purely religious experience. Art acts above all on the
> soul, shaping its spiritual structure.—Andrei Tarkovsky, *Sculpting
> in Time: Reflections on the Cinema*

Cinema and depth psychology are siblings. Not first or second
cousins, they are siblings in the ancient family of image. They
were both born, in their modern incarnation, in Paris in the

Terrill L. Gibson, Ph.D., is a diplomate pastoral psychotherapist, an approved
supervisor for the American Association for Marriage and Family Therapy, and a diploma
Jungian analyst who practices individual and family therapy with Pastoral Therapy
Associates in Tacoma, Washington. He lectures and writes widely on the basic theme of
the integration of psychotherapy and spirituality. He has a passion for film, sea kayaks,
and the blues.

same year at almost the same instant—1893. Sigmund Freud, already filled with the recovered ideas of Mesmerism and unconscious magnetism echoed in the work of his contemporary Charcot, was cementing his revolutionary association technique encoded in repressed childhood memories,[1] while on the other side of town, the Lumière brothers were screening their first narrative and documentary film projects on the brick walls of taverns.

Two lost siblings, almost twins, finding their way back to the same mother—the Mother of Image. And the core of this image, its generative heart and dynamism, its reason for being and its destiny, is the Soul. Arguably, the most important concept in Jungian craft is the Soul/Self concept (what tradition has called the *imago Dei*, the numinous image of the Divine god at the core of the psyche). Arguably, the most important image of film craft is the image of the Soul. And it is the Soul which is the common destiny of both crafts. This essay wishes to tease out a bit of these crafts and the destiny to which they are ineluctably joined.[2]

An Initial Paradigm Sketch

Unus est vas (the vessel is one).
—C. G. Jung, *Collected Works,* 12 § 338

L et me make a few observations and brief amplifications about the paradigm of common Soul and cultural healing as I see it for psychotherapy and film:

• Film is the most readily available vehicle for either genuine escape or genuine therapeutic healing in our culture—the cinema is the most widely attended cathedral in our era. Film gives the Soul hope in much the same way that cathedral, synagogue, mosque, and mystery shrines did for the ancient world. Within the warmth of community and collective image, film soothes the Soul. Film encourages Soul. Film inspires Soul. Like ancient theater, film catharts Soul, heals it, instructs it, and motivates it.

• Film is potentially a medium for awakening, for conscious provocation and integration of the Soul. It is inherently an initiatory medium. Now the cineplex is the sacred precinct where these mysteries are enacted, for entering a dark, cavernous space in expectant silence to watch torch-enflamed moving images on the walls is perhaps the oldest cross-cultural rite known to human consciousness—practiced from the ancient shamanic caves of Altamira and Las Caux to the pictoglyphic caverns of the desert American Southwest. Holy cinema cave mysteries fulfill an "insatiable" human need:

> For more than a century after Henry VIII dissolved the monasteries and broke with the Church of Rome, no churches were built in England. Instead, England built theaters. Alone among European cities, London possessed a multitude of wooden theaters, which inspired wonder in foreign visitors. The English theater became, in effect, a new species of church, a new species of temple. Within the magical precincts of this structure, the rites and rituals of Hermetic mysteries were performed for an insatiable public.[3]

• Film is the fundamental communicator, educator, and translator of living myth in our culture. Film is a tangible collective dream working to resolve our Oedipal/Electral despairs. Often, it seeks the recovery and transformation of the Lost Child—both the archetypal Divine Child and the traumatized personal child. This has always been a primary task of living myth—the recovery of lost innocence, not naiveté, and its suffering-enriched narrative of personal and collective redemption and transformation. Film and film analysis is much more than simply a reductive activity of "decoding" the "Gaze" of cinematic "desire" and "mirroring."[4] The Soul always stands beyond, under, and over such reduction. It is the living Self, the mythic embodiment of the One World of the Numinous.

• Film is deeply sacramental and, like any sacrament, it is enhanced by an attitude of conscious, soulful reception. The Soul only appears if the coast is clear, in a boundaried, safe place. The Soul is shy and fragile. It is vulnerable and hyper-sensitive to violence and trauma. It needs protected space and that is what sacraments do—they create protected space. That is the miracle and mystery of the sanctuary of the movie house alluded to above. In the blink of a frame, a cold, cola-sticky-floored concrete pavilion becomes an ancient initiatory cave.

Then, when the Soul is assured that there is a calmed and receptive body-observer, it can expose the human psyche to all manner of inciting/healing/transforming images. Though the Soul appears fragile, it is profoundly resilient. It is really ego which is fragile and brittle, capable of snapping in the fierce winds of unregulated unconscious assault. It is ego more than Soul which requires such careful sacramental containment in the end.

• Film, like analysis, "works through" individuation by conscious, alchemical, symbolic interaction with the archetypal world of the psyche. It facilitates often rapid regression to early life damage and suggests repair possibilities.

In a typical film construct, there is an ego narrator, a Self-Soul presence, and a plot that creates a dialogue between the split worlds of ego and Soul, a dialogue that suggests and image-lures transformative, healing re-engagement between the ego and Soul. Jungian literature has called this the ego-self axis[5] and suggests that healing regression is perhaps the only way the rent between consciousness and the numinous unconscious can be repaired. Film's powerful regressions usually get us to suspend our disbelief and enter film's story of transforming image within the first thirty seconds of a well-crafted piece of cinema. Though the screen narrative may be about someone else's quest for lost childhood innocence, it is frequently ours that is most implicated. While we weep and thrill and grieve for the actor's success or failure in this journey, it is often our childhood and archetypal wounds of the Lost Child that are being constellated and potentially healed.

• Film is a crucial medium of initiatory ritual and transformative experience—one of the few fully viable such precincts left to us. The Soul seems to awaken and transform through image. Image is the essential alchemy. The Soul moves through image more elementally than through the phenomenal world. Dream, vision, and trance are key image-texts in spiritual and depth psychological experience. Film moves through us like dream, vision, and trance. Film, which is simply an organization and choreography of image, is inherently an initiatory medium, if initiation is defined as entering and being transformed by contact with the living Soul of the world, the *Anima Mundi*.[6] And film, being a primary archetypal medium, is a tool of the Soul and its initiations whether it chooses to be conscious of this alchemy or not.

• Film is living Soul experience and, therefore, needs to be "read" gnostically, alchemically, mythically, and mystically. Film requires profound devotional literacy in these areas to be fully appreciated. Gnosticism, alchemy, mythology, and mysticism are the key recurrent narratives of inner human experience. They form the corpus, the core cannon of exegesis in analytical psychology. They are as important for explicating the inner/psycho-spiritual aspects of things as chemistry and modern physics are for the outer/phenomenal aspect of things. They have served as enormously useful lexicons to crack the code of inner experience—dream, trance, and vision—and hold that same rich potential to similarly crack the image sequence of meaning in film and art.

• Film is the key holder of paradox and the opposites—all "outer"-world film, no matter how grade B and trivial, has inner significance; and all inner-world cinema, no matter how self-absorbed, has outer-world implications. Perhaps Jung's single greatest contribution to modern psychoanalytic discourse was his notion that the unconscious is always in compensatory relationship to the conscious self. The unconscious is trying to integrate that which consciousness most unhealthily avoids—particularly our profound traumas and self-deceptions. Dissociation is probably an archetypal emergency procedure that saves our lives when we are very young and exposed to the sometimes vicious, cruel, projected vagaries of our parental or primal guardians.[7] Back then, we often needed to split off and psychically bury these painful wounds or we would not have survived, so oppressed would we have become by their indigestible darkness within our undeveloped psychic fragility.

But such necessary emergency dissociations become habitual under the awesome dictatorship of the inner Guardians we assigned to keep them under lock and key.[8] They need to be pried loose and aerated if a life-threatening psychic septicemia is not to set in. This is the prying power of the horror film genre, for instance, where our worst terrors are reflexively constellated past our deep denials so as to be hopefully desensitized and digested.[9] Horror films, just like fairy tales, their genre ancestor, are a series of images of the primal ghouls, zombies, vampires, and other unimaginable uncanninesses[10] that abusively devoured our innocence as children. A good film can be a crucial revisiting and integration/individuation through our repressed and introjected shadow-psyche. Analysis and film are both potentially useful and straightforward psychic crowbars to demolish unhealthy barriers between the light and dark sides of our image life. Better to project and sort out this undifferentiated toxic mass onto an animated screen or the animated "screen" of a trained analyst than an unsuspecting spouse, or child, lover, co-worker, or another religion/culture.

• Film plays with paradox. Paradox is the secret core of film's being. Paradox is film's inherent magic. For film really is a static medium masquerading as a dynamic one. Actually, film is a series of image-stills racing by a light source. And so is the Soul. It is basically a static, eternal moment being raced by the light of our deliriously-distracted phenomenal world.

Great directors directly and deliberately play with this paradox in cinema image and Soul. Two examples come quickly to mind. In *Fargo* (1996), almost dead center in its running time, there is an awesome image of an early dawn parking lot after a fresh overnight snow fall. It is Zen-like in its pristine, frozen beauty. All narrative stops. All image stops. We are watching still life there in the silence with strangers in a vast cinema complex cavern. Then there is a little movement. And the scene is marred a bit by tire tracks across the snowy surface. Still awesome, just a bit marred by the inevitable intrusions of our imperfect world. But the memory and impact linger like a visit to a well-crafted Zen rock garden. The film then starts racing through its plot once again, but we remember that quiet snow still life. It gives us hopeful anchor in the often very dark revelations to be endured ahead.

Similarly, Pedro Almodovar etches a still life mandala almost dead center in his recent masterwork *Bad Education* (2004). Boys in a Roman Catholic prep school are in uniform doing undulating Spanish pushups as the over-weight, black-clad priest sadistically beats out the meter with his walking staff. It is almost a quadrilateral still life like the one in the Coen brothers' *Fargo*. And it catches our breath with its contemplative, unnerving, silent peek at the eternity of the Soul under the racing images of literal child-abuse and mayhem in the film.

Again, in both films, the images reveal the dark, almost evil, subplots of their narrative even as they point to a chastening, spirit-beauty and purity beyond. As with all great still lifes, we do not know whether to laugh, cry, or rage, so we settle for simple awe, hopefully a transformative awe that shares the Soul's love of integrative paradox.

> Something happens, you see it happening, you film it as it happens, the camera sees it and records it, and you look at it again afterwards. The thing itself may no longer be there, but you can still see it, the fact of its existence hasn't been lost.[11]

• Film is, most of all, the respectful teller of story and lover of mystery. Mystery is our most permanent condition. Psychology, particularly the hard-science edge of psychology, sometimes forgets this. The best cultural wisdom can do about the ultimate philosophical issues of existence—most urgently, the answers to our incessant questions about the meaning of our lives, our births, and our deaths—is to try and blend rational and irrational, left and right brain, into some form of organically-satisfying whole. This whole should make sense to the mind, as well as the heart, to the body, as well as the Soul. This is what story does best, for, at the end of the day, it is story told round the evening family meal that gives the deepest hint and insight into the Great Mystery that fuels our destiny. Film is arguably the most haunting and aesthetic evocation of this Big Story in our era.

Film is not a representation of the transcendent function[12] but a vehicle for individuation, for psycho-spiritual education, for educating the ego to recognize the transcendent function and the visions of the Self it relays and portrays. The Soul's crowbar, to extend the metaphor used above about tearing down the walls between the Opposites, is what Jung artfully named the Transcendent Function. It often arrives at the most desperate of moments when the agonizing tensions between the Opposites seem to have hardened into a merciless dryness unto death. The tension frequently breaks at this most crushing moment of despair, when an ego fiercely intent on maintaining consciousness no matter the cost fears it finally will be crushed into oblivion. Then, the moist mercy of the Transcendent Function rushes in with the right dream, the right symbol, the right felt-body sense[13] that gives the right illuminating meaning and horizon to the horror too long endured.

The resonant peace and relief of such moments are beyond simple description. They are the living embodiment of the Soul and its promise of meaning. They do not stay very long—we are too soon cast into the oppositional *dynamis* again—but they linger just long enough to leave us a strong impression of their solidity and connection to the ultimate nature of things somehow.

Yet film is not the Transcendent Function, but a vehicle to deliver its presence and action into our very midst—into the depth of our bodies and spirit if we let it in deep enough. Film is the sacrament, the container of process, while the Transcendent Function **is** the process, its enactor. It is important that they are not confused but seen as crucial allies as Jung so wisely observed:

> It must be remembered that the image and the statement are psychic processes which are different from the transcendental object; they do not posit it, they merely point to it (*Collected Works*, 11 § 558).

Such declarations perceive that the connection between film and psyche is not casual or coincidental. It is fundamental.

Two Crucial Recurrent Soul Images

A rguably, the most important concept in Jungian psychology is the Soul/Self concept. Arguably, the most important image of film is the image of the Soul. But how do you locate the Soul in image? How do you define Soul? How can you be sure your image and your definition are genuine and not just manufactured *post facto* to soothe aesthetic and theological taste?

The Soul stalks us, individually and collectively. It is merciless in its demand that we make meaning of our lives. It will haunt and hound until we lift the veils of repression, deceit, and avoidance, until we become accountable to the context and shape of our lives and acknowledge the numinous, non-egoistic ground of our being.

Every age has different patterns of depression and denial, different vehicles of avoidance and escape from the Soul and its merciless demands. In our late-patriarchal age, I see two massively recurrent images of the Soul in contemporary cinema—the Deep Feminine and the Child. It is the innocence of the child and the mercy of the deep feminine which apparently frighten us the most. And it is through these lenses that the soul seems to be stalking us into conscious accounting.

An elegant, vivid, recent example in popular cinema of reclaiming of lost innocence of the Child and the mercy of the Deep Feminine might illustrate. Taylor Hackford worked nearly a decade on his biopic *Ray* (2004) on the life and time of the rhythm-and-blues icon Ray Charles. He structured the film around a series of flashbacks to Charles' poor black sharecropper origins, a poverty that ultimately took his sight when he was quite young.

All through the film, Charles is shown having visionary panic attacks about seeing a tub of scalding wash water that killed his brother, a death he witnessed as a child in that sharecropper shantytown. We mutely, horrifically witness with him as his brother falls into the tub while Charles stands there paralyzed in horror. We stand there with him in abject shame as his mother keens with cataclysmic despair, holding her lifeless son's body and railing at Charles about why he didn't shout or scream so she could have raced out of the house to save the brother's life.

There is a silent hint in these flashback sequences that Ray Charles saw his soon on-setting blindness as a judgment from the gods for his tragic impotence. There is a continuing hint that he became addicted to heroin to sooth the watery terrors of his growing panics.

But eventually, paradoxically, at the pinnacle of his creative life, his addiction drives him into collapse and in-patient treatment. There, he courageously goes cold turkey. But once de-toxed, he stubbornly refuses the mandatory psychotherapy, even though he had been driven into treatment by a pending felony drug possession conviction if he did not cooperate fully with the psychiatric protocol. In the day room, where he is still in-patient confined, he is thrown into a panicky drowning in those terrifying inner waters until he has a vision of his long-dead mother—young, loving, and vibrant on their migrant shack stoop—telling him that she did not raise him, suffer with him into adulthood, to have him capitulate to a dehumanizing addiction. He feels her deep love and her freeing, harsh challenge. And just at that moment, his resonantly alive baby brother emerges smiling from the interior of their shotgun shack.

The salvaged and restored Lost Childhood Innocence through the guiding mediation of the Deep Feminine—there it is—in *Ray* and many contemporary films—over and over and over.

Mira Nair directed an homage to her family legacy, *Monsoon Wedding* (2001). It is a story about an Indian wedding where both local and American family members gather in India for a lavish, multi-day celebration. Well on into the narrative, there is a scene of the father of the bride standing in the midnight bedroom of his two daughters—the one to be wed and the adoptive daughter of his dead brother. We do not see him clearly at first. We see only these two radiant young women in quiet repose, bathed in the soft gossamer moonlight of silvery-sky, dressing gown, and bed linen. Between them is an open book of Tagore poems.

Then the father's voice: "You know, Pimmi [his wife], sometimes when I look at them I feel a love which I almost cannot bear." The camera pans right to his shadowed visage standing next to his raptly attentive wife. This is a man transformed by contact with the Deep Feminine—in him, in his daughters, in his wife, in his ancestry, in his country, in the infinite beauty of the lunar night. We didn't even like him much in his first opening scenes of the film—yelling and anxiously gyrating on his lawn in frustrated alarm at the chaotic wedding orchestrations of his hired wedding event contractor. He is harsh, aggressive, impudent—the quintessential Indian iteration of the universal, intrusive, patriarchal archetype. But here, we peer deeper, we see truer into the silent, vast sea of Soul and affect in him. We are skillfully led to challenge the patriarchal cartoon wherein we first imprisoned him. Mira Nair's film has taken us from solar light into lunar luminescence. The Goddess Soul is more in and among us—father/daughter, mother/son—than we might at first suspect. The cultural change is slow but relentless. She is coming.

The salvaged and restored lost childhood innocence through the guiding mediation of the Deep Feminine—there it is—in *Monsoon Wedding* and many contemporary films—over and over and over.

Cinema in our time speaks not to the conscious or the unconscious, but the in-between realm. It is a living, moving lexicon of image attempting to increase our literacy and interaction with transforming symbol. Film serves the *Anima Mundi*, the spirit of the world.[14] Film seeks to incarnate more and more Soul into our individual and collective worlds, Soul which sees the inherent unity, the one-worldness of things. Jeff Raff is a Jungian analyst who has been doing groundbreaking analytic work in the liminal interface between the human and the Divine.[15] He believes that there is a mutual probing and reaching out toward each other at the core of both human and Divine unconsciousness. He sees a process of co-evolution—that Divine needs human as much as human needs Divine and that the leaven of integrative consciousness is love, human/Divine love enacted at this liminal crossroads. If Raff's careful analysis of western alchemy is the proof text for his claim, then the alchemy of contemporary cinema is at ground zero in this dialogue.

Raff feels the intense multi-decade practice of active imagination (a technique Jung developed out of ancient sources to dialogue with animate unconscious entities and processes) and dream work in his clinical practice have confirmed direct access with these incarnating probes of the Numinous Other. Raff believes he and his patients have experienced immediate interactions with numinal, intermediary Others he calls Allies. These are real beings of the liminal realms who communicate in rich, full-text ways through often lustrous image and intense body-felt sensation. They are wisdom bearers as well as negotiators, imparting wisdom and negotiating further expansion of the numinous Other into our temporal world plane. They are imaginal diplomats seeking psychic treaties of evolving peace and connectedness in the service of the One, the *Unus Mundus*.

I believe film is one of the Allies' most alive arenas of inner-terrestrial encounter with our individuating psychic experience. Film is not just a potentially interactive phenomenon for individual transformation but collective differentiation toward the *Unus Mundus*, the one world of true Soul-in-the-world. The arts have always been the most sacred of precincts for this transformational alchemy, and film is one of its most sensorial and liturgically complete expressions for it involves the participation of the senses in the service of giving full, kinesthetic voice to the Other mediated through the living cells of image-transmission.

> The ally neither creates suffering nor avoids it. It suffers as we do, as we work together to unite and heal the wounds of the Divinity. God is not a perfectly happy Ruler who sends his [her] happy little angels to make us happy. Such a view is as revolting as it is common.[16]

Run Lola Run—A Case-Study into Cinematically-Mediated Soul

> It is rewarding to watch patiently the silent happenings in the soul.
> —C. G. Jung, *Collected Works,* 12 § 126

A central icon of the Soul is the individuation process. Here image is both process and image, a dynamic moving image. The Soul is, paradoxically, both condition and goal, a thing in itself and a thing yet to be revealed.

Run Lola Run (2002) captures this paradox as profoundly as any modern film. It may be seen, in historical retrospect, as a pivotal film in cinematic evolution. It constellates the individuating Soul not just in visual image but aural image as well with its almost shamanic, techno-beat soundtrack. Tom Tykwer, the director, is a genuine *auteur* in the full sense envisioned by the French New Wave theorists nearly a half century ago, for he not only scripted and directed the visual images, he also composed the ground-breaking soundtrack-of-images as well. A German, product of the profound confessional generations following the Nazi horror, Tykwer was a witness with all of us to the almost atoning fall of the Berlin Wall and the endless nights of techno-pop trance dancing by youth from both Germanies—youth night-seeking something deeper than mindless communism or capitalism, something more alive than the living death of ideology and consumption. Tykwer's soundtrack evokes this healing ritual-animism across the surface of Mother Earth's urbanized body. The film's opening credits begin with what feels like a direct evocation of an urban ritual gathering ending in a soccer ball kicked up into the heavens of the emerging film narrative.

The concept of the film is exquisitely succinct. Lola, a young adult still living at home, receives a call from her boyfriend Manni. Having drifted into work as a runner for a local drug lord, he has failed his initiation rite into middle Underworld management by inadvertently switching bags with a street vagrant on a subway, getting the vagrant's pottage, and losing the 50,000 Deutschemarks drop money. He calls Lola in a panic. Can she come up with the money in twenty minutes so he is not executed by the drug lord?

In ingenious visuals, we are invited into her inner world as she searches for a response to this crisis. She shrieks, an ancient harridan's shriek, the shriek of Medea over her dead children. The clock on the wall shatters. Chronos, chronological clock time, is stopped. She races through her imagistic palm pilot—one image keeps racing by on the spinning roulette wheel of fate-karma—dad, mom, friends, dad, dad.

She has it. The ancient incestuous solution still has her. She sets off on her twenty-minute run against impossible fate. She races out of her bedroom and down the stairs, suddenly animated stairs with a big snarling Cerebus-dog half way down. This is the ancient mythic descent—the *descensus*—into the unconscious. With the animation, the director leaves us no doubt.

Three times Lola makes the run. She dies at the end of the first attempt. Everything in her world dies in this first attempt. Her father dies to her. She catches him in the middle of his escapist love affair with a colleague bank executive. He denies her the money. He throws her out on the street after verbally lashing her with the hidden truth that she is the biological progeny of another man—not his child, not then and not now. He is leaving her mother, leaving her for a woman who "really" loves him and will bear him "real" children.

The incest wound is torn open. She is an orphan in the raw, urban despair of Berlin. Lola is paralyzed by the curb in her frozen, hollow, shocked grief. An old Crone comes up to her, "Are you all right, my Dear?"

Shocked back awake, Lola begins her run again. She, or maybe it is just the omniscient camera (we are never really sure), has an almost mediumistic insight into everyone she passes on the streets in her mad dash—menopausal baby abductors, thieves, a parade of nuns-judges, a bicycle thief, a depressed worker. We see their true selves now and the often tragic future of accident, dismemberment, and suffering death ahead. On and on she runs, across a public square labyrinth that is as eerily silent as the runes. With each breath, she almost prays, "Wait, Manni, Wait. . .Wait for me. . . . I'm coming. . . I'm almost there." But he can't. He makes desperate call after desperate call—to his grandmother, to friends. A blind crone hovers protectively outside his public phone booth. An advertisement spiral goes round and round behind him as the hands of the large public clock move relentlessly toward noon, the Solar Noon, Gary Cooper's archetypal High Noon.

Manni pulls out his hidden gun. He will rob the big discount store. There has to be enough there to cover his debt. Lola arrives too late. She haplessly joins the robbery in progress. She takes dark, unexpected pride in a new gun moll's toughness as she disarms a guard. She is now Bonnie to his Clyde. The ancient mythic relational drama—anima rescues animus; animus, anima. She escapes with Manni—the bagged, redemptive loot in hand. Lola is running again. Dinah Washington ironically fills the soundtrack: "What a Difference a Day Makes." But it is too late. A police cordon across both ends of the street. The surrendered money and hope. An accidentally discharged officer's gun. Lola crumbles, sinks down to the pavement, and dies there in an urban, postmodern hell.

The screen fades to black, then deep crimson. Manni and Lola are in a lover's bed. She is asking if her loves her, really loves her. It is an ancient discourse of lovers—full of doubt and hope—wary of the capricious gods, clinging to the only thing at hand, the warm body next to us, but knowing full well that even that body cannot die with us and answer our deepest questions of meaning, passion, destiny.

A red phone cord, then phone, fall like manna from above. It rings. It is Manni in trouble.

Lola's run two begins. She falls down the animated stairs and stumbles into her run again. This time she robs dad; she does not ask. This time Manni dies. Father/lover are asked for their sacrifice—not the daughter/lover. But, ultimately, it too, turns out bad. Fade to black, then red, more archetypal anima[us] pillow talk, this time not about love but about death.

Lola's run three begins. This time it all works out. She relies not on father, but self. She give up logos and finds eros, swaps calculation for intuition, gives up Father Time for Lady Luck. She enters Patriarchy's capitalistic casino, its inner aristocracy of control where the only Deep Feminine image is an elegant ancient woman (or is she an elegant Crone?) with her back turned to us and the whirling roulette wheel—round and round, *acta contra naturam*—acts against nature, as Lola shrieks again and cleans them out. She has it all shoved impromptu into a plastic bag.

Lola arrives on time. But she is ultimately unneeded. Manni has had to find his own inner resources of intuition and eros. He has had to confront and transcend his own inner violences and Mother Incest Wound. He has had to accept help from the Blind Crone and pass her mercy on to the street beggar self. He gets his own ill-gotten gain back to the Mob men. Lola waits, lonely, at the crossroads, turning, as in a Lakota Sioux sweat lodge, to slowly address all four directions before Manni arrives. They walk off quietly together into normal everyday time again. He asks offhandedly, "What is in the bag?" Fade to credits.

Same old time but also new time. This had been an initiatory sequence. The ego has died and been reborn. The youth has died. The adult woman emerges.

Joseph Henderson, drawing on the work of social anthropologists, suggests that deep initiatory experiences involve three rites:

Rites of Separation/Submission
Rites of Transition/Transformation
Rites of Immanence/Incorporation.[17]

The first rite of is one of pre-liminality. It is that distorted infantile time when we cling to our denials and repressions, awash in our childlike, unconscious ennui. It is a day at the shopping mall and all its consumerist lies. It is all Jack La Lane and pre-fall Martha Stewart. It is the Fox News Network world.

Then, by a sudden and abrasive twist of fate, we are violently thrown into our vulnerable mortality and utterly naked exposure to the storms and vicissitudes of the cosmos—liminality. Here we are thrown into Alice's Wonderland where all the norms we borrowed from our Patriarchal culture to control those cosmic savageries are exposed for the frail contrivances that they really are. Up is down, left is right, Manni is Lola, daughter is father, youth is Crone, seeing is blindness, High Noon is Deep Midnight, sun is moon.

Ego is thrown on the mercy of the psyche and must surrender to new humble intuitions and body-whispered wisdoms it has too long ignored. If it is earnest and sincere enough it just might survive this dark night of the soul transformed into a broader new dawn than ever before experienced and treated to a more calm, grounded expanse of beauty-and-Soul presence than ever before comprehensible. This is the post-liminal return, a return that all too quickly reverts to old patterns and ways of being but with a deep cellular memory of that different space and time that will survive a lifetime and beyond. That is Lola's initiatory accomplishment—it is her long-distance runner's soulful victory. There in the hush of that crossroads, rotating quietly through all the ancient four directions of the Soul's compass, there at precisely that moment of seeing Manni and quietly walking back home—there, then she is Returned, the same but somehow ineffably changed, different forever.

The Soul both wants to move and it wants absolute stasis. In *Run Lola Run* both these polar tensions find voice.

Everyone who becomes conscious of even a fraction of his [sic]
unconscious gets outside his own time and social stratum into a
kind of solitude. C. G. Jung, *Collected Works*, 14 § 258.

The Crone and the Soul: The Triplets of Bellevue

Cinema is an old whore, like circus and variety, who knows how
to give many kinds of pleasure. Besides, you can't teach old fleas
new dogs.[18]

F ilm images favor the poor, the impoverished, the orphan, the Lost
Child. *The Triplets of Bellevue* (2003) describes how the ancient
crones are still alive in the impoverished bowels of our cities of despair
seeking to replenish our lost reserves of soulful compassion and mercy
for the poor, lost, orphan children of the inner and outer psyche.
Sylvain Chomet's animated story tells of a dogged grandmother's efforts
to bring her orphaned grandson back to life after the trauma of losing
his parents (for reasons never fully explained but poignantly implied).
She tries everything—toys, activities, a dog—nothing avails until she
notices his taking to a bicycle. Imaginatively and creatively grasping,
as Crones are wont to do, at any slender thread thrown up by fate, she
becomes his road-cycling coach. She enters him in what looks look a
Tour de France event. Though he slogs far, far away in the very back of
the field, he nonetheless slogs on. Silent—but slogging. He is silent
and overwhelmed throughout the entire film. But slog away he
faithfully does, that is, until he is snatched from the race by Mafia
guys in a sinister van.

I won't trouble you with the incredible details of how our invincible
Crone impounds a recreational pedal boat to follow across the seas the
giant freighter carting away her beloved grandson. But I do want to
have you join me as we see her peddling into the harbor of Bellevue—
a very thin analogy to New York City and our post-911 crisis. She and
her faithful dog find no food, friends, or fellowship in this bustling,
manic place whose Chronos (clock-time) pace hides its homeless Kairos
(soul-time) sorrows. Darkness falls and the starving pair hovers under
a bridge abutment around a fire she has scratched up from the earth.
A ship glides by and sounds it harbor horn—wooonnnggg,
wooonnnnggggg. She likes the sound. She picks up a bent Chronos
bicycle wheel, sights it twisted edges. Then she picks up two sticks

and mimics the sound—woooonnnnnk, wooooonnnnnnkkkkk. She begins a little rhythm. Soon a nice, breezy spoke-reggae is whirling magically from the now-transformed Kairos wheel.

Shadowy figures are drawn to the light and the music. Big, dark feet begin to tap. The camera rises up slowly to see the visages of three, tall, lithe ancient Crones. They begin to snap their fingers and intone. It is the harmony of the reggae gods. It is crone street doo-wop, and we are transported. There in the bowels of our feckless postmodern urban hells, crones still have the courage and body to sing and boogey joyously. That is what initiated people do for lost cities and cultures. That is what I hope they are doing for us as we struggle to find our way to Kairos, divine time, the pure heart of love and peace in our sometimes very dark times.

The Crone is the initiating mentor. She offers us an opportunity for a redemptive martyrdom. She ask us to let our self-and-other contempt die. She asks us to convert our contempt into wonder, awe[19] . . . into song and fire under a lonely inner city bridge. She is our collective therapist. She contains our contempt. She fixes her compassionate fierce gaze right on our contempt and melts it down into a redemptive, moist sorrow. This is her alchemy of healing witness and therapeutic presence.

Initiation, Her initiation, offers syn-thesis, [20] something more than just uniting the twin poles of the opposites (e.g., life and death, masculine and feminine). Initiation offers the potential hopeful visitation of the *tertiam non datur,* the third unseen, the Crone.

But it is clear that the coming world is Her world not His. I just saw *Batman Begins* (2005), a nice, dark-tinged tale. But it is His tale. It is a man fighting Patriarchally-generated evil with violent patriarchal tools of death and destruction. She fights differently. She knows how to play dirty but in a soul-moist way. Patriarchy is all dry and dead. The new World will be Her world, Her gift of Soul, if we survive. Can we hold on to Her compassionate, cinematic visitations in recent years and not convert it back to our old defensive rages and terrors, both personally and culturally? The Gods are eagerly awaiting our reply.

NOTES

1. Jeffrey M. Masson, *The Assault on Truth - Freud's Suppression of the Seduction Theory* (New York: HarperPerennial, 1992).

2. Some of these ideas are not new—see Patricia Berry, "Image in Motion," in Christopher Hauke and Ian Alister, eds., *Jung and Film: Post-Jungian Takes on the Moving Image* (London: Brunner-Routledge, 2001), 70-71.

3. Michael Baigent and Robert Leigh, *The Temple and the Lodge* (London: Arcade, 1991), 227.

4. Ann E. Kaplan, ed., *Psychoanalysis and Cinema* (London: Routledge, 1990).

5. Edward Edinger, *Ego and Archetype* (New York: Penguin, 1972).

6. Robert Sardello, *Facing the World with Soul* (New York: Perennial, 1994).

7. Donald Kalsched, *The Inner World of Trauma: Archetypal Defenses of the Personal Spirit* (London: Routledge, 1996).

8. *Ibid.*

9. Barbara Creed, *The Monstrous Feminine: Film Feminism and Psychoanalysis* (New York: Routledge, 1993).

10. *Unheimlick* as S. Freud referred to it in "The 'Uncanny,'" in the *Standard Edition* 17 (London: Hogarth Press, 1959).

11. Wim Wenders, in Robert Craig, *The Art of Seeing Rescues the Existence of Things: Notes on the Wenders Road Films and Henri Bergson's Creative Evolution (Part 2).* (http://www.horschamp.qc.ca/ew_offscreen/artofseeing2.html, 2002).

12. Hauke & Alister, *Jung and Film*, 208-225.

13. Eugene Gendlin, *Focusing* (New York: Bantam, 1982).

14. Sardello, *Facing.*

15. Jeffrey Raff and Linda Bonnington Vocatura, *Healing the Wounded God: Finding Your Personal Guide on Your Way to Individuation and Beyond* (York Beach: Nicolas-Haye, 2002) and Jeffrey Raff, *Jung and the Alchemical Imagination* (York Beach: Nicolas-Haye, 2000).

16. *Ibid.*, 93.

17. Joseph Henderson, *Thresholds of Initiation* (Middlebury: Wesleyan University Press, 1967).

18. Federico Fellini, http://www.brainyquote.com/quotes/authors/f/federico_fellini.html, 2005.

19. Rudolf Otto, *The Idea of the Holy* (Oxford: Oxford University Press, 1923).

20. Luigi Zoja and Donald Williams, eds., *Jungian Reflections on September 11* (Einsiedeln: Daimon-Verlag, 2002), 36.

THE FEMININE PRINCIPLE IN FILM:
REFLECTIONS ON FILM AND ITS RELATION TO THE HUMAN PSYCHE

INGELA ROMARE

Introduction

L et me briefly introduce myself. I have been a film director for almost thirty-five years. I received my training first at the Swedish Filminstitute's Filmschool, where Ingmar Bergman was the inspector, during 1965-1968. I was accepted as the first and at that time only woman. I mainly went to film school so that I could become a fiction film director, but for different reasons I have ended up dedicating most of my work to documentary films instead.

For several years I travelled all over the world and made about fifty documentary films together with my former husband. We went to Vietnam during the war, and we wandered in the jungles of Mocambique and Guinea Bissau, devoting most of our film work to describing the liberation struggles in the world.

Ingela Romare is a Jungian analyst (IAAP) trained at the C.G. Jung Institute in Zürich, who has had a private practice in Malmö, Sweden since 1992. She is also a film director trained at the SwedishFilminstitute's Filmschool, and has made about fifty documentary films about political, social, and existential questions. Her film *On the Dignity of the Human Soul* explores how the imagination helped a man survive torture and imprisonment. Her latest work is a trilogy about *Faith, Hope, and Love*.

In 1975 there was peace in Vietnam. There was peace in the former colonies of Portugal. That was also the time that my husband and I divorced. Two things happened for me in film making then: I took up the camera myself. Earlier my husband had held the camera, I the tape recorder. Now I started to make my images myself. The second thing that happened was that instead of directing the camera outwards towards the conflicts of the world, I now also directed it inwards towards what happened within the human psyche.

I made a film titled *Courage to Live,* which was a film about the last five months in life of a young woman named Pia and our meetings during that time. This film, among other things, led me to the C.G. Jung Institute in Zürich. I realized while working on the film, and afterwards when I discussed the film with the audience, how interested I was not only in film making but also in *meetings* with people around existential questions.

For one and a half years I was present at each showing of the film and invited those in the audience that were interested to join in a conversation about the thoughts and feelings that arose within them in response to the film. During this time I became especially interested both in the ethics and the aesthetics of filmmaking. I was by necessity confronted with questions like:

How is it possible to direct the camera towards a dying person without exploiting the situation?

How is it possible not just to talk *about* things but create a situation where people are moved on a deeper level and can share their experiences?

How is it possible to create a deeper dialogue around the questions of life and death instead of just making a "story"?

During my investigations of the film medium which took place both on the practical and the theoretical level, I was brought closer and closer to the questions: *Is there a feminine way of making film? How does the feminine principle manifest itself in film creating?*

Between 1987-1997 I studied Jungian psychology at the C.G. Jung Institute in Zürich. When I first went to Zürich I was struck by the subtle similarities that exist between film making and analysis, between art and Jungian psychology, between the symbol and the "film image."

·I at first thought I had wandered from one world into another new one and was a stranger in it. But I realized that there were no harsh borders between them—at least not in the way I looked upon film making—but rather there were many inspiring and challenging connections.

Now, almost eighteen years later, having the experience of being both an artist and a Jungian analyst, I want to try to discover the points where art and Jungian psychology touch each other. I want to focus on the perspectives where a film as a work of art can have a deeper therapeutic function. Maybe by doing so I can also throw some light on the process of analysis being regarded as an art.

What then is Art?

So how do we grip the essence of art? What is it actually? I will try to discover something. Without capturing the flying bird in the cage. Perhaps art could be described like this: *A way to search for and try to reveal—to yourself and your fellow-beings—something about the very conditions of human existence.*

That would mean that art is one way for us to get to know about reality—outer and inner. Science would be another. What science is doing is working with facts that can be scientifically proved. What art is doing is playing—playing with words, with images, with sounds, with things—taking us into a symbolic understanding of the world, a symbolic *relation* to the world. That means that we can approach and understand the world—and ourselves—in two ways, the scientific way and the symbolic way. Which to choose…? I think man has to walk on two legs. It gives him a beautiful opportunity to move.

I turn around and listen to other artists. This is what Andrei Tarkovsky, the Russian film director, says about art in his book *Sculpting in Time*:

> An artistic discovery occurs each time as a new and unique image of the world. It appears as a revelation, as a momentary, passionate wish to grasp intuitively and at a stroke all the laws of this world — its beauty and ugliness, its compassion and cruelty, its infinity and its limitations.
>
> Through the image is sustained an awareness of the infinite: the eternal within the finite, the spiritual within matter, the limitless given form.

If I translate these lines by Tarkovsky into Jungian language, it would mean that art is trying to find out about and mirror the archetypes.

I turn to another artist—Leo T. Hurwitz, one of the great documentary film directors in the United States, a pioneer and one of the great artists among film makers. I have made a film about him called *On Time, Art, Love and Trees — a meeting with Leo T. Hurwitz.* In this film I asked him, "What is the very essence of art?" and this is his answer:

> I have done a lot of thinking about that. And a lot of trying to condense it into something simple and not mysterious and not mystical, although the creation of art and the response to art *is* a mysterious phenomenon on a certain level, it's no doubt about that. But the function of art and what art is is not so mysterious I think. At least it can be spoken of.
>
> I think fundamentally what it is — whether you are dealing with a painting, a poem, a novel, a movie, a play — you are dealing with *finding a form to hold experience.* Experience in itself is an ever nascent thing, it flows and it disappears. It's held partially by memory, but much of it disappears and it has very complex interactions. By experience I don't mean any narrow aspect of experience, because experience is a very wide thing. It moves from dream and nightmare to that we are sitting here with a cup of coffee and talking. There are whole ranges of the stuff of experience. And fantasy is of course one of them!

What Leo Hurwitz says is that on one level the creation of art and the response to art is a mysterious phenomenon, not accessible to our rational descriptions. On another level it *is* possible to talk about it, to talk about what art is and about its function.

I think it's exactly the same thing with analysis. To some extent we *can* talk about it, its character, and its function. At the same time we have to be conscious about—and respect! —its mysterious nature. This is the place where Jungian psychology comes close to art and has its unique strength. I think we must be brave enough to defend this place from invasion from our rational thinking. To keep the paradox… To move gently on two legs…

"What art is dealing with is *to find a form to hold experience,*" Leo Hurwitz says. And what would be the purpose of holding experience by giving it form? It gives us a possibility to *share* it — even over time and distance—which in turn opens up the possibility for someone else to mirror his or her experience in ours. And in the moment those experiences given form in a work of art have reached archetypal depths, the spectator too is given the opportunity of going to those depths. We are given the opportunity of getting to know something more about ourselves, about unknown life, and about our common humanness. This is what I would call the *mirror function* of art.

On Film as a Unique Form of Art

Film as a medium is very young, just about one hundred years old. When the very first moving images were shown by the brothers Lumière in the Grand Café de Paris in 1895, the director of Folies-Bergères at once offered 50.000 Francs for the exploitation rights to this new medium. He immediately saw the commercial potentiality that was inherent in it.

Since then film has lived its life in the tension between being on the one hand, a commercial, industrial product (where the most important aim is to bring in money) and, on the other hand, being a very rich, and to some extent yet unexplored, form of art.

Film is a very powerful medium, one of the most powerful there is. Why is it so? Let's look at that very first showing of film, of moving pictures in 1895. Different short sequences were shown with titles like "The child having breakfast" and "The workers leaving the factory," sequences about eighteen seconds long. One sequence was called "The train arriving at the station" and showed an engine with wagons arriving at a railway station in Paris. It has been said that people in the audience became very frightened. They took shelter behind the chairs; they ran out of the room.

We may laugh today because we are so used to moving pictures. We may laugh at the first movie-watchers' naiveness, we may laugh at their believing that the train could hurt them, could run over them. But I think that we should reflect a little bit about the reason why they reacted as they did. The significance of their reaction was that this new medium—moving pictures—gave such an impression of reality that it could hardly be separated from it.

This is one of the reasons that the film medium is so strong. I would like to add here that I often wish that we still had some of this same immediate reaction towards the film medium—and to all mass media—that people had in the beginning. I wish that we could still feel a sense of danger and an urgent need to protect ourselves because I think that we many, many times are run over in a very destructive way by the pictures—if not our bodies—at least our souls. That might be even more dangerous, as we often are not aware of it. There is no obvious blood around.

Another reason why this medium is so powerful is that it potentially is a very intricate system of manipulation. A film is a very complicated combination of images and sound, images with images, and sound with sound. There are many choices made on different levels before the film reaches the audience. This is inherent in the medium. This is necessarily so. But what gives the medium its power is that it is not possible for the spectator to see what most of these choices are. They enter him, so to say, on the unconscious level.

What we mostly see and talk about is what happens on the conscious level in a film or in a mass media sequence, on the content level or the level of action. We are much too unaware about what is there below the surface—in the form itself or on the level of telling. Most of the objects for the camera—people, animals, things, events— can be looked at and described in two quite opposite ways. Either they are seen with care and respect, or they are used and exploited for some other purpose. The attitude of the film maker and how it influences the film lies on a level that most of the time remains unconscious for the audience but which nevertheless is strongly transferred to it.

This is an area which I think deserves much attention. How will it affect our psyche in the long run, that we are being exposed, day in and day out, to images and sounds against which we are not aware enough to defend ourselves?

And Now to the Anglo-Saxon Dramaturgy

Before I discuss the feminine principle in film, I would like to describe what is called the "Anglo-Saxon Dramaturgy," a particular way of telling a story which was introduced about thirty years ago in Sweden. Sometimes it is also called the Aristotelian Dramaturgy, borrowing its name from the Greek philosopher, Aristotle. It started among a small group of film makers and script writers, but later spread like an epidemic to all the institutions of mass media, including television and journalism institutes, so that practically everyone who worked actively with the mass media participated in courses about it. Later, that was not enough. Even the chiefs, the decision makers, and the administrators of mass media institutions had to know about it.

So what was it about? Very briefly, it is a way of making a film, telling a story, which is common in the Hollywood tradition and which can be described like this: We have a *main conflict*. The conflict is the starting point of the action. It is introduced in the first scene and is then presented in more detail, deepened, and accelerated until a *climax* occurs, where the conflict is resolved and the story winds down and ends.

The action, built on a conflict, is driven forward in a *logical chain of events* and a *linear progressive time.* The spectator is bound in eager expectation which keeps him asking the question: What will happen? What will happen? How will it end—this conflict? The whole expectation is built on *the movement forward,* forward towards the goal which is the conflict resolution, and then the story is "over." One sequence leads to the next which leads to the next. Everything that doesn't immediately and logically belong to the main conflict and the movement forward has to be removed. Everything that can build up the excitement about the conflict has to be included.

With this model there are a whole arsenal of tricks and ways of telling to *catch* the spectator, take him or her to where you want, get him to think, feel, and experience what *you* want him to think, feel, and experience.

I have to confess that in the beginning this was very stimulating to learn about. We film directors acquired a language for what we did and did not do. There were efficient and goal-oriented tools we used when we made a film that we wanted to be successful.

But what is also involved in this dramaturgy is of course the *power* of language. This is not a way of creating a dialogue with the spectator or an opening for a relation with him. This model of building a film very easily results in the opposite. Added to the power I as a film maker or mass media person already by necessity have, I now also have a whole arsenal of deliberate *tools of manipulation* to catch and bind the audience. And this is on a level which to a great degree is unconscious for the audience.

What is most obvious with this dramatic structure and the consequences of it within the mass media world is the absence of the *meeting*, the absence of the *space in between*, the absence of the *respect for "the other."*

The Feminine Principle and The Feminine Principle in Film

Now I would like to say something about the feminine principle. And, when I talk about the feminine principle, I also must say something about the masculine principle. I do not have the space here to go into long definitions of each concept, so I will just give you some words that I associate with each one. The masculine principle I associate with *efficiency, goal orientation, moving forward (towards a goal), analysis, Logos.*

The feminine principle I associate with *holding, carrying, nourishing, creating space, synthesis, Eros,* and, above all, *relating* — inwards and outwards—towards the psyche and towards your fellow-beings.

I mentioned in the beginning that I was interested in the question of whether there was something one could call a feminine way of film making.

For some years I was chairwoman of the Women Film Directors' Association in Sweden. This was in the late 70's, long before I went to the C.G. Jung Institute. It turned out that resistance to the more and more prevalent and efficient Anglo-Saxon dramaturgy slowly grew and was first formulated among women.

It started with a feeling... We women film makers felt more and more closed in and pressed in. There was something that did not get its space—its room—its time in this structure where everything had to be better and better, faster and faster, and more and more efficient.

At that time we invited a Danish woman author and dramaturgist, Ulla Ryum, to give a seminar around the question "Is there a feminine dramaturgy?" There were three overbooked seminars. And what did she say? She said that if we wanted to do something other than merely tell "a story" in an efficient way with conflict acceleration, conflict solution, and conclusion, then we had better look out! We had to find another *movement!*

She used a very special word, which does not really exist either in Swedish or in Danish, "*på tvärran.*" It indicates both that you oppose the conventional, the expected way of moving—forwards towards a goal—and also that you move laterally, in the direction of your fellow-beings.

At that time I was working on my film *Courage to Live,* mentioned earlier, which is about the last five months in the life of a young woman named Pia. I was stuck. I couldn't find my way through it. I hadn't found the adequate structure for the film. In front of me on the editing table I had just a "story," which I was trying to make efficient.

But it was not a "story" that I wanted to make. It was not a conflict with an acceleration, a climax, and an end. I wanted to do something else. At the same time as I told about Pia's last five months in life, I wanted to raise questions in the film, questions that touch all of us. Questions about how we *relate* to life, how we *relate* to death, how we *relate* to time.

I went home and I thought about what kind of different movement I could find. What could be behind this expression that Ulla Ryum had used, "*på tvärran*"? How would I apply it in this very case?

I realized that it had something to do with time, with the *time construction of the film.* So, what other construction of time is there if you don't want to use a linear, causal one which leads towards a goal?

I think there *is* another kind of time, which moves in a circle. It starts at one point and then slowly turns around this point. Or it starts in the periphery and moves inwards in the searching for a kernel. A conception of time that allows a telling that rather than putting the question "what will happen, what will happen?" quietly wonders how is it — *really?*" A time that gives space for searching and finding out about the questions of man's existence in this world. A time that allows a movement towards the archetypes.

These thoughts led me intuitively to include a sequence at the beginning of the film which I hadn't used so far. It was one that I had filmed intuitively, but I hadn't found a place for it, so I had put it aside on a shelf. The sequence is a three-minute-long image, unbroken, non-edited, of a sunset in Greece, with mountains in the background, and the sea in the foreground. The young woman, Pia, was born of Greek parents and was buried in her mother's home village in Greece. Now the film opened up for me.

Time…What is it that happens in the relation between the image and the spectator when time comes into the picture? After about three seconds we have taken in, apprehended, the content of the image. We have water, we have mountains, we have a sun which is setting behind the mountains. We have a sunset.

If we keep this image for ten seconds then we have *quite a long* image of a sunset. If we then keep it for twenty seconds we have a *very long* image of a sunset. Maybe we get anxious. What kind of film is this? We have now seen this image, give us a new one! We know it is a sunset. Doesn't she know how to edit?

After about thirty seconds, maybe our worry gets worse. But maybe it might also be that our eye starts moving in the picture, that we see that there are more things to discover, the movement in the water, the changes in the light.

And when the image stays on the screen even longer — one minute, two minutes — then there may be something more happening. It is not just an image of a sunset, but also an image of time. And in that time there is created *a space*, a room, for us as spectators to stay in, to be in. There is a possible relationship created between the film and us, a relation to sunsets, to our own memory of sunsets, to ourselves. Having started in this way, creating a space for a possible relationship, the film opened up for me and was possible to complete.

Is this now a feminine film language? This other way to relate to time and space and goal orientation? A tendency rather to ask questions than to present answers and conclusions? A wish to create relationships and to surrender power? A wish to give respect to "the other"? A wish to create a movement towards the archetypal structure of the psyche?

Today I am prepared to say "yes" to this question, I would describe it so, that there is an attitude, where the feminine principle is at hand. At that time in Sweden in the late 70's it became a question of sex, of men and women film makers, and there was a hard and fruitless debate around those things. I then preferred not to talk about it in terms of feminine or masculine but more in terms of the power play in film language. But after having studied Jungian psychology, I am more ready to talk about it again in terms of the feminine principle, the feminine principle in film making.

We live in a world today where most people get as many impressions from mass media images as from life, if not more. I think that we need a much deeper understanding and awareness about what is happening in this field. It highly affects our psyches.

What we need is above all a *balance,* a balance between the masculine and the feminine principle. We need a balance to safeguard our bodies, to safeguard our minds, to safeguard our souls. I say it as a woman, as a film maker, and as a Jungian analyst.

We have reached up to the moon — what a goal! What efficiency! But how do we *relate* to nature — around us and within us...?

WHAT MAKES MOVIES WORK: UNCONSCIOUS PROCESSES AND THE MOVIE-MAKERS' CRAFT

CHRISTOPHER HAUKE

T his paper is a small part of my work-in-progress on a book of the same title which is to occupy the next two years of my life. This writing and researching, however, will have to fit around a schedule that includes completing a screenplay in collaboration with someone else — the actor, in fact, who will take the lead role when it comes to actual production, which I also plan to complete during the same period. In addition I have made a documentary called *On The Money* — about money, creativity, and the feminine and what flows where and how — which is already in pilot form and will now need pitching to producers for Channel 4 in the U.K. And I say all this not to convince you I am busy or talented — God forbid — or short on sleep (that part is true) but to put my ideas and writing in context. I am no longer an armchair viewer of movies.

Christopher Hauke is a Jungian analyst in private practice in Central London and Lecturer at the University of London, Goldsmiths College. His publications for Routledge include *Jung and the Postmodern: The Interpretation of Realities*, *Jung and Film: Post-Jungian Takes on the Moving Image* (co-editor), and his latest book *Human Being Human: Culture and the Soul*, due out this fall, 2005. Chris is now working on a new documentary film, a screenplay, and a new book called *What Makes Movies Work? Unconscious Processes and the Movie-Makers' Craft*.

Affordable pro-quality digital video-cameras, professional editing software, helpful books, and larger, cheaper hard-drives all make the technical side of movie-making within the reach of anyone who, like me, is happy to keep driving a fourteen-year-old car (a Volvo station-wagon, naturally) to afford it.

I realized a while back that if I was to start writing about what happens to any one of us on the movie-making team — whether writer, director, actor, cinematographer, production designer, gaffer, or caterer — I was going to have to go hands on. Making movies myself not only helps me to talk with filmmakers far more professional than I am, and share a language and discover what they do and what they think, it also gives me a taste of some of the experiences that arise.

Like, for example, when I was filming my forty-five minute feature *Losing Dad* in New York and the two boys (my twin sons aged twelve at the time) were in Central Park. Two balloons, a red one and a green one, were floating loose, and one boy chased the green balloon, kicking it back in the air until it drifted off, while the red balloon stayed in a tree and refused to come down. I knew the scene would be good for the point in the story when we see the boys alone and sad they have failed to find their Dad. Old films like *Le Ballon Rouge* came to mind with its scenes of a boy of the same age. And, once I began editing, looking at the other footage I had shot, there were several shots of the boys walking down a New York street with balloons tethered and floating above them. All of these were "unintentional" shots when it came to the balloons. Finding them, piecing them in the right emotional spaces through the editing, and then adding evocative music, all brought out meaning for this aspect of the story.

I felt I was following the great film editor Walter Murch's recommendation that editing decisions are best made with these proportions of intent in mind: 51% Emotion, 25% Story, 10% Rhythm, and the rest just about the reality of the eye tracking in three-dimensional space — the reverse of the hierarchy they teach you in film-school, apparently.

But back to this paper. I have several assumptions I make and even more questions I ask in my investigations. First I am assuming that unconscious processes can be found in a highly structured art form like movie making, just as they can be found in the novel or painting. But when it comes to creating the movie, just what is the relationship between successful planning and the successfully unplanned, between conscious intentions and the "happy accident"? In such an expensive, time-consuming, over-populated enterprise, just how do artists, technicians, directors, and producers manage to incorporate new creations stemming from "intuition" or "happy accidents," which may often involve the sacrificing of earlier decisions? For instance, in a recent talk the director/writer Anthony Minghella spoke of how he had labored over the writing of the movie *Truly, Madly, Deeply*, and when it came to production, he rehearsed one scene with two actors for three days. On the day of filming it suddenly struck him to tell the actors to play the whole scene without any of the words. They were dumbfounded, they had sweated over those words and now they were all being taken away. But they filmed the scene with only the woman playing the piano and the man playing the cello, and not a word was said. This unplanned, inspired idea gives us one of the most powerful moments in the movie.

Many involved in the industry confirm how great creativity is more likely the better planned and secure the movie production is. I say more later about the comparison with psychotherapy where structure and boundaries also work to enable unconscious contents to arise, to be seen, and to be accepted and included.

But when it comes to movies, this begs the question of who are the major *contributors* to this spontaneous creativity? Actors? Writers? Director? Focus puller? Catering? Drivers? (The answer, many have told me, is it could be any one of them). But after this, w*ho decides* on the fate of unconscious and unanticipated contributions? Is it a high level (studio/producer) decision, or can it get by and get accepted at the actor/director level as part of the overall vision?

Last, but not least, when it comes to the psychology of all this, what is the *source* of these contributions stemming from the unconscious? Is it individual genius — the *Auteur* — or is there a collective, more *archetypal process at work* that supercedes any single individual and expresses something all can recognize but none could have dreamed up on their own?

No one, no writer, director, actor, or cinematographer can claim it to be "their" movie like the author of a novel or a painter can claim sole creator rights over their work (leaving aside the "audience creating the work" argument for the moment). Movies are such a collaborative art form the psychology of creativity in this case must involve shared processes. These collective events might be as unhelpful as a complex, or they might be as deep and rich as the expression of an archetype which all may be moved by. Whatever we say — and I refer to Jung's ideas on the "author" of a creative work in a moment — movies are a highly collective activity, thus offering material for a psychology that has an understanding of both collective and individual processes as a distinguishing feature — the psychology of C.G. Jung.

Structure and Enabling the Unconscious

In a recent interview for BBC radio, the director Michael Apted spoke enthusiastically of those who notice aspects of his movies which he had not consciously intended. Personally, he says, "part of my life is carefully examined in therapy" and adds that, of course, "a lot of art is unconscious." Therefore we should not be surprised when movie-making produces elements of which the makers were unaware at the time. He adds:

> a movie is such a collaborative, business-like job....not a pure art
> of being confronted with a blank sheet of paper in a quiet room
> whether you are writing words or music, there's something very
> rough and tumble about doing movies ......and it's wonderful
> when people come in and point these things out to you. I so
> *don't* mind it — I like it! It takes other people to point things out
> to you.[1]

In the book of which this paper forms a part, I intend to "point things out." Movie-making generally involves great amounts of time spent in preparation, development, and conscious decision-making, which results in plans, designs, budgets to fit these, and an overall vision that is then communicated to all involved.

Making a movie, as everyone knows, rarely proceeds "according to plan." More often than not, plans change, compromises are made (often over where cash will be spent or saved in the implication of creative ideas), and the movie staggers forward to post-production, publicity, premiere, and distribution. Throughout the planning and the alteration of plans, everyone tends to maintain the view that all these creative and commercial decisions are made in full conscious awareness.

However, great movies achieve results through many unplanned events. Such movies, of course, do not throw all conscious rationality to the wind, but achieve a greatness which derives from the unanticipated aspects that conscious planning seeks to avoid. These *unconscious* aspects to movie-making, when recognized and incorporated, are often the difference that makes a movie really *work* — rather than ending up as just another "piece of work."

There is a fear of this in the expensive business of film-making. As the cinematographer (director of photography or DP) Gordon Willis said of his experience filming *The Godfather* for Francis Ford Coppola,

> I like to lay a thing out and make it work, with discipline. Francis's attitude is more like, "I'll set my clothes on fire — if I can make it to the other side of the room it'll be spectacular." You can't shoot a whole movie hoping for happy accidents. What you get is one big accident.[2]

In psychology we avoid terms like "happy accidents" — and indeed, I will address the language the movie-makers prefer shortly, but what do *we*, as analytical psychologists, mean by "unconscious factors and processes"?

What do we mean by "unconscious factors and processes"?

When it comes to movies, a great deal has been written about the unconscious processes in the minds of the audience — how movies are affecting them. As I have said, my interests lie on the other side of the camera, with the film-makers themselves.

While some unconscious factors in creative people indeed derive from their personal circumstances (and I will pick up on Jung's views on this aspect of creativity shortly), this perspective is so often overworked it falls into cliché. My preferred angle is to discover disjunctions and unintended results that artists and technicians then incorporate into their work. The aim is to show how these unconscious elements work in cooperation with those that are consciously planned; it is *not* my purpose to claim an understanding of the source of the unconscious elements in a personal, biographical, cause-and-effect fashion. But it *is* my conjecture that in many cases, artistic creativity stemming from collective unconscious processes reaches the audience at a deep level, and that it derives from the film-makers' ability to act as conduits of contents and themes of universal significance that lie outside their own personal, conscious awareness and intention.

Neither do unconscious contributions to the creative process differ from conscious ones in a simple 'rational' versus 'emotional' split. A moment's reflection tells us how rational thinking always has an emotional element charging it, and so the division of 'head and heart' is artificial. I am drawn to C.G. Jung's idea there are two kinds of thinking: not only *directed*, rational thought that seeks its aim, follows a linear form, and uses much psychic energy, but also *undirected thinking*, or fantasy, which is goal-less, free-flowing, uses little energy, and can produce surprising and unanticipated results — especially in film-making. Clearly much human activity benefits from both types of thinking, but artistic activity of all sorts cannot work without the full cooperation of both kinds.

When it comes to making movies, it would be simplistic to say some contributors are working purely rationally (producers, accountants, technicians), while others (actors, writers, directors) are operating with fantasy thinking all the time. Clearly all contributors are using both approaches in varying proportion — imagining solutions and subjecting them to rational scrutiny. Practical applications often start with input supplied by the unconscious. And not only the arts, but the history of science is also full of rational conclusions that were arrived at via irrational means, such as through dream images, as in the famous case of Kekule's discovery of the ring structure of the benzene molecule. Apparently both Einstein and the physicist David Bohm 'felt' mathematical answers to the problems they were struggling with in vague but informative small muscular movements in their bodies.[3] And of course it was Picasso who said: *"Je ne cherche pas: je trouve."*[4]

In addition to individual unconscious effects, it may also be useful to analyze collective unconscious phenomena for their resonance and impact on the creative process. The archetypal theory of C.G. Jung proves fruitful in this aspect, and it is obvious how this has informed Joseph Campbell's work on universal myths which in turn influenced writers and directors of many movies from the *Star Wars* series to *Mad Max*. It is my conjecture that artistic creativity stemming from collective unconscious processes is capable of reaching the audience at a deep level, and that it derives from film-makers' ability to act as conduits of contents and themes of universal significance that lie outside their conscious awareness and intention.

Joseph Campbell's *The Hero With a Thousand Faces* (1949) was the source for Christopher Vogler's influential book (originally a fifteen-page memo that circulated round L.A.) which inspired and enlightened Hollywood film makers about universal aspects of narratives of the hero. At first, this led to an over-structured template for movie stories, but it soon became a crude analytic tool by which studio executives and screenwriting students — perpetually baffled as they all are as to what makes a successful movie — might understand the appeal and success of movies like *Star Wars, Raiders of the Lost Ark, Mad Max, Rocky,* and others. Such a Frazerian *Golden Bough,* universalistic approach is not to my taste; it smacks too much of formula — a formula that restricts the emergence of the unconscious while trying to pose as a revelation. It says what has *happened* but says little about the conditions required for such meaning to arise. So, because they can be so misleading, because they tend to promise more than they deliver, I wish to steer clear of universal, essentialist formulae. This is not to say, of course, that I deny the usefulness of a distinction between individual and collective phenomena. My first intention is to address the limitations of an analysis of movie-making that regards it as a purely conscious activity, and in doing so my approach has more in common with post-structural and deconstructive perspectives. As Brunette says,

> Deconstruction is not a discipline or….a methodology, but rather a questioning stance taken towards the most basic aspects of the production of knowledge. Like Lacanian psychoanalysis, it tends to concentrate on the slippages of meaning, the gaps and inconsistencies, that inevitably mark all understanding.[5]

I would like to add that this attitude is not restricted to Lacanians but one presented by many contemporary Jungians (and of course Freudians) too! In my use of the term, 'unconscious'[6] refers to these slippages of meaning, gaps, and inconsistencies. In common with such an approach, *my intention is to discover the presence of unconscious aspects of movie-making — both individual and collective — and to map their contribution to the creative process as a whole.*

Personal Psychology, Collective Creativity, and the Movies

In his 1930 paper, "Psychology and Literature," Jung notes how the "reduction of art to personal factors....deflects our attention from the psychology of the work of art and focuses it on the psychology of the artist."[7] Looking at the director or cinematographer or writer as personalities with interesting lives may have its place, but we should never compound the two analyses. As Jung puts it, "the work of art exists in its own right and cannot be got rid of by changing it into a personal complex."[8]

Jung likens great art to the dream — despite all the conscious human craft gone into its production — he claims art, like the dream, is *a product of nature* — our "human nature" if you will.

> A dream never says "you ought" or "this is the truth." It presents
> an image in much the same way nature allows a plant to grow,
> and it is up to us to draw conclusions.[9]

Note how Jung speaks of plural "conclusion*s*." There are many so-called "meanings" in our understanding of a creative product; there may well be single intentions on the part of its creators in the case of movies, but once a film is shown, there are many human eyes seeking to find meanings. Jung notes that we realize this "when we let a work of art act upon us as it acted upon the artist. To grasp its meaning, we must allow it to shape us as it shaped him."[10] It is only in recent years that I have found how viewing movies a second and third time, often years apart, has yielded quite different experiences and meanings on each occasion, something which I had never expected when I was younger.

The personal psychology and biographical stories of the creators of film images can be a help, a hindrance, or irrelevant. Film narratives and images frequently go further than the conscious intentions of those who make them.

This is similar to how Jung concludes of the creative artist that, "His personal career may be interesting and inevitable, but it does not explain his art."[11] …. "it has escaped from the limitations of the personal and has soared beyond the personal concerns of its creator."[12] One well-known way in which Jung approaches the issue of human collective imagery is his discovery of mythological phenomena in the modern events of our contemporary stories,

> instead of the eagle of Zeus, or the great roc, there is an airplane;
> the fight with the dragon is a railway smash;.....the earth-mother
> is a stout lady selling vegetables; the Pluto who abducts
> Persephone is a reckless chauffeur, and so on.[13]

Frankly, I am not sure what books Jung has in mind here, but since his writing there have certainly been many movies depicting these powerful collective characters and scenes, often, these days, with even less disguise: giant sharks, just as themselves and not substituted by a "modern" equivalent, were back in vogue just ten years after his death! The San Francisco analyst John Beebe has, for many years, been pointing out contemporary and collective resonances in themes and characters in films as diverse as *Atalante*, Hitchcock's *Notorious* and *Marnie*, and in George Lucas's *Star Wars*.

This type of film analysis follows one of Jung's major themes — how the unconscious produces material to *compensate* for the one-sidedness of our over-rational conscious minds.

> Whenever conscious life becomes one-sided or adopts a false
> attitude, these images.... rise to the surface in dreams and in the
> visions of artists and seers to restore the psychic balance, whether
> of the individual or of the epoch.[14]

But the Jungian attitude to creative arts and, in our case, the movies, goes beyond this initial formulation. It is also about the nature of our creativity itself, what it does for us in the production of arts, and what it does for all of us in the communication of a deeper sense of what it is to be a human being. Although Jung is speaking of writers, I believe the illusion of conscious control of the process applies to the film-makers we will hear from. As we will see, some are more willing to admit this than others.

The cinematographer Mario Tosi, for example, also views cinema in a collective sense. He extends his own individual preferences to embrace the cultural significance of cinematography

> as the ....last medium left in this society, artistically speaking,
> that can be enjoyed by many people. Painting, sculpture, etc.,
> have limited audiences.....I like to paint on the screen. I like to
> create a mood and treat it as an art form, the last art form.[15]

But how conscious are other movie makers of any of this?

In his latest book — titled *Which Lie Did I Tell?* — William Goldman, the Oscar-winning screenwriter (*Butch Cassidy and the Sundance Kid, Marathon Man,* and *All the President's Men*), after offering us a good chunk of his new screenplay, stops to reflect on the work so far.

> I have been continually surprised at what you've read. I don't want that to come off as mystical shit. It isn't. But as I've told you, I don't know what I'm doing, not in any logical way, I'm totally instinctive. ....I think writing has always got to be an act of exploration......
>
> One of the worst parts of being an instinctive writer — of having to go with "feel" rather than logic — is the sense of helplessness that overwhelms me at moments like this.
>
> I am convinced that scene is a proper place to start.
>
> I also have no idea what it is or how to write it.[16]

Did you notice the range of words Goldman uses to describe his non-conscious process? He denies any use of the M word — "mystical" is clearly a slur and taboo — and uses "instinctive" when he may mean intuitive; finally contrasting "feel" (which he places in quote marks) with "logic" (which he doesn't!). I don't think he ever uses "unconscious" or "irrational." We come across an interesting vocabulary (or sliding of signifiers in our psycho-sociological terms) that presents much for discussion as we see what the film-makers have to say.

For example, when the cinematographer, Michael Chapman (*The Last Detail, Taxi Driver, The Last Waltz, Invasion of the Body Snatchers, Raging Bull, Dead Men Don't Wear Plaid*), talks about his craft, he frequently substitutes another word to avoid saying "unconscious." Interestingly he is one of the few who substitutes the word "existential" as a way of avoiding "unconscious" or the dreaded "mystical" or, even worse, "transcendental." In his expression, "unconscious" seems synonymous with "emotion" or "emotional effect," and also with "mystery" and "mysterious," and with "magic" or "magical." Historically, all these terms have been held in direct opposition to words like "conscious," "rational," and "mechanical." It is fascinating to see how language used in the field of movie making — with its mix of conscious rationality and vital intuition — sustains this tension.

The way actor James Woods speaks of the director Oliver Stone suggests a familiarity with an idea of the "non-conscious" and a coining of terms to describe what he means without speaking "psychologically":

> He achieves his desired end as a film-maker by being provocative and yet at the same time subverting his own ego in the process. For Oliver Stone nothing matters but the film and the result that even he may not consciously know he is seeking. Some deep intuition drives him, a majestic demon muse to whom he is but a humble servant.[17]

When describing his process himself, Oliver Stone appreciates the way in which the conscious and the mundane need to be assimilated and incorporated before something else, outside consciousness, can happen.

> I think that directing actors is a very humbling experience…..you have to listen to everybody's gripes and everybody's fears….it's pretty exhausting, but through the medium, through the director, I think something happens, something grows, like in a petrie dish.[18]

(We shall have to gloss over how Stone's regarding of actors as bacteria appears several steps down even from an earlier, damning attitude when Alfred Hitchcock called actors "cattle"!)

Stone also speaks of his relationship with the non-organic elements of movie-making as also partly unconscious.

> I always respected the camera as another actor….I see the actor, I see the camera, and I see myself. I see a triangle. So that the camera…is as much a human participant as I am. It's an interesting relationship. So often the camera will speak to me on the day and say: "Not, this. That." And it will become clear to me.[19]

The 'Mechanics' of Filming and Lighting versus Intuition & Unconscious Knowing

A good place to begin viewing what the cinematographers and camera and lighting technicians have to say is a series of interviews collected in the book, *Masters of Light: Conversations With Contemporary Cinematographers,* and the accompanying DVD, *Visions of Light.*

One theme that strikes the reader and viewer immediately is the tension between the consciously intended *mechanics and math* of lighting and filming, and the unconsciously achieved *magic and mystery* that occurs just when cinematographers are at their most scientific and rational and working to achieve their shot. This really is a case of 'two kinds of thinking' working side by side. Throughout the interviews, the idea of an unknown, unconscious factor emerging and, heaven forbid, this element making all the difference between a professional piece of work and an artistically powerful piece of filmic communication, seems a taboo area of discussion for most of the photographers concerned.

Michael Chapman begins his interview defensively:

> I wish there were some great thing dredged up from my psyche that I could say was the key to all these things, but there isn't. It's a mechanical medium and you've got to do the mechanics and let the mechanics give the aesthetic pleasure.[20]

But Chapman then goes on to give a huge range of examples of unconscious decisions and solutions he has applied in his work. He is clearly uneasy in admitting how this unpredictable factor has a place *alongside* the mechanics of the cinematographer's art in case this assertion should *override* his emphasis on the mechanical. Not to mention how it would make him seem unreliable to his employers if he dared pay attention to anything but the planned mechanics of achieving the shot. But Chapman clearly wonders about the relationship between the two.

> The amount of unconscious material that you're involved with in shooting — I couldn't believe it, when I started shooting, how much there is. .....I can't explain why or how but it's true. I can't explain why, if I'm lighting your face, why the light being here or being there makes a difference but I do know it does. I do know if you have a firm view of the movie and you stay with it, it works.[21]

From this it is clear that Chapman is fully aware that unconsciously derived decisions and results count every bit as much as those arrived at mechanically. When he gets going he lets it all slip out:

> ....I realized that the first time I was a director of photography....
> I found that I was drawing on unconscious sources amazingly
> more than I would have had any idea that I was. Anybody who
> was going to be honest about it would say the same thing.
> Unless they are just hacks. If they are really trying, and trying to
> do something for the first time, then you are using unconscious
> material surprisingly intensely......[22]

Chapman adds in reference to the director he often works with,

> Everything's unconscious to Marty (Scorsese); everything's
> mysterious to Marty.....I can't believe I'm not right about the
> unconscious things for someone who really is trying in some
> way to let some kind of energy loose.[23]

What about camera angles and the link with emotions, characters,
and narrative? Do directors plan such effects mechanically or do they
"reveal" them? Michael Chapman tells us how:

> [Camera] Operating allows you to think about angles, you think
> about what angles do, whether they are efficient, whether they
> work. Operating is great for that.[24]

But he soon shifts to aspects of the camera-work that are far harder to
articulate or plan.

> A lot of times, what angles give you emotionally is puzzling and
> mysterious. I don't have any sense that I understand them.....And
> I think one of the ways unconscious material reveals itself is in
> angles: in what it says about the relations of character and the
> relations of character to place. Or what it says about dominance
> and submission. It's genuinely mysterious.[25]

But now Chapman has unnerved himself and back-pedals rapidly!

> And I don't like mystery. You should never count on anything
> being mysterious or new or wonderful. Or that in the joy of
> doing something, you're going to create something new. I think
> the more planning, the more meticulous, the more anal-retentive
> you are, the better off you are. But there's no sense pretending
> that that mystery isn't there. I don't think you should ever count
> on it or even think about it till afterwards.[26]

The director and writer Anthony Minghella in a series of interviews
says, quite rightly, that the camera, "..... is not watching, it's telling."

Ten different photographers taking the same subject with the same camera would have ten different pictures,

> because the subject and the photographer have some alchemic relationship, and it either produces gold or dross.....I have absolutely no doubt that there is an action involved in photography which changes the subject.[27]

The Editing Process and Post-Production

The film editor Walter Murch (*The Unbearable Lightness of Being, The English Patient, The Talented Mr. Ripley, Cold Mountain, Apocalypse Now, The Conversation*) is highly articulate about his contribution to making a movie.

While editing *The Conversation* — especially Gene Hackman's acting performance as Harry Caul — Murch noticed he was cutting the shots just when Hackman blinked; he suggests that this seems natural as it is where a thought (spoken or unspoken) ends; we unconsciously blink to punctuate our inner and outer phrases of meaning. Murch goes on to mention how the director John Ford said movies were more like thinking than anything else even before Murch noticed this phenomena. (And thinking that does *not* exclude emotion I have to add.) Murch also points out how editing is

> Not so much a putting together as it is the *discovery of a path*........The editor is actually making twenty-four decisions a second: No. No. No. No. No. No. No. No. No. No. No. Yes.[28]

There is an interesting anecdote about *The Conversation* that shows how many choices are arrived at outside conscious decision-making. The Harry Caul character was loosely modeled on Harry Haller of Herman Hesse's *Steppenwolf* novel and called by that name early in development. But during this period, a typist in Francis Ford Coppola's office mistyped the name of the character as Harry *Caller*. Due to the film's theme (Harry is a high-tech audio eavesdropper/industrial spy), the name got changed to "Call" and then spelt "Caul." This then gets echoed in the strange see-through pac-a-mac which is like the 'caul' around a new-born baby and which Harry wears throughout the film.

Last Reel

A photographer I have been talking with maintains that the unconscious and unexpected elements (just to add to the vocabulary, he called it the 'serendipity') are *facilitated* by their exact opposite: a very organized and planned shoot where there is agreement on what the scene needs to say, and where the boundaries of location, lighting, and script are all in place. As I suggested earlier, the security achieved through such planning strikes me a comparable to the effect of the boundaries of time, place, and relationship we find in psychotherapy. In both cases, such a security is vital to the emergence of unconscious factors. On the movie set, as in psychotherapy, it is the safe, boundaried environment which creates the possibility of awareness, and then the use of an intuitive vision stemming from the unconscious that adds so much to a movie scene.

Once the secure environment is in place, the last thing to be done on the shoot is to turn the camera on and to point it in the right direction. The very element the audience does not see — because what they look at is the set and the actors, and what they hear is the dialogue, the music, and the unfolding of the story — is this: they don't watch the camera itself and what it is doing. In all seriousness, I wish to emphasize how the lens is transparent. The camera *is the unconscious element in movies*. It is the view we need not be conscious of (at least on first viewing) because to be so would interrupt the life of the movie.

The vision of the camera that stems from the film-makers' vision is the unconscious vision; this is carried through the materiality of the other elements mentioned, which we witness visually and follow with our hearts and minds. The unconscious is then transmitted directly from them to us through this medium.

NOTES

1. Michael Apted, *Backrow* 'Interview with Michael Apted,' BBC Radio 4, London, 2001.

2. Peter Biskind, *Easy Riders, Raging Bulls* (London: Bloomsbury, 1999), 156.

3. David F. Peat, *Synchronicity: The Bridge Between Matter and Mind* (New York: Bantam, 1987).

4. Margaret Boden, *The Creative Mind: Myths and Mechanisms* (London: Sphere, 1992), 129.

5. Peter Brunette and David Wills, *Screen/Play: Derrida and Film Theory* (Princeton: Princeton University Press, 1989), 89.

6. The fact that anything unconscious is by definition not able to be known about will be tackled early in the research. Suffice it to say that when 'unconscious' is mentioned this refers to an idea, action, or utterance not consciously intended or planned but which, once revealed to consciousness, is assumed to have arisen out of an unknown, unconscious process which leads to artistic creation. The emphasis on *process* is quite different from claiming the source is an unconscious *place* in the mind, I should add.

7. C.G. Jung, *The Collected Works of C. G. Jung,* trans. R. F. C. Hull (London: Routledge and Kegan Paul, 1950), 15 § 147.

8. *Collected Works,* 15 § 147.

9. *Ibid.,* § 161.

10. *Ibid.*

11. *Ibid.,* § 162.

12. *Ibid.,* § 107.

13. *Ibid.,* § 152.

14. *Ibid.,* § 160.

15. Dennis Schaefer and Larry Salvato, eds., *Masters of Light: Conversations with Contemporary Cinematographers* (Berkeley: University of California Press, 1984), 246.

16. William Goldman, *Which Lie Did I Tell?* (London: Bloomsbury, 2001), 407-408, 415.

17. Chris Salewicz, *Oliver Stone: The Making of His Movies* (London: Orion Books, 1997), 56.

18. *Ibid.*

19. *Ibid.,* 73.

20. Dennis Schaefer and Larry Salvato, eds., *Masters of Light: Conversations with Contemporary Cinematographers* (Berkeley: University of California Press, 1984), 99.

21. *Ibid.,* 101.

22. *Ibid.,* 125.

23. *Ibid.,* 125.

24. *Ibid.*, 101-02.

25. *Ibid.*, 102.

26. *Ibid.*

27. T. Bricknel, ed., *Minghella on Minghella* (London: Faber, 2005), 106-107.

28. Walter Murch, *In The Blink of an Eye, 2ⁿᵈ edition* (Los Angeles: Silman-James Press, 2001), 16.

A 'CLOSE-UP' OF THE KISS

MARILYN MARSHALL

I remember my first kiss — it was the boy next door. We were both in 4th grade — he kissed me on the cheek and I felt thrilled. Something Other entered my world — Other than Mom's good night kiss or grandpa's endearing "give me some sugar" kiss. It was not so other in its location, the cheek, but, oh, it did not feel the same! Not long after that, maybe in 6th grade, my dad stole me away for a father-daughter night out at the drive-in movie. As we settled in with homemade popcorn, a jug of grape kool-aid, and a mosquito coil, a must for drive-in viewing on a hot Southern night, I saw a couple in the car ahead of us — arms wrapped around each other, kissing: it was nothing like my neighbor's kiss. I asked my dad what they were doing, and he said with a smile, "Oh, sugar, you'll learn about that when you get a little older." Of course I got older and did learn. I am much, much older now and have probably given and received thousands of kisses, many mindlessly so. But, suddenly I had an idea that came out of the blue about eighteen months ago — 'The Kiss' as the topic for an assignment in my training in the New Orleans Jungian Seminars.

The Kiss — besides a slap on the rear end, we probably first received it as a welcome into this world. We kiss to say hello, good

Marilyn Marshall attends the New Orleans Jungian Seminars as a Candidate-in-Training with the Inter-Regional Society of Jungian Analysts. She is a Licensed Professional Counselor in private practice in New Orleans, Louisiana.

night, and goodbye. We kiss a child's wound to make it better. We blow a kiss to someone who is not in range for a real kiss. We kiss as a prelude and in passion and in passing. We kiss under the mistletoe and we kiss the Blarney Stone and dice. We kiss the crucifix, the mezuzah, the Bible, the Torah, the bishop's ring, the pope's ring, the king's robe. Politicians kiss babies, athletes kiss trophies, priests kiss altars, and various tribal peoples kiss the path on which their chief walked. We write XXXX's for kisses, sing songs about kisses, eat Hershey's kisses, listen to the heavy metal band KISS, wear lipsticks that color kisses, and employ the acronym KISS — keep it simple stupid. We may purchase an orchid named "first kiss;" we may give or receive CPR's "kiss of life;" and, if we live in Toledo, Ohio (as well as in many other cities), we may tune into K – I – S – S, radio 92.5 on your dial. We wait for the words "You may now kiss the bride;" we flinch at the words "kiss my ass;" and if Greenspan suggests a rise in interest rates, that could be the "kiss of death" to the stock market. Klimt painted The Kiss, Rodin sculpted The Kiss, poets imagine the kiss, authors describe the kiss, and filmmakers direct the kiss.

What is it about this physical expression that has so permeated our personal and collective experience? There is a numinous quality to it that moves us, affects us. The image of the kiss is one that can provoke fear or disgust as well as harbor hope or desire; here, a kiss can defy convention and there, defend tradition; in one moment it can deny responsibility and in another define courage. The kiss may symbolize union, faithfulness (or worship), courage, and love as well as possession, betrayal, regression, and death. Contrary to the song, a kiss is NOT just a kiss; it is an image of complexity, an archetypal image imbued with emotional impact and psychological meaning, something deeper than its definition "to touch or caress with the lips as a mark of affection or greeting."

So, where did this 'mark of affection' originate? There are many theories about it but none definitive. Some scientists believe it to be genetic in origin. For instance, Bonobos, a member of the chimpanzee family, use kissing to reduce tension and assuage fear. Every Bonobo, male or female, young or old, seeks and responds positively to kisses. Biological anthropologists suggest that the kiss evolved from the grooming behavior of primates which is viewed as a form of physical affection and often involves the mouth. Others propose that the kiss developed from the sniffing behavior animals engage in to determine whether or not another animal is dangerous — thus some cultures rub noses to kiss. Anthropologists also suggest that primitive peoples, after nursing the infant was complete, may have masticated food and fed the child mouth to mouth and thus the kiss evolved in this way. Others believe that kissing, with its use of lips and tongue, arose in relation to the sucking experience of the infant nursing.

The image of the kiss is found in Assyrian and Babylonian, Greek and Roman, and in the Hebraic-Christian myths, as well as in folk and fairy tales from many cultures. And whether pronounced *cyssan* or *coss* in Old English, *cussian* in Old Saxon or *kussen* in Dutch, *chussen* in High German or *kyssa* or *koss* in Old Norse, all of these words for 'kiss' seem to echo a similar sound. Whereas *The Oxford Dictionary of English Etymology* defines it as a "salute or caress with the lips," the kiss takes different forms in various cultures. There are innumerable web sites that explain how to kiss like the French kiss. In European countries, unlike the handshake in the United States, it is customary for women and men to greet with a double kiss, one on each cheek. And whereas certain cultures, such as the Inuits, Maories, and Polynesians, rub or touch noses to kiss, others, such as the Vietnamese and Mongolian, sniff one another as a kiss.

Whereas we often imagine the cinematic kiss in its connection with sexuality, we can look at the etymology of kiss and flesh out its relationship to nourishment[1] and its invitation to 'enter into' or 'open to.' In Latin *osculum* means "little mouth and kiss;" *osculor* means "to kiss" and *osculatio* is "a kissing." These words have in common the root word *os* which means "mouth, jaws, tongue, lips, and opening." The Latin word for "mouth," critical to one form of the kiss, is *ostium*, which includes as part of its meaning "door, entrance." Therefore, the kiss includes a relationship to the mouth and its function in assimilating nourishment, as well as its image as an entrance or opening to another realm.

The Kiss of Union

Cinema offers us a close-up of the kiss, projecting it onto a screen larger than life and offering us a metaphor for the magnitude of its meaning. One of the most poignant images of a kiss in recent film is the fantasy kiss between Lester Burnham and Angela in *American Beauty*, which won Oscars for Best Picture and Best Screenplay in 1999.

Lester is forty-two years old. Masturbation is the highlight of his day, his wife and daughter see him as a loser, and his job is in jeopardy. As he slumps, dozing in the back seat of the car while his wife drives him to work, we hear his thoughts of feeling sedated, as if he has lost something. At mid-life, things are apt to occur in our lives which force us to become conscious that the contentment and completeness we have sought is lacking. It is here we have the opportunity to make the transition that leads from the first half of life with its biological attitude to the second half with its cultural or spiritual attitude. During this tension between the old and the new attitude, when consciousness sees no solution to a problem, an archetype is explosively constellated and the symbol forms in an effort to transform one's psychic energy.

Enter Angela, a friend of Lester's adolescent daughter. In Lester's initial fantasy of her, she is clothed and sensuously surrounded in vibrant red rose petals. Here we are given a glimpse of the sudden constellation of the anima and the transformative potential of the rose, a symbol that becomes more personal in the fantasy of the kiss:

> He cups her face in his hands and kisses her. She seems shocked, but doesn't resist as he pulls her toward him with surprising strength. He breaks the kiss, looking at her in awe, then he reaches up and touches his lips. His eyes widen as he pulls a ROSE PETAL from his mouth . . . .[2]

Lester's fantasy kiss is an opening, an entrance to another realm, that of the anima and the new life she offers. This kiss also has the quality of union, for Lester takes in the rose, symbol of the love and relatedness the archetypal feminine brings — a relatedness to his soul. This quality of union with, or assimilation of, an aspect of the Other has the potential to nourish psychically and in that nourishment transform. And, in fact, we see Lester's gradual transformation not only physically but psychologically throughout the film, and his redemption in the end.

In watching this scene, I could not help but think of the redemption of Lucius in Apuleius' *The Golden Ass*. Lucius has been changed into an ass but is redeemed when Isis tells him to eat a bunch of roses — the flower with which she is associated — at a festival in her honor. He does so and is transformed back into a man. The image of Lucius' eating the roses and the rose coming out of Lester's mouth after kissing Angela seem to relate to one another. As the symbol of the rose is taken in and assimilated, both men are redeemed; for Lucius it is the culmination of his journey and for Lester a foreshadowing of the redemption in his.

The Kiss of Possession

While the kiss in *American Beauty* is nutritive and reflective of the generation of new life through union, the kiss also may serve as an image that reflects other, quite opposite qualities — for example, it may be vampiric, symbolizing a possession that devours and takes away life from another. J. K. Rowling's *Harry Potter and the Prisoner of Azkaban* depicts such power in the Dementor's Kiss. The dementors are the guards of Azkaban, a prison for wizards who have committed crimes. Dark, Grim-Reaper-like creatures, they seem to be disembodied except that they have shriveled hands and a mouth that sucks the soul out of their victims. Harry Potter faints when he first encounters the dementors on a train which the dementors have entered to search for Sirius Black, a prisoner who has escaped from Azkaban. Harry later learns from Professor Lupin, the professor of the Defense Against the Dark Arts class, that the dementors symbolize fear itself. Lupin describes the "worst weapon" of the dementors as the Dementor's Kiss:

> They call it the Dementor's Kiss, . . . It's what dementors do to those they wish to destroy utterly. I suppose there must be some kind of mouth under there, because they clamp their jaws upon the mouth of the victim and — and suck out his soul.

Harry thinks this means they kill the person. "Oh no," said Lupin,

> Much worse than that. You can exist without your soul, you know, as long as your brain and heart are still working. But you'll have no sense of self anymore, no memory, no . . . anything. There's no chance at all of recovery. You'll just — exist. As an empty shell. And your soul is gone forever . . . lost.

Harry faces the dementors at a lake when he is trying to save the escaped prisoner Sirius Black, who is not only his godfather, but is also innocent of the crime for which he was imprisoned. The dementors fly around the lake like spirits of the dark and "kiss" both Black and Harry, feeding on their memory and consciousness, and then sucking them out as they try to possess Harry and Black's souls. Harry recollects and focuses upon his happiest memory and also uses his wand to ward them off, but these are not strong enough (or so it seems in this part of the film), and both succumb to the kiss. Finally, for Black, there is only his soul left and we see it slowly begin to leave through his mouth. The kiss is almost complete and Black's soul lost, when suddenly the permeating, penetrating light from a white stag across the lake fights off the dementors and makes them disappear; this saves Black just in time and his soul returns to his body.

In *Symbols of Transformation*, Jung states that the spirit of evil is fear.[3] In this context Jung is speaking about evil as regression, the backward movement of libido. In this film, the dementors symbolize this fear. Dementia comes from the Latin word *demens*, "out of one's senses, insane, foolish," and *dementia* is defined as "folly, madness, insanity." The Latin word for sanity is *sanus*, which is defined as "sound, health, whole;" therefore, fear or the dementor is *in*-sanity, *against* wholeness. These descriptions could be used to identify the image and effect of a neurotic complex: through its activation the ego loses its integrity as the complex takes over as an agent of fear. When we meet an external situation in which the old adaptation no longer works, we are thrown out of our sense of reality and into chaos; we may act foolishly, insanely, against our wholeness when touched or possessed by a complex.

It is this fear that faces us with the heroic challenge and task of overcoming it and thereby taking the necessary risk to achieve a new state of consciousness. Jung believes fear to be a basic component of the human condition: in the first half of life we fear life and in the second half, death; consequently, whether the heroic task involves the establishment of an ego identity in its separation from the collective unconscious or the suffering of the ego in the process of individuation, we are all at risk for the Dementor's Kiss. However, we are not at its mercy: *Exspecto patronum!*[4]

Kissing the Gods

In *American Beauty*, the kiss significantly affects the soul through its quality of union, and in *Harry Potter*, possession. The kiss is also frequently emblematic as an expression of faithfulness and betrayal. Job, for example, uses an image of the kiss to argue with God that his faithfulness is reserved only for Yahweh:

> Have I put all my trust in gold,
> From finest gold sought my security?
> Have I ever gloated over my great wealth,
> Or the riches that my hands have won?
> Or has the sight of the sun in its glory,
> Or the glow of the moon as it walked the sky,
> Stolen my heart, so that my hand
> Blew them a secret kiss?[5]

In *Memories, Dreams, Reflections* Jung gives an account of a primitive ritual that reflects a similar meaning and resembles Job's image of blowing a kiss. The men of an African tribe performed a ceremony to the rising sun. They held their hands in front of their mouths and spat or blew vigorously and then turned their palms toward the sun. They were making an offering to the sun divinity, and Jung explains this offering psychologically:

> If the gift was spittle, it was the substance which in the view of primitives contains the personal mana, the power of healing, magic, and life. If it was breath, then it was *roho* — Arabic *ruch*, Hebrew, *ruach*, Greek, *pneuma* — wind and spirit. The act was therefore saying "I offer to god my living soul. . . ."[6]

The film *Equus* (the Latin word for horse) is about a young man who offers his soul to the horse. His communion with, as well as his reverence and passion for Equus, is symbolized by a kiss.

Equus is based on a play written by Peter Shaffer about an actual crime committed by a disturbed young man in England who gouged out the eyes of six horses. Shaffer invents a story surrounding this crime, for he knew none of the details, and names the young man in the story Alan Strang. Alan is a boy of seventeen and rather than send him to prison, the magistrate, Hesther, sends him to a psychiatric hospital and persuades psychiatrist Martin Dysart (played by Richard Burton) to work with him.

The film opens dramatically: a metal spike shines against a black background. On the handle of the spike, a horse's skull comes into view: it has chains in its mouth and a flame that flickers in the socket where an eye belongs. This image slowly changes to a white horse with a dark mane and, so close they almost seem one, a nude boy stands with his arms wrapped around the horse's neck. We hear Richard Burton's voice:

> [They always] embrace. The animal digs its sweaty brow into his cheek, and they stand in the dark for an hour — like a necking couple. And of all the nonsensical things — I keep thinking about the horse! Not the boy: the horse, and what it may be trying to do. I keep seeing that huge head kissing him with its chained mouth. Nudging through the metal some desire absolutely irrelevant to filling its belly or propagating its own kind. What desire could that be?[7]

Alan secretly kisses a divinity and it kisses him. Never mind that he is possessed by the archetype. Never mind the symbol of the horse or the horror of Alan's crime. For our purpose, it is the kiss, its numinosity and meaning, that more than once grips Alan's psychiatrist with the question of his relationship to his own soul.

After a number of sessions, Dysart discovers Alan's love of and relationship with horses and the midnight rides he stole on one of the horses in his care as a stable boy. In the following dialogue, Dysart speaks to Hesther after Alan's disclosure of midnight rides in the nude: we have just seen one of these rides, including its closing ritual where Alan bends down and kisses the hoof of Equus and cries up to him "Amen." Dysart is emotionally moved by and jealous of the young man's experience:

> I go on about my wife. That smug woman by the fire. Have you thought of the fellow on the other side of it? The finicky, critical husband looking through his art books on mythical Greece. What worship has *he* ever known? Real worship! Without worship you shrink, it's as brutal as that ... I shrank my *own* life. No one can do it for you. I settled for being pallid and provincial,

out of my own eternal timidity. . . . Three weeks a year in the Peloponnese, every bed booked in advance, every meal paid for by vouchers, cautious jaunts in hired Fiats, suitcase crammed with Kao-Pectate! Such a fantastic surrender to the primitive. And I use that word endlessly: 'primitive'. "Oh, the primitive world," I say. "What instinctual truths were lost with it!"And while I sit there, baiting a poor unimaginative woman with the word, that freaky boy tries to conjure the reality! I sit looking at pages of centaurs trampling the soil of Argos — and outside my window he is trying to *become one*, in a Hampshire field! . . . I watch that woman knitting night after night — a woman I haven't *kissed* in six years — and he stands in the dark for an hour, sucking the sweat off his God's hairy cheek! Then in the morning, I put away my books on the cultural shelf, close up the kodachrome snaps of Mount Olympus, touch my reproduction statue of Dionysus for luck — and go off to hospital to treat him for insanity. Do you see?[8]

Alan's faithfulness to and worship of Equus includes a passion for which Dysart longs, and his description of Alan's kiss, his "sucking the sweat off his God's hairy cheek," stands in stark contrast to Dysart's compensatory touch of the very god his Apollonian one-sidedness has feared.

At the climax of the film, we see Alan re-live his crime and what led to it: He wanted "to kiss," "to lie with" a young woman but could only see the face of Equus. Unable to betray his jealous God who sees everything he does, Alan fitfully blinds Equus, again and again, so the God will not see. Alan falls to the floor in convulsions of pain, a pain with which we may be familiar if we have ever kissed a God and, like Alan, had no means of mediating its demands. After he comforts Alan, Dysart cries out to Hesther from his own pain, one born of his timidity, his fear to risk the kiss and the passion which it exposes; as Dysart speaks about relieving Alan's pain, his own pain is revealed:

All right! I'll take it away! He'll be delivered from madness. *What then?* He'll feel himself acceptable! *What then?* Do you think feelings like his can be simply re-attached, like plasters . . . . *Look at him!* My desire might be to make this boy an ardent husband — a caring citizen — a worshipper of an abstract and unifying God. My achievement, however, is more likely to make a ghost!

> ... Let me tell you exactly what I'm going to do to him! I'll heal
> the rash on his body. I'll erase the welts cut into his mind by
> flying manes. When that's done, I'll set him on a nice mini-
> scooter and send him puttering off into the Normal world where
> animals are treated *properly*: made extinct, or put into servitude,
> or tethered all their lives in dim light, just to feed them [*sic*]! I'll
> give him the good Normal world where we're tethered beside
> them . . . . He'll trot on his metal pony tamely through the
> concrete evening — and one thing I promise you: he will never
> touch hide again . . . . Who knows? He may even come to find
> sex funny. Smirky funny. Bit of grunt funny. Trampled and
> furtive and entirely in control. Hopefully, he'll feel nothing at
> his fork but Approved Flesh. I doubt, however, with much
> passion! . . . Passion, you see, can be destroyed by a doctor. It
> cannot be created.[9]

A contrasting image of Alan's kiss of faithfulness and worship is
Judas' infamous kiss of betrayal. Whether in Franco Zeffirelli's *Jesus of
Nazareth* or the more recent controversial film by Mel Gibson, *The
Passion of the Christ*, Judas' kiss is a pivotal image. In the first film,
Jesus responds with, "You betray your Master with a kiss?" And in the
second film, "You betray the Son of Man with a kiss?" We discussed
above Job's use of the kiss as an image of faithfulness to Yahweh and
Alan's as one of faithfulness to Equus. Jesus' question acknowledges
the use of a kiss for a different purpose. And so it is that we see another
of its dark qualities — betrayal.

A modern image of Judas' kiss of betrayal, also known as the kiss of
death, is yet another in *American Beauty*. It is the kiss between Lester
and Colonel Fitts. Colonel Fitts is portrayed as homophobic. He disdains
and degrades homosexuals and beats his son when he thinks he and
Lester have had a sexual experience. Fitts is rigid, controlling,
suspicious, and angry, and the catatonic state of his wife portrays the
state of his anima. This kiss is indicative of what Jung calls an experience
of enantiodromia — its vulnerability, confusion, and desperation
express the unconscious compensation for Fitts' one-sided conscious
attitude: there is a god within Fitts who demands to be acknowledged.

It is dark and raining outside and Lester is in the garage doing
pull-ups on a bar when he sees Colonel Fitts through the garage door
window, standing in the rain looking at him. Lester drops down and
opens the garage door.

Lester: Jesus, man. You're soaked.

The Colonel walks inside, slightly disoriented.

Lester: You want me to get Ricky? He's in Jane's room.

The Colonel just stands there, looking at Lester.

Lester: You okay?

Colonel: Where's your wife?

Lester: Uh . . . I don't know. Probably out fucking that dorky prince of real estate asshole. And you know what? I don't care.

Colonel: Your wife is with another man and you don't care?

Lester: Nope, our marriage is just for show. A commercial, on how normal we are. When we are anything but.

He grins and so does the Colonel.

Lester: You're shaking.

He places his hands on the Colonel's shoulders. The Colonel closes his eyes.

Lester: We really should get you out of these clothes.

Colonel: (a whisper) Yes.

He opens his eyes and looks at Lester, his face filled with an anguished vulnerability we wouldn't have thought possible from him. His eyes are brimming with tears. Lester leans in concerned.

Lester: It's okay.

Colonel: I . . .

Lester: Just tell me what you need.

The Colonel leans in and hugs Lester. [Lester holds this and we see the concern and tenderness in his eyes.]

The Colonel [withdraws the embrace, looks at Lester and then] kisses him on the mouth. Lester is momentarily stunned, and then he pushes the Colonel away. The Colonel's face crumples in shame.

Lester: Whoa, whoa, whoa. I'm sorry. You got the wrong idea.

The Colonel stares at the floor, blinking, and then he turns and walks out the open garage door into the rainy night.[10]

We might imagine Fitts' kiss as an openness to the homosexuality he has unconsciously repressed and projected onto Lester; we could also imagine it as an unconscious desire to assimilate the shadow Lester represents for him — a masculine attitude very different than his own, one that has struggled with and begun to integrate unconscious aspects of his nature and to relate to his soul. However, none of this matters for, whatever Lester represents for Fitts, the kiss does not assimilate or nourish; it does not open Fitts to a new realm of feeling and relatedness, both of which Lester movingly portrays in his response to Fitts' hug and finally, the kiss. Instead, it becomes the kiss of death: Fitts returns shortly, puts a gun to Lester's head and pulls the trigger, committing a physical and psychological murder of a masculine Fitts desperately needs but cannot take in.

The Kiss of Courage

Whereas the kiss between Fitts and Lester in *American Beauty* leads to death, a tender kiss between Laura and Kitty in the recent film *The Hours* leads to new life. Laura, one of the three women upon whom the film focuses, is pregnant with her second child, and it is evident that she is depressed. The starkness of her loneliness is depicted in her vacant, dutiful responses to her husband and young son; however, this alienation seems to have begun much earlier — we see a black and white photograph of her on her wedding day where her facial expression reveals the same sad feeling tone.

The kiss takes place when Laura's neighbor Kitty comes to her house to ask Laura to feed her dog. After initial pleasantries about making cakes, social life, husbands, and the book Laura is reading (*Mrs. Dalloway* by Virginia Woolf), Kitty reveals to Laura she has a growth on her uterus and that she will be away for a few days because she has to go into the hospital. Her fear and helplessness dissolve her confident persona. She presumes that the growth is the reason she can't conceive and tearfully shares with Laura her belief that a woman is incomplete unless she has had a child. It is in this tender moment when Laura tries to assuage Kitty's fear that the kiss occurs. Laura makes soothing comments to Kitty, then kisses her first on the head and then on the mouth. In this context we can explore the kiss and its quality of courage.

It is courage that delivers from fear and we often see this courage offered through the kiss — whether to assuage the fear or pain of the child or to 'en-courage' the soldier we send off to war. Laura's kiss offers courage to Kitty. Yet it goes further — Laura is nourished by the kiss she gives. Whereas Kitty carries a somatic symptom of her inability to conceive, Laura suffers a psychic symptom of the same, for she has been unable to conceive the new attitude she needs to discover her own wholeness. Although Laura's initial response to the kiss is to betray herself through suicide, the psyche responds with a dream image that jolts her to consciousness; consequently, she assimilates the kiss. From this perspective, we can say that Laura finds the courage to leave her husband and children, keeping her vow to do so after the birth of her daughter: regardless of her sexual orientation, the deeper awareness is that she is dying in the conventional roles of wife and mother and chooses instead, as she explains at the end of the film, to live. From another perspective, if Laura, like Colonel Fitts, has repressed her homosexuality because of the cultural milieu of the 1950's, we might imagine that her kiss opens her to an awareness of her sexuality and, unlike Fitts, gives her the courage to embrace it.

The Kiss of Love

I saved for last the quality of the kiss we most often associate with the cinematic kiss — love. However, before exploring the kiss of erotic love, I want to begin with the kiss as an expression of filial love. One of the most moving portrayals of this kind of kiss is found in *Whale Rider* in the kiss between Koro, a New Zealand tribal chief, and his son Porourangi, when Porourangi returns to New Zealand after a twelve-year absence. Twelve years earlier, Porourangi's wife died in childbirth delivering twins — a boy and a girl. The boy twin died too, but the girl survived. Grief-stricken by the death of his wife and his baby, Porourangi leaves his New Zealand coastal village and his new-born daughter, refusing to fulfill his father Koro's expectation that he succeed him as chief of their people. During the two men's twelve-year estrangement, Porourangi has followed his own path, establishing himself in Germany as an artist while Koro has helped rear Porourangi's daughter and begun the search for the new chief.

The kiss takes place when Porourangi returns home and greets his father. It is the Maori kiss; as Porourangi and Koro's heads reverently come together, their noses touch and they linger in an intimate image that communicates what words cannot. We can hear the sound of their inhalation as they take in one another's breath, and we can sense through this kiss an offering and a reception of respect and love.

The kiss of erotic love evokes a very different quality. Whether it is the kiss of tragic love between Romeo and Juliet in *Romeo and Juliet* or of young love between Jack and Rose in *Titanic*; the kiss of unrequited love between Rhett and Scarlet in *Gone With the Wind* or of forbidden love between Almasy and Katharine in *The English Patient*; or the kiss of 'lost' love between Rick and Ilsa in *Casablanca*, this kiss takes one beyond familial bonds and deeper than shadow's layers, for its image unites the masculine and feminine in an outward portrayal of an inner potentiality that brings the unknown, contra-sexual Other, the anima/animus, into relationship with consciousness. It is this kiss that moves us out of the security of the known into the vulnerability of the unknown; out of the protection of defenses and into the risk of self-revelation.

Cinema gives us the 'close-up' of the kiss; it is up to us to look closely at its image, for it has a purpose, a quality, a meaning. The kiss opens us to and nourishes us with the lost and unknown aspects of ourselves in order to give them their places in the interior life of the soul. In the Gnostic Gospel of Philip, Christ describes it in this way: "For it is by a kiss that the perfect conceive and give birth. For this reason we also kiss one another. We receive conception from the grace which is in one another."[11]

I realize that the psyche does not give an idea — the Kiss — unless through its image I will be taken deeper into my own soul. And I realize through these cinematic images of the kiss, I have revealed aspects of myself — the shadow qualities of the feminine that have demanded my conscious assimilation and opened me to a fuller experience of my nature; the masculine qualities that have desired redemption and have opened me to the Other in myself. And I too have sucked a God's sweaty cheek and am grateful that Jungian analysis has been able to mediate what Dysart could not.

Eighteen months is not such a long time to live with an idea, to let it kiss you in the many different ways it can; show you the beauty in and the betrayal of your own soul. How is it that a kiss can do so much? I sit here at my computer and finish this article for today's deadline and the dementors are flying around, but last night I dreamed of a kiss — *Exspecto Patronum*!

NOTES

1. C.G. Jung, *Collected Works*, 5 § 652.

2. Alan Ball, "The Shooting Script of *American Beauty*" (New York: Newmarket Press, 1999), 15.

3. C.G. Jung, *Collected Works*, 5 § 551.

4. D. Heyman & C. Columbus (producers) & A. Cuaron (director), 2004, *Harry Potter and the Prisoner of Azkaban* [Motion picture]. USA/ UK: Warner Brothers.

5. *The Jerusalem Bible* (New York: Doubleday & Company, 1966), *Job* 31: 24-48.1.

6. C.G. Jung, *Memories, Dreams, Reflections*, A. Jaffe, ed. (New York: Random House, 1961), 267.

7. Peter Shaffer, *Equus* (New York: Penguin Books, 1977), 17. (I have noted the pages in the published play since the dialogue in the movie follows it exactly.)

8. *Ibid.*, 82-83.

9. *Ibid.*, 107-108.

10. Alan Ball, "The Shooting Script of *American Beauty*," 88-90.

11. *The Nag Hammadi Library*, J. M. Robinson, ed. (New York: Harper Collins, 1978), 145.

LOOKING FOR MOTHER:
THE POWER OF THE MOTHER COMPLEX
IN THE FILMS OF INGMAR BERGMAN

INGMARIE MCELVAIN

A s a teenager in the fifties growing up in Sweden, I was moved by Ingmar Bergman's early films without quite understanding all the psychological subtleties. By the early sixties Ingmar Bergman had become a recognized, world-famous director. By then I had married an American and moved to the United States, where I saw and was greatly taken by his films, *Wild Strawberries* and *The Seventh Seal*, among others. I felt proud that Ingmar Bergman was from Sweden. Much later, in the nineties as a Jungian analyst, I initiated several programs for the community branch of our institute in Santa Fe, New Mexico, where we showed and discussed his work. My perspective had changed. I still admired the depth and complexity of his films, but I had become particularly interested in his female characters, how they were presented, and the effect of Bergman's own psychology in his shaping of them. I came to see that his difficult relationship with his mother, his negative mother complex, and the working through of

Ingmarie McElvain grew up in northern Sweden and moved to the United States in 1963. She is a graduate of Syracuse University School of Social Work. She received her training as a Jungian analyst through the Inter-Regional Society of Jungian Analysts and graduated in 1995. She is in private practice in Santa Fe, New Mexico, and a member of the C.G. Jung Institute of Santa Fe.

this complex have played a large part in how his female film characters have been presented over the years.

Ingmar Bergman has directed more than forty films over the last fifty years. From the script to the choice of actors, to the directing and the editing of the finished film, each film bears his imprint. He writes his own film scripts, which are inspired by his memories, dreams, visions, fantasies, and people close to him. He directed all of his films through *Fanny and Alexander* (1984). After that, he continued to write film scripts, which others directed. Billie August, his son Daniel Bergman, and Liv Ullman, for example, directed *Best Intentions* (1996), *Sunday's Child* (1998), and Faithless (2000), though Bergman was still actively involved in the process, supplying written notes and directions for the actors. In the fall of 2002, at the age of eighty-two, he once again directed, this time the film *Saraband* from his own script. *Saraband* reintroduces the divorced couple from *Scenes from a Marriage* (1974), which he had written and directed thirty years ago, with the same actors from the earlier film, Liv Ullman and Erland Josephsson, in the leading roles. This film was shown on Swedish television in late 2003 and released in the United States in July, 2005.

Ingmar Bergman has had a stable of actors who performed at the theaters where he was the director. In the summer, when the theaters were closed, these actors were unemployed and available to act in his films. He developed close personal and professional relationships with many of them—including romantic relationships with several of his featured actresses—so that not only did they act in his films, they also sometimes served as inspiration for his film characters. Having married five times, he has ten children with his wives and lovers. In 1974 he married Ingrid von Rosen, his fifth wife, who died in 1995. Since then, he has not remarried. Talking about Ingrid in a 2004 interview on Swedish television, he said, "Ingrid was grounded in reality."[1] She was a steadying influence, a good mother and manager, and through her, all his children met together for the first time. He had had little contact with most of them, and spoke in the interview of his shame over his neglect of them.

Women are often the main characters in Ingmar Bergman's films. He has said, "My ceaseless fascination with the whole race of women is one of my mainsprings."[2] This fascination has had, however, a strongly negative aspect. Frequently women in his films are portrayed as passive with little sense of self-esteem and agency, as lustful bodies who leave mates and children behind as they blindly respond to the selfish, immature, and crazy men who appear in their lives. Neither questioning their hasty decisions, nor thinking of the consequences, they seem to be driven by instinctual gratification and the need to take care of their worthless paramours. Other women characters are frozen emotionally, sexually conflicted, denying or punishing their sex. Some are unrelated, dry, and defended by their intellect. Still others are spinsters with sick wombs or lungs, repugnantly and deathly ill.

For a long while I saw Ingmar Bergman as doing injustice to women. I did not want to recognize these women, so blindly self-destructive and so stuck in their miseries. I did not like them. However, my feelings were tempered when I realized that the energy of my own mother complex was activated by Bergman's women characters. It was not just righteous indignation at what I perceived as his mistreatment of women that fueled my interest. By focusing on Ingmar Bergman's mother complex as reflected in his female characters, I was also looking at and digesting issues around my own mother complex. My mother complex has a different content, as I am a woman, grew up somewhat differently, and with different genes. But I did grow up in Sweden in the forties and fifties in a middle-class family that in some respects behaved similarly to Bergman's own. I recognized in his portrayals of women a certain way of non-being, a way of erasing oneself, and the destructive consequences of this, which is painfully familiar.

I had been looking for, and missing, a balance and wholeness in his women characters. It was not there, and could not be there, since these women were Ingmar Bergman's projections of his own inner images of what he believed women were like. I realized that they held pieces of his negative mother complex, and they alerted me to his ambivalent relationship with his mother and the feminine. They documented his inner psychological world, filtered through his particular, patriarchal, middle-class background in Sweden and his genetic makeup. The mother complex thus provided an unending source of fuel for his creative process.

Ingmar Bergman's Mother Karin

Ingmar Bergman's mother Karin was a complicated and intelligent woman who had married his father Erik, a young, struggling minister, in part out of attraction, in part out of pity, and in part to spite her own mother. She soon realized that she had made a mistake but attempted without success to make the best of it. Divorce was not much of an option in those days, particularly not if you were married to a minister and had children. The marriage lasted until Karin's death when she was in her late sixties. It was an unhappy one, full of conflict, with toxic emotional fallout for the three children.

Ingmar Bergman's autobiography, *The Magic Lantern,* was published in 1987, when he was sixty-nine years old. It ends with a quote from his mother's diary, supposedly written in July of 1918, shortly after he was born.

> I have been too ill to write in recent weeks. Erik has had Spanish flu for the second time. Our son was born on Sunday morning on July 14. He immediately contracted a high temperature and severe diarrhea. He looks like a tiny skeleton with a big fiery red nose. He stubbornly refuses to open his eyes. I have no milk after a few days because of my illness. He was baptized in an emergency here at the hospital and given the names Ernst Ingmar. Ma has taken him to Varoms, where she found a wet nurse. I lie here helpless and miserable. Sometimes when I am alone, I cry. If the boy dies, Ma says she will look after Dag, [her eldest son] and I am to take up my profession again. She wants Erik and me to separate as soon as possible...I don't think I have the right to leave Erik. He is overwrought and his nerves have been bad all spring...I pray to God without confidence.[3]

Several years later, Karin Bergman's diary and letters from 1907-1936, *Den Dubbla Verkligheten* (*The Double Reality*), was published in 1992 in Sweden. (It has not yet been translated into English and translations from the diary are mine.) When I read Karin's diary entries around the time of Ingmar Bergman's birth, I could not find the one quoted above by Ingmar Bergman in his autobiography. Instead, her diary indicates that though her marriage had been troubled for several years before Ingmar was born, it was relatively amicable at the time of his birth, which the couple had longed for. Karin writes in her diary,

> Ernst Ingmar born on July 14, 1918. No one has come as early to
> our house "Varom" as Ingmar, who came here when he was just
> 14 days old. He was baptized an August evening at sunset in the
> flower corner of the big room.[4]

This diary entry has a different and more positive tone than the one
quoted at the end of Bergman's autobiography. Was the entry Ingmar
Bergman refers to in his autobiography taken out of his mother's actual
diary before it was published? Was her actual diary entry changed, or
did Ingmar Bergman create it himself to end his autobiography on a
sad note? Whatever the case, the reader of his autobiography is left
with the impression of his mother as ill, unhappy, and unable to nurse
and to nurture him. Whether this is the literal truth or not, it appears
to be Ingmar Bergman's psychological truth. It highlights his difficult
relationship with his mother and how unresolved this issue still was
for him at the time he wrote his autobiography. Bergman's perception
of his mother is also reflected later in the book *Bilder*, published in
1990, where he writes, "I thought I was an unwanted child evolved
out of a cold womb and given birth to in a crisis both physical and
psychological."[5]

A child's earliest and most significant connection with the feminine
is through its mother. The child needs a good connection, needs to
feel nurtured, cared for, encouraged, seen, and heard by her. In a child's
development with a psychologically healthy mother who is able to be
present with her child, the child learns to hold the tension between
the image of the bad, abandoning mother and the good, present mother.
Mother comes to be seen as good enough of the time. This did not
happen for Ingmar Bergman. His mother Karin, because of her
personality and psychic wounds, in addition to her unhappy marriage,
was not able to be there for her son; and when she was present, she
was too intrusive and controlling.

Karin's later diary notes and letters show that her marriage again
deteriorated after Ingmar's birth. She writes,

> Sometimes people crowd me so terribly...especially those closest
> to me. I know that they all have a right to me, and I want to give
> of myself to them. But I can only give of myself freely and not be
> forced, which happens too often. Then I feel hunted with no
> space of my own to withdraw to. It is for those times that I have

created my own inner world, to which no one, no human being, has the key. And it is so lovely to be able to escape to this place. When I am there it is amazing how little what is happening outside touches me.[6]

And in a later entry she writes,

I walk around with a great tiredness, that is not only physical, but mostly spiritual. I want badly to do things right but I cannot. What my tiredness comes from I am not clear about. I think at times that it has to do with my whole marriage to Erik. Even when things are working at their best it is as if there was something false in it.[7]

In a letter to her mother she writes,

I have never said this to you before in my letters but I have hardly ever had more difficulties as during the last couple of months after you left. I realize that it mainly has to do with Erik. I am beginning to clearly understand that I am not in love with him, that I can only remain with him as the children's mother. I can try to the best of my ability to fulfill the role of his wife by being his good friend only and Erik does not want to accept this.[8]

In 1925, when Ingmar Bergman was seven years old, Karin became involved in an important love affair with a younger man, a theology student and a friend of the family. She was happy with him and considered him to be her soul mate. She wanted to leave Erik, and after several years, finally got up the courage to tell Erik about this relationship. When she did, he fell apart and threatened to take the children away from her if she left him. Karin turned to her mother Anna, her long-time confidant, for support, but Anna, even though she had been against Karin marrying Erik and had little regard for him, now admonished her to do her duty and stay in the marriage. Karin followed her mother's advice, but still secretly continued her forbidden relationship, occasionally meeting her lover and writing to him. The relationship did not end until 1931, when he married another woman.

There was a high emotional price to pay. Erik felt Karin's rejection, clung to her desperately, spied jealously on her, and forced himself on her sexually. She cried bitterly afterwards, something witnessed by the children. Erik also suffered serious depressions and appeared almost psychotic at times. Both Karin and Erik suffered nervous breakdowns, and each spent months in rest homes several times a year. Karin's mother then stepped in to care for the children. Karin repeatedly resolved to love her husband, but she never succeeded. She was also severely burdened by her responsibilities as a minister's wife. She had to manage a busy household that was open to the parishioners; her home was a stage where she and Erik performed when parishioners or guests were present. They performed well, but the children saw and felt the unhappiness brewing underneath their—to outsiders—correct and welcoming home. Eric was a well-liked minister, but he doubted his abilities and suffered anxiety attacks when he was preparing his sermons. He was a harsh and narrow-minded father, who sometimes suddenly erupted with violent anger about minor infractions. A sadistic disciplinarian, he meted out punishment through confinement and beatings. Karin watched unhappily but did not interfere with his disciplinary practices or protect Ingmar and his siblings from him. (The bishop in *Fanny and Alexander* is likely modeled after Bergman's father.) Erik became for Ingmar Bergman the representative of a weak, despotic, and despicable masculine.

Ingmar Bergman's imagination provided an escape from his unhappy family life. He made up plays that he and his siblings performed. His fascination with film started early, and he went to the movies as much as he could afford to. When he was eight years old, he obtained a primitive movie projector and began making films, combining old film scraps to create his own stories. He sometimes went to the movies with his maternal grandmother, visiting her in her big apartment and spending happy hours there as a child. She was a positive female in his life, but she could also be sadistically punitive. She was the one who locked him in the closet, an incident that he referred to in his autobiography and in his films. She was also unable to protect him and his siblings from the fallout from his emotionally turbulent family. (The nurturing grandmother in *Fanny and Alexander*, which was released in 1982, is perhaps modeled after her).

Conflicts with his father continued through his growing-up years and after a physical fight with him at age eighteen, Ingmar left home never to return to live there again. By then, he had already begun his theater career on an amateur level, something his parents strongly disapproved of.

Ingmar Bergman left his family physically; however, psychologically he could not escape. In the introduction to the autobiographical movie script *Private Confessions*, he writes,

> What does the truth look like? ...how were the thoughts, the feelings, the tendency towards anxiety of the main actors, twisted and shaped and deformed.... You wound me mortally. I wound you mortally. The psyches of the main characters are violently shaken up — it is like a nature catastrophe. Is it possible to describe this, and most importantly: is it not the long term consequences in bodies, souls, moods and facial features that only gradually, perhaps long after the breakdown itself, become visible? Is a confrontation like this on a verbal level? ...Maybe not in the so called reality, where this event is stretched over weeks, months and years in a grinding monotony, occasionally broken by truces and illusory reconciliation and pathetic assurances about a final peace... How do I describe the poison that unnoticeably fills the home like a nerve gas and that corrodes everybody's spirit for a long time, perhaps forever?[9]

In his autobiography he writes,

> Were we given masks instead of faces?... Were we given shame and guilt instead of love and forgiveness? ...Why did I live with a never-healing infected sore that went right through my body? ...Why was I incapable of normal human relationships for so long?[10]

The Women in Ingmar Bergman's Films

The women in many of Ingmar Bergman's films have characteristics in common, whether they are portrayed as weak, beautiful heroines, unreliable mothers, amoral, exhibitionistic women, physically ill, hysterical, barren, angry, intellectual, or frozen women. They are bound to their physicality, whether they are enslaved to their bodies, or have attempted to flee from their bodies, or their bodies are killing them. Their bodies define and imprison them.

Emily in *Fanny and Alexander* (1982) and Marianne in *Faithless* (2000) are portrayed as women who sacrifice their children for new relationships with men of questionable character. Emily is Alexander's and Fanny's mother in the film *Fanny and Alexander* — a beautiful woman, a leading actress, and the wife of the director of a family-owned theater. When her husband dies suddenly, she is courted by the rigid and punitive bishop that had officiated at her husband's funeral. She quickly accepts his marriage proposal, not considering her own or her children's welfare. Her sexual needs that were not met by her first husband seem to have, in part, motivated her, and she soon becomes pregnant. Her children are mistreated, kept captive, and ill fed by the bishop and his mother, his housekeeper, and his sister, three representatives of negative and sadistic mother energy. Emily also is badly treated and becomes a victim, unable to defend herself and her children, unable to leave the bishop.

However, all ends well in this film. The children are magically spirited out of the bishop's house by a Jewish friend of their grandmother. The bishop dies in a fire. Emily is, at the end, back in the bosom of her extended family, nursing her new baby and running the theater as seemingly capable as she was at the beginning of the film. Emily's fateful attraction to the bishop rings a bell in the context of Ingmar Bergman's parents. It is an exaggerated version of Karin's unhappy marriage to Erik, as the bishop, another weak and rigid man of the cloth. However, Emily, unlike Karin, escapes.

Ingmar Bergman wrote the script for *Faithless* (2000), which was directed by Liv Ullman, his former lover and a major star. It is an autobiographical story of an old director, named David Bergman, who looks back, with teary regret, at an affair he had with his best friend's wife, Marianne. Marianne is a successful actress, supposedly happily married to her composer husband with whom she has a nine-year-old daughter, Isabel. What is striking in this film is Marianne's suddenly awakened desire for David after he has casually asked her to have sex with him while spending the night at her house when her husband is away. She says "no" that night, but nonetheless invites him to sleep in her marital bed, and soon begins to pursue him without regard for the welfare of herself, her child, and husband. David responds, and they begin a relationship in which David early on becomes pathologically jealous and physically abusive. Marianne still decides to leave her husband and daughter for him. Although she expresses pain over her treatment of her daughter Isabel, she appears driven to abandon her for David. She says to Isabelle, "I am in love with David. I can't live without him. I am going to live with him and you are going to live with grandmother."[11] Marianne and David marry. Her former husband commits suicide. David continues to be abusive. Marianne puts up with this until she discovers that he has been unfaithful to her with a young actress in his new film; only then does she leave him. She later dies in a drowning accident. The director is left to cry about his mistreatment of her. (Liv Ullman related in an interview with Charlie Rose that Ingmar Bergman liked women like Marianne.[12])

Others female characters in Ingmar Bergman films, although they are portrayed less sympathetically, share similarities with Emily and Marianne. (Marianne expresses remorse, at least, for her actions in *Faithless.*) These women's bodies move them into relationships, which they enter without apparent concern for themselves and others. They allure with their seductive beauty, but they also repel with their hysteria and instinctual, amoral willing bodies, their inability to relate and feel empathy for their mates and children.

For example, Maria, played by Liv Ullman in *Cries and Whispers* (1971), is a beautiful, vain woman, constantly looking for confirmation of her beauty in the mirror. She has pursued a loveless affair with the visiting doctor, who after a while has scorned her. His rejection appears to make him even more attractive to her. One wonders what does she sees in him, a cold, cruel, and cynical man, shown in the film shoveling food into his mouth? She has a daughter that she uses as a playmate, but she does not have the ability to nurture and care for her or for her husband. (He is admittedly no great catch either, an unattractive and weak man.)

Anna, in *The Silence* (1962), is traveling by train with her son and sister Ester. They stop in a country seemingly on the eve of war, where they do not speak the native language. Anna, a lush, sensual woman, is shown ministering to her body with lotions and baths. She is overcome by lust watching a couple have sex in a movie theater and picks up a sleazy waiter for violent, unrelated sex that highlights their different status and their inability to understand each other's languages.

These women are portrayed as unhappy and driven, run by their bodies and disrespectful of themselves and those close to them. They have little ability to think and reason when in the proximity of a man whom they want sexually or who wants them. They seem to seek degradation and there is a strong element of aggression towards women in these portrayals. They also hold pieces of Ingmar Bergman's negative mother complex.

The negative mother complex is seen from still another perspective in other women characters in Bergman's films. These women, unlike the ones discussed previously, reject their traditional female sexual roles. Some are consumed by rage and appear to be stuck in emptiness.

Ingmar Bergman focuses on two women, Alma and Elisabeth, in the film *Persona* (1965). Elisabeth has retreated into stubborn, angry silence, rejecting her roles of mother, wife, and actress. She tears up a picture of her son and refuses to see her husband. After a hospital stay, she is sent to her psychiatrist's country house with the nurse Alma as her companion. Alma's nurturing nurse persona gradually breaks down during their stay. The initially prim Alma confides to Elisabeth her ecstatic participation in an orgy with two young strangers and her inability to recapture this excitement in her sexual relationship with her fiancee. She reveals her own ambivalence about being a mother to Elisabeth, telling her about an abortion she has had. However, at the end of the film, Alma puts on her chaste uniform and catches the bus to return to the hospital and her old nurse role. Elisabeth is left behind, still silent.

In *Cries and Whispers* (1971) Karin, one of three sisters, is an emotionally frozen and barren woman, married to an unpleasant man. She takes revenge against her sex and her husband through mutilating her vagina. As he comes to her room to claim his conjugal rights, she greets him smiling with vaginal blood smeared on her face.

These women, who attempt to deny and turn away from traditional, nurturing female roles, are full of rage towards themselves, their children, and their mates. They bear a likeness to the women discussed earlier, the ones who so promiscuously use their bodies, but the rage is more out in the open. Their method for dealing with their bodies is different, but the underlying message, that the feminine is not worth much, is the same. The sisters Maria and Karin in *Cries and Whispers* represent opposite sides of the same coin. Maria does not value herself and her sexuality and manifests this in her seductive pursuit of the rejecting and unattractive doctor. Karin expresses her loathing of her own female sexuality and the feminine more directly through her self-mutilation.

There is no movement towards wholeness. These women do not develop, do not move towards becoming more centered in themselves. They do not become better able to be in a relationship, or to truly mourn the nonexistence, or loss of, the relationship. They are stuck in their afflictions, pain, and anger, the way Ingmar Bergman's mother Karin was stuck. Karin, the sister in *Cries and Whispers* who mutilates her vagina, can be seen as an extreme version of Ingmar Bergman's mother Karin, a version where the wife finally shows her rage at being trapped in a miserable marriage.

Women's Illnesses

Women in Ingmar Bergman's films are sometimes plagued by physical or psychological illness. There is a lack of sympathy in his portrayals of these women's ailments, from lung disease, uterine cancer, psychopathology, or psychosis. Agnes, the dying unmarried sister in *Cries and Whispers* (1971), suffers horribly from what seems to be uterine cancer, coughing and throwing up with a distended belly and cramping legs. She slowly dies a painful death. The mannish and lonely Esther in *The Silence* (1962), masturbating in her hotel room, is dying from a mysterious lung disease and suffers from painful and violent phlegm-filled coughing attacks. In *Through a Glass Darkly* (1960), the only female character in the film is an increasingly disoriented, young, lonely, childless woman who at the end of the film is taken away by helicopter to to be committed to a mental hospital. Liv Ullman, as Anna in *The Passion of Anna* (1968), portrays a hysterical, pathological liar, who may have murdered her husband and son and may be trying to murder her lover. Her murderous rage was precipitated by these men's felt betrayals. Eva, another female character in this film, a former lover of Anna's boyfriend, suffers from migraines and the inability to sleep. She is stuck in a loveless marriage to a sadistic man who takes photographs of her when she is in the throes of a migraine attack.

These physically and mentally ill women hold Ingmar Bergman's severely wounded inner feminine, a feminine wounded to death. They also give voice to his aggression and rage towards the feminine, as shown by the harshness and lack of sympathy in his portrayals of them, as well as his anger towards a world so impossible for the feminine to thrive in.

Women's Relationships

I ngmar Bergman's view of relationships between men and women is pessimistic. There is no comfort or safety to be found in them. Instead they deteriorate to indifference or dissolve in acrimony. Women and men are alone in the world. Bergman's perspective has not changed. Happiness is transitory and related to the ecstatic, early part of a relationship, and then is followed by regret and withdrawal. This mirrors the relationship between Bergman's mother and father, where their happiness was brief, early in the relationship, and followed by life-long regret. It also mirror's his own life where one relationship followed another until his last marriage.

The strong women in Ingmar Bergman's films are usually women alone without men. Suzanne, the main character in the film *Dreams* (1954-55), runs a successful modeling agency. She is involved in a love affair with a married businessman, who ultimately rejects her. She is almost driven to suicide by his rejection, but then she seals off the pain and hardens her career persona. We see her laughing at the end of the film, smoking a cigarette as she gets ready for a new fashion shoot. With her lover she was reduced to tears and begging for his time; only when she is alone is she strong.

The female lead character Marianne in *Scenes from a Marriage* (1972) finds peace at the end of the film in occasional trysts with her former husband, Johan. Both have remarried and speak condescendingly about their new spouses. Their contentment is found in brief, secret interludes with each other. It is a relationship unhampered by marriage or commitment. Marianne is stronger now than when she was married to Johan and subjected to his betrayal. However, her strength is bought at a steep price; loneliness and the lack of sustained companionship and intimacy.

Women's relationships with other women are portrayed as superficial, ambivalent, unrelated, or hostile. In *Persona* (1965) the two main characters, Elisabeth, the mute actress, spies on the initially kind nurse, Alma, and writes catty letters about her to her psychiatrist. Alma finds out about this betrayal and sadistically inflicts pain on Elisabeth, watching as Elisabeth steps on broken glass she has scattered about. Anna's communication with her dying sister Esther is hostile and withholding in *The Silence* (1962). At the end of the film Anna gets on the train to go home with her son, leaving her sister Ester to die alone in a foreign country. The sisters in *Cries and Whispers* (1971) have a few moments of peace as they read to the dying Agnes or when shown in flashback walking in white dresses in the castle garden, but they mostly talk superficially to each other or avoid each other. Moments of closeness are brief and denied or defended against.

Mother's Ambivalence

Mothers are ambivalent or overtly rejecting of their children in Ingmar Bergman's films. They have characteristics in common with Ingmar Bergman's mother, who wanted to be left alone in her private world, as she found no way to leave her marriage and felt she had sacrificed her happiness for her children. When physically present, she was mostly absent emotionally. Ingmar Bergman writes in his autobiography that he desperately loved his mother and tried to get her attention, but she would send him away, telling him to go and play with his toys. This maternal rejection is played out in his films. Elisabeth in *Persona* (1965) is disgusted with her son's desperate search for attention from her. Alma, the nurse in the same film, speaks of her lack of desire for children. Anna in *The Silence* (1962) has little time for her son, and when she relates to him, she relates in a sexual manner. Maria in *Cries and Whispers* (1971) uses her daughter as a playmate when it suits her. Her dying sister Agnes speaks about their mother, who was not available to her, who would not listen to Agnes but would be bored and tell her to go away. Marianne in *Scenes from a Marriage* (1972) pays cursory attention to her two daughters who are never seen in the film. In *Faithless* (2000), Marianne, who is shown initially as loving towards her daughter, suddenly leaves her marriage for her new lover with little consideration for how this will effect her daughter.

These women's lack of nurturing ability is also present in Ingmar Bergman himself. He left his wives alone with their young children and was not part of their lives as they were growing up. The few times he spent with them he could be distant, critical, and rejecting. His daughter Anna writes,

> In my unconscious I carry the memory of something that happened to my two year older brother Jan who was a bit clumsy and a dreamer as a child. Our father Ingmar often got irritated with him. Jan got in his way and disturbed his thinking. Ingmar

was always working, always creating. He disliked us children, the four of us, he had had in his marriage to Ellen. We got on his nerves. We disturbed him.[13]

This is a sad book. Anna Bergman seems to have spent much of her life desperately and fruitlessly looking for love and approval from her father and father substitutes.

Ingmar Bergman describes at the end of his autobiography a vision of his mother he had several years after her death. In this vision, he is back in his parents' old apartment, sees his mother Karin, and talks to her. He addresses her in the third person as 'Mother', never directly as *'Ni'* or the less formal *'Du'* or by her name. Addressing his mother with the title, 'Mother', exemplifies the distance and formality of the relationship. (And I recognize this. I refer to my ninety-three-year-old mother as 'Mother', never *'du'* or even *'ni'*!) Ingmar Bergman was seventy-two years old when he had this vision. However, with his mother, he becomes in the vision a subservient and needy child as he speaks:

> Don't be angry now Mother!... I want to ask Mother something urgent. Several years ago I was sitting in my workroom in Faro...I was reading and listening to the rain. Then I felt that Mother was very near me, beside me.... It wasn't that I had fallen asleep. I'm sure of that and it wasn't even a supernatural event. I knew Mother was with me in the room, or did I imagine it? I can't make it out. Now, I'm asking, Mother. "It probably wasn't me, she says calmly. I am still far too tired. Are you sure it wasn't someone else?"[14]

His response to his mother's answer to his question is to feel let down. He feels that he has trespassed by asking her a question. One could imagine that he could be angry with her for not giving him anything of herself, not even admitting her presence. But how could he allow himself to be angry with his tired, martyred mother? How could he possibly have confronted her? And thus, how can there be a possibility for healing and for reconciliation? Instead, the anger and hurt at his mother's betrayal has found expression in his negative portrayals of women and their miserable fates.

Healing of the Feminine?

In two later biographical scripts, *Best Intentions* (1991) and *Private Confessions* (1996), directed by Billie August and Liv Ullman, the lead female character in each film is inspired by Ingmar Bergman's mother and portrayed with more sympathy and balance than the women in his earlier scripts. The first film tells the story of Bergman's parents' marriage before his birth and the second tells us about what happened later. We see the marriage deteriorate and this woman trying and trying with little success to understand and love her narrow-minded, severe husband. She remains in the marriage held by duty and cultural demands. Ten years into this unhappy marriage she becomes involved with a friend of the family, a seminary student, and enters into a new, happy extramarital relationship which she keeps secret for several years. She finally confesses her infidelity to her husband and asks for a divorce, but her husband, her mother, and also her lover, thwart her attempt to leave. She struggles with the loss of her relationship but attempts to be a good wife and mother. She now knows what happiness is and what a loving relationship is like, and her unhappy marriage becomes even more difficult to bear. This woman comes across as a real person, someone who is able to feel joy and also pain. She is someone who knows what a good relationship would be like, someone who is able to relate intimately with her lover and express pain when she loses him. One can understand and sympathize with her predicament.

Saraband, the first film directed by Ingmar Bergman since *Fanny and Alexander* in 1982, was released on Swedish television in December of 2003, and just released as a film in the United States this summer. I read the script when it was published in Sweden. In it, Marianne, the wife from *Scenes From a Marriage* (Bergman's earlier film produced thirty years ago), pays a surprise visit to her ex-husband Johan, whom she has not seen for more than thirty years. He is living in isolation in a house in the country. Marianne is now sixty-seven years old, and her ex-husband is eighty-four. Henrik, age sixty-three, Johan's son from an earlier marriage, and Henrik's daughter Karin have been staying in an adjacent cottage belonging to Johan. Henrik keeps Karin virtually captive, both of them practicing cello together. Henrik hates Johan, who rejected him as child, and they never see each other. Marianne becomes a catalyst for change, helping to break up their frozen distance. Karin talks to her grandfather for the first time during Marianne's visit. Marianne helps to thaw Johan so he is able to express his care for his granddaughter. (She literally thaws Johan by letting him come into bed and lie next to her when he is having an anxiety attack.) Marianne also becomes a witness to Henrik's unresolved grief over his wife's death, which has been expressed in his incestuous and abusive relationship with Karin. Karin is finally able to leave her father and find a place for herself in the music world. Henrik tries to commit suicide, but by then Karin has gone abroad to her new job, and she is not called back.

I recognized here themes from older Ingmar Bergman films—the characters' isolation from each other and the abuse of the feminine. The initial inability of Karin to even question her situation is familiar, as is her putting up with abuse. But there is an important difference here. Karin, as representing the abused feminine, does not have to die as her mother had to. With the help of Marianne, Karin is able to leave her father and free herself from the abusive relationship. She leaves for a career in music and to be with young people her age. Henrik also admits his own guilt to Marianne.

I see this film as illustrating a lightening-up of the mother complex for Ingmar Bergman. Henrik, speaking to Marianne about his dead wife, says,

> If you talk about Anna I start to cry. That is the way it is. Anna has been gone for over two years. It still hurts. To live has become a ritual. There are no words for this. I have become an invalid. Anna gave my life meaning. I often think about death now. I imagine that Anna is waiting for me. This is how I imagine it: I am walking on the forest road by the river. It is a fall day, foggy, wind still, silent. I see someone walking by the gate. She is wearing her blue jeans skirt and blue sweater and is barefoot. She has her hair in a thick braid. She is walking towards me. It is Anna who is coming towards me. And then I understand that she is dead. Then the strangest thing happens. I think is it really that simple! We go through life wondering about death and what will or will not come after death. And then it is so simple.[15]

This could be Ingmar Bergman speaking about his wife Ingrid to whom *Saraband* is dedicated. He referred to this quote in the 2004

interview on Swedish television cited earlier, saying that this is how he
imagines dying. He imagines that Ingrid will meet him. I was struck
by his gentleness and peacefulness in this interview as he talked about
himself, his past, and present. Ingrid, the steadying, calming influence
to whom he was married from age fifty-seven until her death in 1995
when he was eighty-two, helped him begin to heal his wounds around
the feminine. He has also been helped by his long film career and his
opportunities to look at the wounded feminine from many different
angles.

The young feminine can now be allowed to live in *Saraband*. Karin
escapes alive, unlike Ingmar Bergman's mother Karin. There is in
Saraband, as in *Fanny and Alexander*, also a nurturing, older, mature
woman, Marianne, who steps in to help Karin leave. Ingmar Bergman
can at age eighty-four present both the positive, nurturing, older
feminine, as represented by Marianne, and the younger, trapped
feminine, represented by Karin. Karen can now be allowed to escape
the clutches of the negative masculine with the help of the nurturing,
older feminine, Marianne—unlike Karin Bergman's mother Anna, who
would not, or could not, assist her in leaving her unhappy marriage.
This film points to a shift in Ingmar Bergman's negative mother
complex and his wounded feminine. The complex is no longer as
negative as before. Some healing has taken place. The work is not
finished for him (or for me) as the work never ends. The energy around
the complex may become less negative, but there will always be energy
left to be activated to give us opportunity to do more work until we
die.

NOTES

1. Interview with Ingmar Bergman on Swedish Television, July,
2004.

2. Stig Bjorkman, Torsten Manns, & Jonas Sima, *Bergman on
Bergman*, trans. Paul Britten Austin (New York: Da Capo Press, 1993),
188.

3. Ingmar Bergman, *The Magic Lantern: An Autobiography* (New
York: Penguin, 1988), 289-290.

4. Birgit Linton-Malmfors, *Den Dubbla Verkligheten, Karin and
Eric Bergman i dagbocker och brev 1907-1936* (Stockholm: Carlsson,
1992), 89 (my translation).

5. Ingmar Bergman, *Bilder* (Stockholm: Norstedts, 1990), 17 (my translation).

6. *Den Dubbla Verkligheten*, 94.

7. *Ibid.*, 97.

8. *Ibid.*, 128.

9. Ingmar Bergman, *Den Goda Viljan, Sondagsbarn, Enskilda Samtal* (Stockholm: Norstedts, 1998), 61-62 (my translation).

10. *The Magic Lantern*, 284-285.

11. Ingmar Bergman, *Forestallningar, Trolosa, En Sjalslig Angelagenhet, Karlek utan Alskare* (Stockholm: Norstedts, 2000), 78 (my translation).

12. Interview with Liv Ullman on Charlie Rose, February 23, 2001.

13. Gun Arestad, *Anna Bergman berattar for Gun Arestad* (Stockholm: Bra Bok, 1987), 5 (my translation).

14. Ingmar Bergman, *The Magic Lantern*, 283.

15. Ingmar Bergman, *Saraband* (Stockholm: Norstedt, 2003), 59 (my translation).

SEARCH FOR THE SOUL: THE CINEMA OF KRZYSZTOF KIEŚLOWSKI AND *THE DOUBLE LIFE OF VÉRONIQUE*

LINDA SCHIERSE LEONARD

I'm somebody who doesn't know, someone who's searching.
—Krzysztof Kieślowski

Fifteen years ago, while lecturing in Manhattan, I happened in on a special showing of the cinema of new Polish directors at the Modern Museum of Art. Because it was my last day in New York, I saw only two of the films. I left the theatre astounded. I couldn't pronounce the name of the director, but I knew it was the work of genius. The films were two of a series of ten hour-long films — *The Decalogue*—and were made for Polish public television. Each explored one of the Ten Commandments. Set in a Warsaw housing block in the 1980s, the characters were struggling for their souls—each in the midst of a moral dilemma so profound and perplexing that the exact commandment was left uncertain for the viewer. The films provided

Linda Schierse Leonard, Ph.D., is a Jungian analyst and the author of six books: *The Wounded Woman, On The Way to the Wedding, Witness to the Fire, Meeting the Madwoman, Following the Reindeer Woman: Path of Peace and Harmony,* and *The Call to Create.* This article is part of her upcoming book, *Finding Meaning at the Movies.*

no answers, only questions to ponder for the rest of my life. The director was Krzysztof Kieślowski, unknown in America at that time.

I have been in love with foreign films for nearly half a century. I write about them in my books because they touch the deeps of archetypal understanding. The films of Ingmar Bergman, Federico Fellini, Robert Bresson, Carl Dreyer, François Truffaut, Yasujiro Ozu, Akira Kurosawa, Zhang Yi-Mou, Im Kwon-Taek, Bernardo Bertolucci, Pier Paolo Pasolini, Rainer Werner Fassbinder, Vitorrio de Sica, Luis Buñuel, Jean Cocteau, and Andrei Tarkovsky are a few of my early passions. But after seeing only two of Kieślowski's films, I fell deeply, madly, passionately in love with this new mysterious movie muse.

For a long time I searched for showings of Kieślowski's films in America but to no avail. Then, in 1991, while lecturing at a conference in Melbourne, Australia, I discovered that three of his films were showing at a film festival there. The films turned out to be lengthened versions of the very two I had seen in New York—*A Short Film About Love* and *A Short Film About Killing*—in addition to a new one, *The Double Life of Véronique*. Once again I left the theatre thrilled and ecstatic.

I was determined to find everything I could about this director. Kieślowski was born on June 27, 1941, in Warsaw during the war years in Poland, a country disrupted by Hitler and Stalin. His family was poor. His father was a civil engineer who suffered from tuberculosis. Unable to work, his father was sent from one sanatorium town to another. His mother supported the family by working as an office clerk and moved frequently to be with her husband.

Kieślowski's health was poor as a child. Because of this, his family's meager finances, and their many moves, he and his sister were sent to various sanatoria for children. Although he spent much time in convalescence, he was able to play with other children when he was well. However, books became his most intimate friends. His favorite authors included Dostoevsky, Camus, Shakespeare, the Greek dramatists, Faulkner, Kafka, and Vargas Llosa. He felt that great literature was able to achieve a fuller description of what lies within us than film. When he was young he was rarely able to see films because there was too little money. Sometimes he would climb up on a roof and peer through a vent to see part of the screen.

Like many young artists, Kieślowski was bored at school and didn't like to study, although he read profusely at home. Since he admired his father's wisdom, he followed his father's suggestion to attend school to train to be a fireman; his father knew instinctively that after three months his son would be ready to study. His parents asked a distant relative to arrange for him to attend an arts school in Warsaw where he was exposed to theatre and the cinema—a world with different values from the everyday world that emphasized money and comfort. Kieślowski fell in love with theater and aspired to be a stage director. Later, he was determined to study at the acclaimed film school in Łódź where he applied three times before he was accepted. He said that his persistence to get into the film school was due to his own tenacious nature and also his desire to fulfill his mother's wishes for his career in film. He graduated in 1969 and thus began his film career.

Inspired by the early films of Fellini and Bergman, Kieślowski said that Ken Loach's *Kes* was the first film to affect him deeply because of its compassionate simplicity. Fellini taught him about surrealistic poetry and Bergman about probing rigor. He admired the films of Orson Welles, Andrei Tarkovsky, Robert Bresson, Bo Widerberg, Robert Flaherty, Ivan Passer, François Truffaut, Charlie Chaplin, and Tony Richardson.

Kieślowski's early films were documentaries. As a student he was politically active, so making documentaries about ordinary people in conflict with state institutions was a way he could bring social conscience to cinema in a repressive regime. Although his film career was threatened continually by political and economic change within Poland and by political censorship, Kieślowski made some thirty black and white documentaries. Then, after political censorship was abolished, he had to deal with the economic crisis and the lack of funds in Poland to make films. Kieślowski pointed out that in many ways it was easier to trick the censors than to deal with the profit-ridden mandates of commercial filmmaking.

His first consideration in making documentaries and feature films was to focus on the portrait of the individual. Later he became concerned about the way in which documentaries could be invasive of a person's life, so he turned to creating characters for feature films because he thought they could delve more deeply into the interiority of human life. *The Decalogue* brought him to the attention of international audiences. He followed *The Decalogue* with his colorful, elegant, intimate, and spiritual films that were co-produced in Poland and France: *The Double Life of Véronique* and his trilogy, *Three Colours: Blue, White, and Red*, which received an array of international awards.

Kieślowski was neither a Catholic nor a Communist. He hated organized movements. But he did believe that an absolute point of reference exists—a mysterious energy that is lasting, absolute, and evident. He would not have called this greater spiritual force God in the traditional sense. He searched for God but instead found the divine energy in people. Although he despaired about injustice and inhumanity in the world, he created films that helped people seek out goodness.

His films offer us an I-Thou experience. They invite us into a sacred space in which we can discover ourselves. Like all great works of art, films can carry spiritual energy, revelation, grace, and transcendence. Films have a silent invisible potency, a chemistry that affects us and can change us. When this happens the movie theatre is like the ancient alchemical vessel, a crucible for transformation.

Andrei Tarkovsky, the great Russian film director whom Kieślowski admired, believed that creative films—such as Kieślowski's—offer spiritual awakening and community to their recipients. He expressed the I-Thou relationship made possible by cinema in this way. He wrote:

> Touched by a masterpiece, a person begins to hear in himself that same call of truth which prompted the artist to his creative act. When a link is established between the word and its beholder, the latter experiences a sublime, purging trauma. Within that aura which unites masterpieces and audience, the best sides of our souls are made known, and we long for them to be freed. In those moments we recognize and discover ourselves, the unfathomable depths of our own potential, and the furthest reaches of our emotions.[1]

Many people take movies on a literal level only, taking everything at face value, and thus losing the depth and richness of symbolic life that a masterpiece can express. The I-It attitude toward film is literal minded and unimaginative; it confuses archetypal living symbols with signs that are fixed, flat stereotypes. People who approach films with the I-It orientation are likely to want prescribed plots, conventional characters, and happy predictable endings that do not challenge them to question the meaning of their lives.

Commercial movies are often made to provide the audience with easy answers because they make money. Manufacturers of formulaic films—those whose only object is to make money—treat viewers as "objects," thus demeaning them to the status of "It." If they are presented only with hackneyed movies, audiences tend to become accustomed to them. Thus their approach to cinema becomes controlling; they want movies that make them comfortable and become threatened by films that challenge them. Movies that are predictable rob the audience of going through their own process. As filmgoers, the more we rely on easy mechanical plots and stereotypical characters, the more we lose our opportunity to discover, understand, and learn about our own complexities and the mystery of being human.

For transformation to take place, however, we must respond with an I-Thou attitude. If we relate to the film as an object from which we want to obtain a specific end, we lose our chance to find the sacred in film.

Kieślowski's hope in directing was to try to create films in which people find themselves. He constantly honed his skills, hoping to come as close as he could to showing the soul's complexities in a way that would speak to other human beings. Kieślowski *cared* for the spiritual life of the audience and hoped that his films could illumine someone's fate or help them to make life changes.

In the following story, he described what makes the arduous process of filmmaking worthwhile for him. Once a fifteen-year-old girl approached Kieślowski in Paris and said that she had gone to see *The Double Life of Véronique* several times. She wanted to thank him. Seeing the film enabled her to realize something she hadn't known before—that the soul does exist. Kieślowski said:

> There's something beautiful in that. It was worth making *Véronique* for that girl. It was worth working for a year, sacrificing all that money, energy, time, patience, torturing yourself, making thousands of decisions, so that one young girl in Paris should realize that there is such a thing as a soul. It's worth it.[2]

Another time a woman about fifty recognized him in Berlin where *A Short Film About Love* was being shown. She told him that she had seen the film with her daughter. Although they shared a cramped apartment, neither mother nor daughter had been able to share their real feelings for several years. They had been quarreling and could talk only about superficial things. After seeing the film, the daughter suddenly kissed her mother for the first time in five years. Kieślowski surmised that the film had helped them to realize the real reason for their conflict. "It was worth making the film for that kiss, for that one woman," he said.[3]

He preferred to call himself an artisan rather than an artist. "The artisan finds knowledge within the confines of his skills," Kieślowski once told an interviewer. Known for his modesty and sardonic humor, he was aware of the many pitfalls of getting to the top. "I don't like the word 'success,'" he reiterated. It suggests a static state in which we are likely to forget human pain and what it means to suffer and to hurt. This results in failing to care about ourselves and others. Humility is at the core of the search for the soul.

Creating, Kieślowski emphasized, is an arduous and continual process of small steps that take him nearer to his goal: to capture on film that which dwells within us—a goal that he considered rare, perhaps impossible, to reach.

> For example, I know a lot about lenses, about the editing room, I know what the different buttons on the camera are for. I know more or less how to use a microphone. I know all that, but that's not real knowledge. Real knowledge is knowing how to live, why we live ... things like that.[4]

Kieślowski described the daily work of filmmaking, deflating the overblown exaggerated image of the celebrity and the dramatic events that go with it:

> Filmmaking doesn't mean audiences, festivals, reviews, interviews. It means getting up every day at six o'clock in the morning. It means the cold, the rain, the mud and having to carry heavy lights. It's a nerve racking business, and, at a certain point, everything else has to come second, including your family, emotions, and private life. Of course, engine drivers, businessmen or bankers would say the same thing about their jobs. No doubt they'd be right.[5]

He believed that the elusive spirit of a film is born in the editing room. Shooting the film—an act that filmgoers sometimes mistake for the entire art—is only a first stage in which the director collects material and creates possibilities. Craftsmanship requires him to attempt to cut out everything that is not necessary to the film.

In addition to his emphasis on the importance of craft, Kieślowski's advice to young filmmakers was to examine their own lives and to develop by looking within to see what brought them to direct a particular film. "If the artist doesn't understand his own life," Kieślowski asked, "how can he understand the lives of the characters in the stories and the lives of the audience?" A director must learn to find the inner moral compass in himself or herself. The process of self-discovery requires suffering. Going through pain builds human nature and helps us learn to care about others. The easy life does not lead to understanding others.

Kieślowski enjoyed the art of improvisation and collaboration with the whole production company. He co-wrote scripts with Krzysztof Piesiewicz, his long-time fellow-writer, and collaborated with the cinematographer, Slawomir Idziak, and the composer, Zbigniew Preisner. He considered the music and the cinematography to be essential parts of the text. Kieślowski loved actors. He talked with them and asked them about their dreams the night before and shared his dreams with them too. He asked the actors for their ideas about a scene and often put them into the script. Their intuitions, feelings, attitudes to the world contribute to the film. In filmmaking,

> ... the whole point is to motivate people to think together, to solve things together. And that's how I work with lighting cameramen, soundmen, composers, actors, grips, and stage-hands and script-girls and everybody .... Besides there's something like intuition which always varies a little from person to person. It can inspire much better solutions and very often does.[6]

The luminous Irène Jacob, who starred in *The Double Life of Véronique* and *Red*, described his approach to filmmaking as follows:

> He preferred not to explain his ideas of a film on the set, but to keep a constant process of discovery open—not already codified, framed, but fresh for interpretation.[7]

Kieślowski also hoped the producer would be a fruitful collaborator. Most of all he hoped the audience would collaborate by participating in the process of discovery by entering into their emotions and opening to the mystery of the soul.

After finishing his trilogy, *Blue, White, and Red*, Kieślowski surprised the cinematic world by announcing at the premiere of *Red* in Cannes that he was going to retire. He suffered from weak lungs and a serious heart condition. He said he preferred to retire in solitude to his country house in Poland to read books, to chop wood, and to smoke (he was an inveterate chain smoker). Later, however, he started a new project with Piesiewicz and Preisner, a trilogy to be called *Heaven, Hell,* and *Purgatory*. They planned to go to sacred sites around the world where they would first present their projects. However, fate deemed otherwise. Only part-way into the script of *Heaven*, Kieślowski suffered a heart-attack. He chose to go to a local Warsaw hospital for bypass heart surgery, refusing offers from specialists in New York and Paris and two specialized open-heart surgery centers in Poland. He said he was an ordinary Pole and did not want special treatment. He died after surgery on March 13, 1996 at the age of fifty-four.

Towards the end of his life Kieślowski commented:

> I'm confirmed in my pessimism that things are getting worse and worse in the world. Precisely because I don't see any hope, I have to be passionately, desperately looking for it. If I find it anywhere, I think I'll find it in people, because everybody has a little light inside themselves, and you have to look for that. It's important to remind people of certain simple truths like what St. Paul said 2,000 years ago: that love is important. We have a tendency to forget that in our haste to simplify our lives.[8]

Kieślowski found that light through creating the characters in *The Double Life of Véronique* and later in his trilogy, *Three Colors: Blue, White, and Red*. His films are a testament to his hope for people and to his search for the light of love that lies within the human soul.

* * * * *

My encounters with Kieślowski's films seemed to be synchronistic. Each one addressed something pressing in my own life, something I was writing about and trying to understand in myself and others. I did not know then that Kieślowski was to be hailed as the filmic master of synchronicity. A major theme of *The Double Life of Véronique* is precisely synchronicity—the seemingly chance but meaningful meeting of two women whose souls reflect one another. The film also deals with the archetypal motifs of the double, the mystical feminine, and the I-Thou relationship.

When I first saw *The Double Life of Véronique*, I was transported into a timeless realm that was breathtaking. I felt I had entered the mystical field of the feminine—a sphere to which I had been trying to give expression ever since writing my first book, *The Wounded Woman*—, in which I concluded that the integration of gentleness and strength is essential to healing the wounded woman as well as transforming the lack of integration of the healthy feminine in western culture. In a subsequent book, *Following the Reindeer Woman: Path of Peace and Harmony,* I described my vision of this instinctual and spiritual feminine power. I believe we need to acknowledge and draw on a new feminine energy—one that is gentle, caring, and strong but not controlling or fearful. We need to find a feminine force that is wildly ecstatic yet resolute and tenacious enough to move through the World's Dark Night.

Synchronistically, while writing the book on the Reindeer Woman, I saw *The Double Life of Véronique* for the first time. I felt the film portrayed a courageous, compassionate young woman who is able to see the dazzling light and to sing its passion for the divine despite the background of the dark night—to live in the unity of light and dark. This way of being is described by the mystics as the movement of the whole person, freely and unfettered, into the whole heart of the great "*Mysterium tremendum et fascinans.*"

Expressing the mystery of the soul is a problematical task because the rational mind wants to reduce everything to transparent explanations. Yet the realm of mystery eludes clear concepts and logical thought; it threatens those who fear loss of control. *The Double Life of Véronique* throws the viewer into the sphere of mystery; it leaves the audience with questions rather than answers.

In an interview Kieślowski commented that *The Double Life of Véronique* is an attempt to show the soul on celluloid, albeit an impossible task.

> Showing this on film is difficult. If I show too much the mystery
> disappears; I can't show too little because then nobody will
> understand anything. My search for the right balance between
> the obvious and the mysterious is the reason for all the various
> versions made in the cutting room.[9]

He added that *The Double Life of Véronique* is a film about
"sensibility, presentiments and relationships which are difficult to name,
which are irrational." It is a film about the feminine.

> Women feel things more acutely, have more presentiments, greater
> sensitivity, greater intuition and attribute more importance to all
> these things. *Véronique* couldn't have been made about a man.[10]

It is challenging to portray a person who can express ecstasy and
affirm the light without sinking into sentimentality. Kieślowski
accepted this challenge in his portrayal of the women in *The Double
Life of Véronique*. Kieślowski, who was greatly influenced by Dostoevsky,
aimed to express the feelings and sensitivity of inner life. Before him,
Dostoevsky struggled to depict such a sensitive person—a
compassionate man with a pure and beautiful heart, "a wholly beautiful
individual,"—in his novel *The Idiot*, and later through his character,
Alyosha, in *The Brothers Karamozov*. Dostoevsky said: "I believe there
can be nothing more difficult than this, especially in our time."[11]

Like Dostoevsky, Kieślowski attempted to bring to light the
emotional states and moods of the soul.

> *Véronique* is a film about emotions .... What else is there other
> than emotions? What is important? Only that. I play on them so
> that people should love or hate my characters. I play on them so
> that people should sympathize with them. I play on them so
> that people should want my characters to win if they're playing
> a good game.[12]

To bring people into the realm of emotions, he created atmosphere
and mood through music, color, use of camera, silence, and the presence
of his actors. The expressionistic style of his cinematographer, Slawomir
Idziak, and the music of his composer, Zbigniew Preisner, revealed
the most personal moments of his characters and the greater spiritual
forces at play in their lives. He chose Irène Jacob (who won the Best
Actress award when the film premiered at Cannes) to play the leading

roles because he had been touched by her shyness, tenderness, and loving nature. Her natural warmth lights up the two Véroniques. Kieślowski used camera close-ups and emphasized her warmth by using red, a color in which she is often clothed, and he shot the film with a basic golden yellow filter to create a sense of warmth and to effect uniformity for both sections of the film. The dominant golden color that suffuses the film shows a world that "… appears far more beautiful than it really is."[13]

Kieślowski hoped that the audience would be able to enter into the soul's journey through feeling, through listening, and through waiting with the character in her process. To understand Kieślowski's films one has to dive into the deeps with him. Thinking about *The Double Life of Véronique* in a linear analytical way obstructs one's experience.

* * * * *

It is essential to pay attention to the first frames of a film because they prepare us for the developing story. The opening shots of *The Double Life of Véronique* present two tiny girls. The first shot begins with a caption, "Poland, 1968." We hear delicate music play lightly as we see the marveling eyes of a two-year-old girl and hear a woman's voice in Polish, presumably that of her mother, tell her to look up towards the stars shining in the night sky that show the start of Christmas Eve. In the next shot, captioned "France, 1968," a little girl looks down with delight as a woman's voice in French bids her to inspect the veins and the very soft down of the first leaf of springtime. The singing birds announce springtime, and all the trees have leaves. This is our first encounter with the Polish Veronika and the French Véronique. In each shot the mother says to her daughter, "Look." In this way Kieślowski invites us to look and listen to the wondrous beauty of life.

The title sequence follows and the onlooker is thrown into a liminal moment through the camera's viewpoint. On reflection, the lens seems to be behind a magnifying glass, thus distorting the imagery. We see the vague moving shape of a young girl. As she enters a city square she seems to have been jostled. The papers she carries have been knocked to the ground and she bends down to pick them up. The mood is ominous, unsettling to the viewer, and contrasts to the earlier shots of the little girls and the scene which follows next. In effect, the audience is thrown into the unconscious realm via Kieślowski's method of shooting through glass, thus creating a sense of mirroring and doubling.

After this, about two and a half minutes into the film, we see a clear close-up of a sensuous and spirited young woman singing in the rain. Her luminous face turns upwards to the heavens as though to greet the raindrops. Although she is with some other girls who run from the rain as an imposing statue of Stalin passes by them on a truck, Veronika sings the last note to the fullest, enjoying her communion with the rain and inviting us to join in her ecstasy.

Next we see Veronika kissing her boyfriend passionately in the pouring rain. They go into her apartment and make love. During the erotic love scene, Veronika sees a large photo of herself on the wall, intimating the larger image of the feminine Self that she comes to symbolize.

From these early scenes we can see that Veronika loves life and is open to it. She embraces nature (water and sky) and sexuality along with her spiritual love of music. She is natural toward others and herself. When her boyfriend, Antek, and later a teacher, comment on the beauty of her voice, she acknowledges her gift, saying, "I know." Veronika is open and unafraid, gentle and strong. The adult Veronika is the grown-up little girl with the upturned face whom we saw in the first shot of the film. It is Poland in 1990, just after the fall of Communism, a still turbulent time that is evidenced later in the film by a commotion during which Stalin's statue is removed from its pedestal. Veronika's way of being is a stark opposite to the patriarchal, tyrannical Stalin. She portrays the feminine embodiment of the creative spirit.

Veronika lives with her widowed father and the two have a warm, affectionate relationship. After waking up suddenly from a dream she sees a picture of a small village with a church, a picture that her father is painting. She shares a deep presentiment with her father, saying, "I have a strange feeling that I'm not alone." Then she asks him: "What do I really want?" Although her father does not understand the deeper level of what she tells him, he accepts her feelings. She tells him to say goodbye for her to Antek and goes to Kraków where she visits her ailing aunt. Veronika passes the landscape in the painting on the train to Kraków and looks at it through a small crystal-like ball that reflects the church upside down along with some stars.

Veronika is concerned about her aunt, who laughs in response, mentioning that both her own and Veronika's mother supposedly died in good health. Veronika notices a dwarf-like lawyer enter the house; her aunt has hired him to make a will.

In Kraków Veronika contacts a girlfriend who invites her to a musical rehearsal. Veronika finds herself spontaneously singing along. The teacher is struck by her unusual voice and asks her to join a singing competition. She happily accepts. But dark moments begin to intrude. As she walks sprightly to rehearsal, singing joyfully to herself and bouncing the crystal ball, she is knocked down in the central Kraków square. The scene is a repeat of the earlier unsettling scene during the credits. Caught in the midst of a political scuffle—a fracas that reflects the unrest in the city—her pages of music fall to the ground.

She bends down to pick up the music. As she gets up she sees a young French woman boarding a tourist bus, then taking pictures through the window. Veronika is astounded. The young French woman is wearing a black coat and red gloves just like she is and looks exactly like herself. Although the French woman does not see her, Veronika begins to smile with recognition as she sees her own image in the woman on the bus. This recognition was presaged when Veronika told her father that she had the strange feeling that she was not alone. We, along with Veronika, begin to realize that she has just encountered her double. On reflection it seems possible that the scene during the credits was shot through the bus window by the French woman. The French woman, whose name is Véronique, is the grown-up tiny girl shown looking at the leaf in the early shot that is captioned France 1968. The momentous scene of this mysterious synchronous meeting is at the center of the film. It is the only scene in which the two women cross paths.

Veronika continues to the music teacher's house where she sings, twisting a black string that binds together the music. After she leaves, another ominous event occurs. Veronika suddenly falls to the ground on some dead leaves, clutching her heart. When she looks up she sees a flasher on the street. During the fall she experiences the early warnings of a heart condition from which her own mother died when she was a child. Despite the warning sign, Veronika auditions and wins the competition to sing in the concert. However, one of the judges has voted against her, a woman who is dressed in a black hat and coat and who looks forebodingly at Veronika.

After the audition she goes home on the bus and sees her boyfriend riding a motorcycle. He has followed her to Kraków to give her a Christmas present and to tell her that he loves her. She jumps off the bus and runs to embrace him. He ask her to call him at the Holiday Inn where he is staying in room 287. Veronika cares for him, but she has made a choice. Her prime commitment is to her music.

Back at her aunt's house to dress for the performance, Veronika tells her aunt that she is almost afraid the audition went too well. As she gets dressed she looks out of the window and sees an old woman struggling with her bags. She calls out to help the old woman, but she continues on her way.

At the concert Veronika sings the haunting music of the two-hundred-year-old Dutch composer, Van der Budenmajer. Her singing is ethereal. After a long section in which she sublimely sings lyrics by Dante, she gasps for breath and clutches her heart but decides to continue singing. Then, in a shocking moment, Veronika suddenly collapses from a heart attack and dies before the performance is over.

The last scene of the first section of the film shows her funeral, and we see dirt being shoveled onto the glass top of the coffin in which Veronika lies dead. Immediately the camera flashes to France the same day; as the sounds of the dirt falling on the coffin continue. At the very moment that Veronika is being buried, the French Véronique is making love with her boyfriend. However, Véronique's lovemaking is disturbed by a baffling feeling of loss. She tells her boyfriend: "It's as if I was grieving for someone I don't know." Véronique tells her boyfriend she wants to be alone, as the aria that Veronika sang plays in the background.

Like Veronika, Véronique is a singer. Unlike Veronika, Véronique decides to stop singing. She tells her music teacher: "Why, I don't know. But I know I have to stop." He tells her that a person with so much talent has no right to stop, and she replies, "I know." Later she goes to the hospital to have her heart checked. Instead of pursuing her singing career, she decides to teach music to children.

One day a puppeteer comes to the school and performs a story for the children. He opens a red box and takes out a beautiful ballerina who dances exquisitely, then falls to the ground seemingly dead (just as the Polish Veronika did in her performance). An older woman covers the dead ballerina in a white cloth that looks like a cocoon. To the music of the aria, the ballerina is transformed into a butterfly. Véronique is fascinated by the exquisite show and by the puppeteer.

In music class she tells the children to look at the blackboard where she has written the name of her favorite composer, Van der Budenmajer, whose music the Polish Veronika was singing when she collapsed. As the Dutch composer's music plays, Véronique looks out the window and notices a truck with a butterfly (a symbol of the Psyche) painted on it; the driver is the puppeteer. Véronique tries to find out who he is.

At home she answers a mysterious phone call; an unknown man has called her and she hears a woman singing the music of Van der Budenmajer in the background. As she listens she sees an image of Veronika singing, then collapsing, emerge from a red and golden background. The golden light disappears and only the red remains.

Véronique visits her father and tells him she's in love, but she doesn't yet know who the man is. She also confides in her father that she has a strange, sad sensation that she is not alone. Her father replies knowingly that someone has disappeared from her life. Véronique asks her father if he felt the same way when her mother died. But her father says: "I had you. I held your hand." Véronique smiles, saying, "Yes, you held my hand." Later, during another visit to her father, she shares a dream image of a road lined with houses and a red brick church in the background (similar to the painting by Veronika's father).

On the way home she meets with a girl friend to ask her about the puppeteer. During their next meeting the friend tells her that the puppeteer writes children' s books; one has a story about a ballerina as well as a charming story about a shoelace. Véronique finds the book and reads it.

She also agrees to help her friend out by testifying against the friend's former boyfriend in a court case. But when she subsequently meets the boyfriend she tells him she is sorry.

In the meantime, Véronique has been receiving mystifying packages in the mail: a black shoelace, an empty cigar box, and a cassette with sounds that are hard to decipher. She stretches the shoelace (similar to the one that the Polish Veronika had held when she sang for her teachers) to trace the outline of a hospital printout of her electrocardiogram, a sign that she too has a heart condition. Back at school, while she has her students practice Van der Budenmajer's music, she looks out of the window and wishes she could help an old woman whom she sees struggling to walk with her cane.

Véronique finally traces the sounds on the cassette through a letter stamped with a postmark for the Sainte-Lazare train station in Paris. She goes to the station and passes by a woman dressed in a black hat with a foreboding stare; then proceeds to the café where she encounters the puppeteer. He has been waiting for her. He tells her that he is writing a novel about a woman who responds to the call of an unknown man. He wants to see if it is psychologically possible for a woman to follow the signs a man gives her to find him. Although Véronique is drawn to the puppeteer, she is concerned that he might be using her to write his book. She runs out of the station and slips and falls on the street.

Confused, Véronique goes to a hotel to rest. She is assigned to room 287 (the same room number in which Veronika's boyfriend stayed in Kraków.) The puppeteer follows her there and eventually the two make love. She falls asleep and dreams once more of the red brick church that is upside down.

When she wakes up the puppeteer tells her that he wants to know everything about her so she opens her purse. A small crystal ball (like the ball with which the Polish Veronika played) drops out. The puppeteer recognizes it and says that he knows why he chose her; it was not because of the book. She replies: "I now know why you were calling me. All my life I felt I was in two places at the same time. Here and somewhere else. I always sense what I have to do." The puppeteer looks at the contents of the purse and finds a photo page taken while Véronique was in Poland. He points to the photo and says: "Look at you." But Véronique is astounded because the photo is not of herself; in actuality, it is the photo of the Polish Veronika. Overwhelmed by the picture, Véronique cries in amazement. She intuits it is the picture of her double. The puppeteer makes love to her as she continues to be haunted by the picture of her double, the Polish Veronika.

Later, Véronique visits the puppeteer at his home and discovers he is making two puppets of her with the likeness of her face. "Why two?," she asks him. He tells her it is because the puppets are fragile and might be damaged during a performance. Then he reads the first pages of a novel he is writing about two girls born on the same day. He tells her they were born on November 23, 1966 at 3 a.m. in the morning in two different cities in two different countries. Both had dark hair and brownish green eyes. When both were two years old and knew how to walk, one burnt her hand on the stove. A few days later the other reached her hand out to touch the stove but instinctively pulled away. Yet, she could not have known she was about to burn herself. "Do you like the story," he asks? "I think I'll call it 'The Double Life of ...' I haven't yet decided what names to give them."

Véronique is disturbed by the puppeteer whom she now believes is using her for his book. She leaves him and goes directly to the house of her father, an artist-craftsman who is a stable, loving man. When Véronique arrives she places the palm of her hand on the trunk of a tree outside the house. Inside her father is listening to the music they both love as he cuts a sculpture out of wood. Hearing a sound, the father looks up at the same time Véronique touches the tree as the music they both love plays. He comes out to ask if she is cold and Véronique runs to him.

While creating *The Double Life of Véronique*, Kieślowski considered making as many versions of the ending as there were cinemas in which the film could be shown. For Paris he wanted to make seventeen versions. But money and clock-time ran out. Nevertheless Kieślowski made two—one for Europe, in which Véronique simply touches the tree at the end, and one for America, in which her father comes outside to greet Véronique, who runs to embrace him. The European ending hadn't been clear to the Americans at the New York Film Festival premiere.

Perhaps the choice between art and life that the Polish Veronika and the French Véronique face was the excruciating choice that Kieślowski faced too. Like Véronique, who stopped singing for her health and wanted relationship, he decided to retire from film-making and to be at home. But like Veronika, who chose art over health, he returned to his art only to suffer another heart-attack.

* * * * *

The parallels between the two women are striking. Veronika/ Véronique look identical. They were born at the same moment, on the same day, in the same year, although in two different places. Both singers love the music of Van der Budenmajer (a fictitious figure invented by Kieślowski; the music is actually composed by Zbigniew Preisner). Both have heart conditions inherited from their mothers, who died when they were young. Both have affectionate relationships with their widowed fathers, who are artistic and sensitive to their daughters. Both face choices with respect to their art and their love relationships. Both are sensuous and spiritual. Both are gentle and compassionate. Both want to help the old women they see struggling to walk. Both are strong and independent women, who make their own decisions. Both are left-handed. Both have similar objects—a ring they use to rub their lower eyelids, a plastic crystal-like ball through which they see reflections, lip balm, red gloves, black string. Both are connected to a hotel room numbered 287. Both encounter a dark foreboding woman; Veronika at her rehearsal and Véronique in the train station. Both see the same landscape with a church—Véronique sees it in a dream while Veronika sees it while riding the train to Kraków; it is a landscape that Veronika's father has been painting. Both are intuitive and have presentiments of the existence of each other. The beautiful haunting aria that Veronika sings is the evocative music that Véronique hears throughout the course of the film. Both Veronika and Véronique live and love in the dual realm—the everyday world and the numinous sphere of mystery.

The doubling brings to mind the archetypal Doppelgänger motif that is found in Dostoevsky's *The Double*, Conrad's *The Secret Sharer*, and the stories of E.T.A. Hoffman. The Doppelgänger is an apparition, or a spirit, or a living person that looks exactly like someone else but is not a relative. In mythology, the double, or the twin, represents some other aspect of the self. Often it refers to a shadow aspect that is evil, but it can also be a semi-divine being or a human soul-mate. Sometimes it refers to a phenomenon in which one catches one's own image out of the corner of the eye. The double can also be an omen of death, or an indication of approaching illness, or a health problem. The double has a haunting quality; it signals other realms.

In the *Double Life of Véronique,* the Double expresses the deepest layers of the Self. Veronika and Véronique are soul-mates; neither feels alone because each intuits the mysterious presence of the other. Seeing Véronique forewarns Veronika's impending death; the feeling of grief that she has lost someone is a sign to which Véronique unconsciously responds when she decides to give up singing in deference to her heart condition. Is Veronika a double who prepares Véronique for survival just as the first two-year-old girl in the Puppeteer's story somehow enables the second not to touch the stove which burnt the first girl's hand? Are we all, in some strange way, doubles for each other, doubles from whom we learn about existence? Could this be one of Kieślowski's central messages?

Kieślowski emphasizes the importance of love and the incredible task that human beings face: how to be in harmony with oneself and others. In his view, we live in a finite world tainted by grief, loneliness, and suffering. The only way to achieve spiritual peace is by acknowledging that we share with all humanity a desire for fuller life. If we are overly concerned with ourselves and with the past, we will cut ourselves off from life. Instead we must reach out to others through love, compassion, and understanding and accept that there are bonds between us and even something greater, bonds that we may not comprehend. To accept this mystery is to accept our destiny.

The Double Life of Véronique invites us into the mystery of relationship—the sacred bond that Martin Buber describes in his book, *I and Thou*. Buber contrasts true, unconditional love relationships with those that are oriented primarily toward ego-ends. The "I-Thou" attitude speaks from the whole of our being, from the depths of what Jung calls the Self and honors that in the Other. In contrast, the controlling "I-It" attitude is ego-oriented and dominates practical life. Whereas the I-It frame of mind is goal-oriented due to the human need for survival, the I-Thou perspective has no specific end; it takes its stand in awe before relationship whether the "Other" is human or divine. As Buber expresses it: "When Thou is spoken the speaker has no *thing*; he has indeed nothing. But he takes his stand in relationship."[14]

The Thou cannot be found by seeking; rather we meet the Thou only through grace. Every means or attempt to control that we use to find or obtain the Thou is an obstacle. From the Thou we obtain "nothing." The I-Thou outlook respects the Other as an end-in-itself—the prerequisite for true friendship and love, according to Aristotle who contrasts pure friendship with relationships based on using the Other as a means to an end (Buber's I-It attitude). The meeting of I-Thou is direct and occurs in a mysterious moment that cannot be fixed as in the mystical moment when the paths of Veronika and Véronique link. Similarly, in relationship to the divine, the I-It attitude prays to God for things while the I-Thou orientation sings out in praise of existence just as Veronika sings ecstatically in the rain.

As humans we cannot avoid the I-It orientation that inevitably makes use of the Other whom it treats as an object. We need it to survive. The I-It attitude separates, takes distance, organizes, uses, and makes life comfortable and secure. But it reduces the whole person to an "it," to the status of a thing, to a controllable object that can be dealt with in the practical world. Thus we live in the paradox of the worlds of I-It and I-Thou—seeking the Thou which cannot be sought, trying to hold fast to this meeting which cannot be held. Here is one of the great dilemmas of human relationship. We need the I-It attitude in order to survive; yet we long to be accepted and to love and be loved unconditionally.

Veronika and Véronique relate to the world primarily in the I-Thou mode. When they learn about each other, they do not try to explain the mystery away. They simply accept the experience with awe; they ask "no-thing" from it. They are in tune with something greater. Their I-Thou orientation emanates in their relationship to others—to their fathers, to their lovers, to the old women they would like to help; it radiates in their relationship to music and to nature.

However, Véronique succumbs to the I-It orientation when she decides to bear false witness in the divorce case against her friend's boyfriend. Then she is directly confronted with the paradox of the I-Thou and I-It relationship when she meets the puppeteer. The mysterious way in which he calls her to him and the poetic stories he creates show that he honors beauty and understands the I-Thou realm that she reveres. But using her to write his novel shows his calculating I-It attitude. The puppeteer is an agent of change for Véronique. He has shown her the picture of her double, Veronika, and has intuited its importance for her. But she cannot stay with him because he wants to use this intimate secret for his own ends. Véronique has to refuse being manipulated so that she can find her own true Self. Veronika, on the other hand, seems oblivious to the political I-It world going on around her in Kraków. She also ignores the signs of her finitude by disregarding her health which leads to her death.

The Double Life of Véronique calls us to be present to the mystery of time. To understand the ineffable paradox of time, we can turn to Martin Heidegger's analysis in his seminal work, *Being and Time*. Heidegger, in his re-visioning of the question of being, emphasizes the mystery of time and being at our core. Our important "moments," he says, are not those we calculate or control, not those that follow from cause to effect. Rather they are moments that break through and come toward us from a vast and mysterious future, thrusting us back on our past as they gather us into a moment of presence—an ecstatic moment ("ec-stasis") in which we stand out from our ego-selves and are present to all that is. We experience ecstasy in times of love, creation, visions, and awe before art or nature. This is one of the great gifts of our existence. It includes all the dark and all the light as one great revolving cycle of unity. Rilke calls it the "point where it turns," the center of stillness that is the center of creative transformation.

When we live by "clock-time" to deal with practical affairs, we often count the passing time in boredom, frustration, or resentment. But when we are devoted to what we are doing, we experience time quite differently. When transported by a symphony or the passion of lovemaking, an hour of clock-time may be like one ecstatic moment. In contrast, ten minutes of a boring duty may seem to last interminably. This ecstatic moment transcends linear clock time. It is a cosmic moment that breaks through our ego's version of events. In ecstatic time we "stand out" beyond our ego concerns and are fully present to the mysterious happening in the moment. The temporal movement now comes toward us from the "future," i.e., the unknown regions of our being, gathering us up in all the past history of our lives and moving us into a mysterious moment of presence in which we are open to all that is. This moment of opening and presence to what is happening is ecstatic, for we are dwelling in a whole and holy realm that is greater than our ability to control. This moment of presence transports us. In such a moment we are inspired because we feel the holy presence, even in the ordinary.

Both Veronika and Véronique are open to the sacred mystery of time. They relate to life with awe and wonder. Throughout the film, each woman accepts the ecstasy of music, love, and nature. If we share their sensitivity, if we feel what they experience, we, too, share in their bliss. In the synchronous moment in the Kraków square, the

Véroniques meet each other and enter in some uncanny, strange, and inexplicable way into each other's lives. Their futures come towards them to intertwine. Veronika is conscious of the meeting and knows it is meaningful. Although she cannot understand it in causal terms, she already experienced the presence of Véronique when she had the feeling that she was not alone in the world. Later, at the moment of Veronika's death, Véronique experiences her presence and feels the mystifying loss of someone, a loss she cannot understand on the rational level.

Veronika personifies the naturalness and spontaneity needed to be open to such a moment. She is receptive. When the rain falls she accepts it joyfully, singing its praises. She acknowledges her gift of song without restriction or qualification. She takes the offering of love from her father, Antek, and her aunt, returning it in kind. She does not seem to feel abandoned by the early death of her mother. Rather, she accepts the embrace of Mother Nature as she sings in the rain. She auditions with confidence and accepts winning the part with grace. Although Veronika might have faltered by responding with fear to the stares and rejecting vote of the dark woman judge, she continues with confidence. She does not allow cynicism and self-doubt to interfere with love, creativity, and spirituality and that prevents being in the moment. When she sees her mysterious double, Véronique, she welcomes the meaningful encounter.

Although Kieślowski emphasizes the beauty of the mystical I-Thou world of Veronika/Véronique, he presents an implicit caution in the film. Veronika consciously chooses to follow her artistic instincts rather than to continue the relationship with Antek. She willingly accepts the tensions intrinsic to art despite the warning signs of her heart condition. However, the shadow of the practical world invades her world of beauty through the political commotion in the Kraków square. It is a reminder of the I-It aspect of reality. The looming figure of Stalin symbolizes the menacing side of masculine tyranny that threatens the gentle, receptive feminine. The sinister side of masculine sexuality appears through the figure of the flasher. The dark face of finitude intrudes during her audition when she sees the frowning look of the woman jury member who has voted against her, a figure that suggests the shadowy face of the feminine and the lady of death. Veronika chooses the I-Thou relationship to life over these dispiriting aspects of the I-It domain, but dies as a consequence.

Veronika's death enigmatically primes Véronique to survive. Véronique is faced with the choice of whether or not to take the same path as Veronika. But she is alerted by her unsettling sense of the loss of another. As though she were warned by Veronika's death, Véronique acknowledges her heart condition, and chooses to stop singing. She re-directs her musical gifts toward teaching children. At first she is seduced by the magic of the puppeteer in her hope for true love. But when she recognizes his manipulation (a sign of masculine exploitation and domination) she realizes he is using her as a means for his book, thus reducing their relationship to the status of I-It. Instead Véronique turns to the I-Thou love she experiences with her father. She touches the tree of life, and thus affirms her sacred bond with nature.

When I saw Véronique touch the tree, I was reminded of the Reindeer Woman. For the arctic reindeer people and other shamanic cultures world-wide, the tree unites the three realms of the lower world: the unconscious, the mid-world of humans, and the spirit-world of the divinities. The antlers of the reindeer are like the branches of the tree. When people die in the reindeer culture, their bodies are placed in the branches of a tree along with the antlers of their special living reindeer in the belief that their spirit reindeer will carry them to the realm of the divine. The reindeer people also believe that the Reindeer Goddess, whom they worship, will return to earth in human form to teach the people how to honor the reindeer if they have forgotten to do so—a teaching that brought to mind the double relationship of Veronika and Véronique.

Care for the sensitivity of the soul, care for the mystery of existence, care for each other, care for the audience's spiritual life—*care* is the hallmark of *The Double Life of Véronique* and the cinema of Krzysztof Kieślowski.

NOTES

1. Andrei Tarkovsky, *Sculpting in Time*, trans. Kitty Hunter-Blair (New York: Alfred A. Knopf, 1987), 43.

2. Krzysztof Kieślowski, *Kieślowski on Kieślowski*, ed. Danusia Stok (London: Faber & Faber, 1993), 211.

3. *Ibid.*, 210.

4. *Aspen Film Fest Notes*, 1994.

5. *Kieślowski on Kieślowski*, xxii.

6. *Ibid.*, 200.

7. Quoted from Irène Jacob's foreword to Annette Insdorf's insightful book, *Double Lives, Second Chances: The Cinema of Krzysztof Kieślowski* (New York: Hyperion, 1999), xv.

8. Quoted in an interview by Judy Stone, *San Francisco Chronicle Datebook*, January 2, 1994, 24.

9. *Ibid.*, 173.

10. *Ibid.*, 173.

11. *Selected Letters of Fyodor Dostoevsky*, eds. Joseph Frank and David I. Goldstein, trans. Andrew MacAndrew (New Brunswick, N.J.: Rutgers University Press, 1987), 261-262.

12. *Kieślowski on Kieślowski*, 189.

13. *Ibid.*, 187.

14. Martin Buber, *I and Thou* (New York: Scribners, 1958), 4.

THE PHANTOM OF THE OPERA:
ANGEL OF MUSIC OR DEMON LOVER?

SUSAN OLSON

Introduction

In 1911 the French writer Gaston Leroux published his novel *The Phantom of the Opera*,[1] which was soon adapted into several films, including a 1924 silent movie starring Lon Chaney and a 1943 musical starring Claude Rains. Sir Andrew Lloyd Webber's hit musical opened in 1986 and was released as a film in 2004. This romantic tale of a beautiful young soprano and her brilliant but disfigured "Angel of Music"[2] has enjoyed widespread popularity for almost a century, suggesting that it touches something deep in the individual and collective psyche. Recent ads for the touring stage musical feature the Phantom's trademark mask and provocative questions such as "Remember your first time?" and "He's coming to Atlanta!" Who is the mysterious Phantom, and what is his great appeal to the collective imagination? Is he an Angel of Music who delights and inspires us, or a Demon Lover who carries us down into his dark kingdom and seeks to hold us captive there? In this paper I will explore both sides of the Phantom's power as it relates to the process of feminine individuation.

Susan L. Olson, M.A., L.C.S.W., holds degrees in English from Smith College and the University of Wisconsin, and in Social Work from the University of Georgia. She graduated from the C. G. Jung Institute in Zürich in 1992 and is in private practice as a Jungian analyst in Atlanta. A founding member of the Georgia Association of Jungian Analysts, she is also a training analyst in the Inter-Regional Society of Jungian Analysts.

Beauty and the Beast

The Phantom's story belongs to the genre of "Beauty and the Beast" tales such as Perrault's La Belle et le Bête, the Grimm brothers' Snow White and Rose Red, and the Greek myth of Persephone's abduction by Hades. (Interestingly enough, the Disney version of Beauty and the Beast has also become a movie and Broadway hit among the younger generation. Young girls know the story by heart and readily identify with Belle's love for the Beast). In these stories a beautiful ingenue encounters and eventually redeems or transforms a dark, wounded masculine figure who first appears as a beast or monster. Beauty sees beyond the Beast's frightening appearance and learns to love him; Snow White hides from the Bear, but later sees the gleam of gold beneath his fur and realizes that there is more to him than meets the eye. In these stories, the Beast and the Bear are really enchanted Princes who are finally freed from their spells and restored to their rightful states. In the Persephone myth, Hades is not redeemed (the God of the Underworld must remain himself, after all), but does soften his position and allow his bride to spend nine months in the upper world with her mother Demeter, provided that she spends the rest of the year with him. Persephone consumes a few pomegranate seeds (the symbol of her erotic bond with Hades) in the Underworld; through her liaison with him she undergoes her own transformation from *puella* to woman, maiden to wife. In these tales, Beauty needs what the Beast represents: he awakens her sexuality, her instinctive "bestial" side, and her creative power.

The Two Worlds

The story of Christine and the Phantom follows the same pattern, with variations befitting its musical theme. In this tale the worlds of consciousness and the unconscious are represented by the upper and lower levels of the late nineteenth-century Paris Opéra, an opulent building formerly used as an arsenal and prison. The upper floors are now the setting for gala performances, lavish parties, political intrigues, and elaborate masquerades. At the pinnacle of the roof is an angel sculpture, and high above the orchestra gleams an elaborate chandelier. The Opéra shimmers with light and is replete with all the wealth and glamour of turn-of-the-century Paris. But a dark presence haunts this glittering world. It is rumored that once, in the middle of performance, the chandelier fell into the crowd and killed a woman in the audience. Rumor also has it that an elusive Opera Ghost had something to do with the "accident." He is said to dwell seven stories below the Opera in an underground labyrinth near a lake in which bodies were discovered after the war. Thus he is defined, at the beginning of the story, as the nineteenth century equivalent of Hades, the Lord of the Underworld. Even the seven levels of his underground realm recall the circles of Hell in Dante's *Inferno*.

As in many fairy tales, the world "above" and the world "below" symbolize the "upper" world of consciousness and the "lower" realm of the unconscious. At the beginning of *The Phantom*, there is little contact between the two: in Jungian terms, there is no transcendent function to bridge the gap between them, and they exist in an uneasy state of psychological polarization. Consciousness fears and longs for "the darkness of the music of the night," while the unconscious fears and longs for "the garish light of day."[3] Something must happen to bring the two worlds together — and, as in any good fairy tale, it soon does. As the story opens, a temperamental diva named Carlotta is rehearsing a grandiose choral scene. Suddenly a backdrop crashes to the floor, cutting her off in mid-aria. She exits in a huff, and a young chorus girl named Christine Daaé fills in as her understudy and is hailed as a *tour de force*. We soon learn that Christine has secretly been taking voice lessons from an "unseen genius"[4] who visits her in her dressing room. Of course, this is the Phantom, who has conveniently arranged for the backdrop to fall so that his protegé will be discovered. Thus a figure from the unconscious breaks into the world of consciousness, lured by the maiden's beauty and innate but undeveloped talent. She is the Siren whose voice captures his heart, and he is the spirit whose presence she feels when she sings. Their attraction proves to be inevitable, irresistible, and very nearly fatal.

Beauty's Dilemma

Christine, an orphan, is susceptible to the Phantom because she is naive, impressionable, and vulnerable in her grief. Many "Beauties" lack one or both parents, and this Beauty is no exception. The absence of a parent in a fairy tale indicates that the archetypal energy embodied by the mother or father is undeveloped in the heroine's psyche. In Christine's case, both parents are missing: her mother died when she was a child, and she was raised by her father, a talented but impoverished violinist. Then he died, promising to send an Angel of Music to take his place as her guide and tutor. Lacking the containing and guiding energies of the mother and father archetypes, Christine's psyche is wide open to the Phantom's advances. He knows of her father's promise and uses it to bind her to him. Calling himself her Angel of Music, he takes advantage of her vulnerability and encourages her to project the father archetype onto him and to accept him as her "guide and guardian."[5] At the same time he offers to protect and contain her as a mother would. But behind these promises lurks a powerful sexual attraction which he conceals at first, just as he conceals his true face behind his mask. The erotic element reveals itself gradually as the story unfolds, in music and lyrics such as:

> Floating, falling, sweet intoxication!
> Touch me, trust me, savor each sensation!
> Let the dream begin, let your darker side give in
> To the power of the music that I write —
> The power of the music of the night...[6]

The Beast as Protector/Persecutor

Who is the Phantom in a woman's psyche? Disney movies of fairytales such as Beauty and the Beast, Cinderella, Sleeping Beauty, and Snow White demonstrate that even now, girls still believe that some day their Prince will come and carry them off to "happily-ever-after" land. The "Prince Charming" archetype has to do with a young woman's awakening to her own sexual nature and creative spirit. If relationships with actual men in the outer world are positive and life-affirming, her inner Prince Charming will be positive as well and she will form a strong bond with her own creative Animus. But most women are aware that Prince Charming has another face and can turn against them in rage, indifference, or possessive jealousy. In fairy tales this side of the archetype is found in Bluebeard figures who capture, torture, and murder their victims. If a woman's close relationships include emotionally or physically absent or abusive men, her inner man will show his Bluebeard face as well. In dreams he may appear as an intruder or rapist who terrorizes and attacks her. In her waking life he may whisper (in an voice that sounds exactly like her own) that her creative work is worthless or that her "real-life" male partner is weak, clumsy, or stupid. The Phantom, the man behind the mask, embodies both sides of the archetype: he is the Angel of Music *and* the Demon Lover. Jungian writers Esther Harding and Marion Woodman explore the origin and function of the "ghostly lover" (Harding) or the "daimon-lover" (Woodman) in a woman's psyche. According to Harding, he often appears in women's dreams as a figure "who is not of this world but belongs, instead, to the spirit or ghost world." He "is portrayed as the ghost or as the still-living influence of an actual man with whom the heroine had had a real relationship."[7] He can function constructively, as a woman's creative daimon, or destructively, as the spirit who lures her away from reality into a fantasy world. In Harding's words,

> She projects onto him some important element from her unconscious and then is attracted or repelled by that which she sees in him, quite unaware that it has originated deep within her own psyche.[8]

A woman's task is to recognize that the ghostly lover represents an aspect of her own psyche, and then to withdraw her projections onto the outer men in her life, none of whom can measure up to her inner ideal. She must find his creative and spiritual energy within herself and then consciously integrate it into her own psychic structure. Marion Woodman[9] points out that women are especially vulnerable to the negative daimon-lover complex in compensation for "inadequate internalization of the mother owing to a failed psychosomatic bonding [with the] mother in early life."[10] It is not difficult to interpret Christine's attraction to the Phantom as a defensive compensation for the early loss of her mother and an imagined fulfillment of her father's deathbed promise.

Donald Kalsched's *The Inner World of Trauma* sheds further light upon the formation of the "Protector/Persecutor" complex. When the ego suffers unbearable anxiety and trauma, psyche comes to the rescue in the form of an inner guardian or protector figure. Dreams, fantasies, myths, and fairy tales abound with images of angels, spirits, fairy godmothers, and helpful animals who lead the hero or heroine (the developing ego) to safety and protect him or her from beasts, monsters, and other menacing figures representing powerful negative affects such as rage, terror, and envy. But the inner Protector has a sinister Persecutor aspect as well. This side of the complex appears when the ego grows beyond its primitive defenses and decides to risk something new — for instance, a new relationship or creative endeavor. Then the inner Protector responds as if all of its alarm bells, red flags, and warning whistles were being sounded at once: "Stop! No! Don't go there! Danger! You'll die if you try that!" it screams. It seems to perceive every new endeavor as a repeat of the earlier trauma, which must be prevented at all costs.

The Phantom is such an inner Protector/Persecutor figure *par excellence*. He protects and guides Christine when she is weak and vulnerable and unable to fend for herself. He teaches her to sing like an angel and makes her an overnight success. But he wants to possess her completely and to ensure that she sings for him alone. When she falls in love with Raoul, her childhood friend and the Opéra's new patron, the Phantom shows his vicious, destructive, even murderous, face. Christine's early trauma (poverty and the loss of both parents) pales in comparison with his: the "loathsome gargoyle"[11] behind his elegant mask is the face of unbearable physical and emotional suffering. Born with a horribly disfigured face, the Phantom was rejected by his mother and made to wear a mask to hide his deformity. His brilliance as a scholar, architect, inventor, and composer is eclipsed by his monstrous appearance. The film version of his story includes an excerpt not included in the stage musical, showing him as a freak in a circus, his face covered by a rough sack. One day he escapes from his cell, kills the man who has been tormenting him, runs away, and is rescued by Mme. Giry, the Opera's ballet mistress. This brief scene humanizes the Phantom by emphasizing the pathos of his situation, but it also reveals the envy and murderous rage smoldering within him. As an image of Christine's negative Animus, he embodies the unconscious affects concealed behind her beautiful mask. As part of her individuation task, she must integrate his positive and creative power, and (at least to some extent) come to terms with his dark and destructive energies as well.

Christine's relationship with the Phantom develops in a series of meetings which can be interpreted like a sequence of dreams. In them the Phantom functions as Protector by teaching Christine and advancing her career, but then shows his Persecutor side by exploding in jealous rages and insisting that his narcissistic demands be met. When he lures her and Raoul down to his lair for their final confrontation, an unexpected transformation occurs and frees the three from their diabolical *menage à trois*. In the remaining sections of this paper I will discuss each stage of the process in which this naive, gullible Beauty learns to accept the dark masculine Beast as an essential, if complex, aspect of herself.

The Music of the Night: The First Encounter

Christine's initial meeting with the Phantom occurs after her first triumph, when she sees his face in her dressing-room mirror. He sings to her,

> Flattering child, you shall know me,
> See why in shadow I hide!
> Look at your face in the mirror —I am there inside!

and she responds,

> And do I dream again?
> For now I find the Phantom of the Opera is there —
> inside my mind...[12]

The Phantom breaks into Christine's consciousness like a dream image — first as a disembodied voice and then as a masked figure who calls himself her Angel of Music. But even in this first encounter we hear his demonic voice as he rebukes Raoul, who has recognized Christine and come to her dressing room to congratulate her, for interfering in "*my* triumph."[13] Such figures often appear in women's dreams in the form of robbers, rapists, threatening strangers, or dangerous animals. This usually happens at the beginning of the individuation process, when it is very difficult for a woman to recognize the intruder or monster as an aspect of her own psyche. But Lloyd Webber's lyrics and staging make it clear that Christine and the Phantom are mirror images of each other. He reaches for her through her mirror and she takes his hand, passes through the looking glass, and disappears. Next they travel by boat to the Phantom's lair, like souls of the dead crossing the River Styx into the Underworld. When they arrive, he sings the seductive "Music of the Night" and then leads her to his mirror, where she sees a waxen image of herself wearing a wedding gown. This makes it clear that she is a ruling image in his psyche, just as he is a ruling image in hers. In other words, the Animus desires her, just as she longs for him. He sees her as his soul image, his inner bride. At first this knowledge is more than Christine can bear, and she goes unconscious, fainting dead away in the Phantom's arms. But the next morning she is ready to see his real face, sneaks up behind him, and tears off his mask. Instantly he switches into Persecutor mode, cursing her and calling her a "little demon" and a "little viper." Then he reverts to a more plaintive tone and refers to himself as a "monster," a "repulsive carcass, who seems a beast but secretly dreams of beauty, secretly, secretly…"[14]

After this encounter, he suddenly returns her to the upper world of the Opéra, where she goes into seclusion. And no wonder: the ego's first experience of the unconscious can be overwhelming, and it needs to withdraw, rest, and reflect upon what has just occurred.

This first meeting of Beauty and the Beast sets the stage for everything else that follows. The Phantom finally breaks into consciousness to meet a real woman, not the waxen image he has made or the disembodied voice he has heard. Christine, too, encounters a real man rather than her idealized Angel of Music. When she dares to approach and unmask him, he discovers that she is curious about him and has a will of her own. She sees the man behind the mask and learns that he is a man of many voices: seductive, vindictive, wretched, but always compelling. He has entered her world and she has entered his. The idealized relationship between them is over, and a real relationship has begun.

That's All I Ask of You: The Animus Split

Christine and the Phantom do not share the stage again until he hides on the roof of the Opéra and spies as she and Raoul pledge their love to each other. But in the meantime, he breaks into the world of the Opéra in a series of notes to the new managers, who make the mistake of denying his existence and ignoring his requests. The more they flout his demands, the more enraged he becomes, until he finally murders an old stagehand who has made fun of him. This sequence of events highlights the disastrous results of denying and repressing the unconscious as it seeks its place in the world of consciousness. Christine and Mme. Giry take the Phantom seriously but the rest of the world does not, and he retaliates like a repressed complex, erupting in threats and violence.

Christine responds to the murder of the stagehand with fear, beseeching Raoul to protect her and fleeing with him to the roof of the Opéra. Her flight represents the embattled ego's attempt to escape and "rise above" the eruption of its own narcissistic hate, rage, and envy. If the Phantom is an aspect of Christine's psyche, then these feelings are really her own — perhaps her envy and rage at being passed over for Carlotta, the reigning diva. Christine cannot yet claim these emotions and turns to Raoul, her emerging positive Animus, to defend her from them. But like the Opéra managers, he responds with denial and insists that "there is no Phantom of the Opera."[15] By assuming the role of Protector, Raoul identifies with the positive Animus and relegates the negative side of it to the Phantom. This split is a crucial step in Christine's development because it differentiates the two sides and makes it possible to relate to them separately, rather than as a single double-sided entity. But if Christine is now conscious of both aspects of the Animus, she is not yet able to integrate them. Her love duet with Raoul emphasizes his world of daylight, freedom, and summertime, in contrast to the Phantom's world of darkness, solitude, and despair. By pledging herself to Raoul, Christine aligns herself with the positive side of the Animus and attempts to suppress the negative side. This repudiation is more than the Phantom can bear. Lurking in the shadows, he hears her and Raoul sing "Love me — that's all I ask of you..." and responds with his own sinister version of their words:

> You will curse the day you did not do
> All that the Phantom asked of you![16]

Christine returns to the stage in triumph, but the Phantom fulfills his curse by sending the chandelier, the Opéra's great symbol of light and beauty, crashing to the ground at her feet. Now neither she, Raoul, the managers, nor anyone else can deny that he exists. He has penetrated the world of consciousness and revealed himself as a force to be reckoned with. In a woman's psyche, the Animus split occurs when she becomes conscious of the presence within herself of two opposing "inner men" — a menacing spirit who attacks and berates her, and a helpful man who guides and protects. They may appear in dreams as a harsh figure (a judge, "bad cop," or critical father) and a friendly (but at this stage ineffectual) brother, companion, or "nice guy." In her outer relationships, she may be torn between her feelings for two men — one charming and irresponsible, the other decent but boring. Or she may find herself trapped in an abusive relationship with a man who can be violent and destructive one minute, remorseful and apologetic the next. At this point it is very difficult to see that her outer dilemma reflects her inner state, and that both figures are really aspects of her own emerging masculinity. Claiming them as her own is the chief task of her individuation process.

Masquerade: The Split Deepens

Six months pass before Christine and the Phantom meet again. In the interval she and Raoul have become secretly engaged, the Phantom has gone underground, and a new chandelier has been installed. Perhaps this period corresponds to what Jung termed "the regressive restoration of the persona,"[17] in which the ego responds to an onslaught of unconscious material by attempting to restore its mask of social propriety and respectability. The "persona" image is emphasized in the gala masquerade ball in which the entire cast appears in bizarre masks and elaborate costumes. But as they sing, "Masquerade! Hide your face so the world will never find you!"[18] the Phantom suddenly appears, dressed in crimson and wearing a death's head mask. He has not disappeared after all, but has been working on an opera which he haughtily presents to the company. Then he beckons to Christine, rips her engagement ring from its chain around her neck, and declares:

> Your chains are still mine —
> You will sing for me!"[19]

The Phantom's appearance before the entire company indicates that while Christine has been consolidating her alliance with Raoul, the dark side of the Animus has been working in secret to accomplish his own purposes. His trickster qualities — his awareness of everything that goes on at the Opéra, his ability to appear and disappear at will, and his parody of the "masquerade" theme — become stronger as the upper world continues to hide from him. The title of his opera, *Don Juan Triumphant,* hints that his creative and erotic energy is increasing as well, and that in his work Don Juan will succeed in seducing the object of his desire. If this energy is really Christine's own, perhaps her secret engagement to Raoul is an attempt to mask the erotic energy that she cannot yet face or handle in herself. But the Phantom is too wily for her and will not allow himself to be concealed. In terms of Animus development, the masquerade scene represents an intensification of the Angel of Music/Demon Lover split in a woman's psyche. It is clear that the conflict between the two is escalating and that a confrontation is inevitable. The developing feminine ego is caught between them and must find a way to bear the tension until the impasse is resolved. In her outer life, a woman may find herself emotionally "chained" to a man who is caught in his own Angel/Demon complex and hides his violent and abusive side behind a helpful and protective mask. In her fantasies, she may imagine a heroic knight in shining armor who will rescue her from her predicament. In dreams, the Angel may appear as a wise man or a helpful animal, while the Demon takes the form of a terrorist or mass-murderer. The psychic pressure increases until, like Christine, a woman feels that she is about to go mad. In the ensuing scenes, Raoul becomes something of a trickster himself and cooks up a scheme to use Christine as bait to trap the Phantom. By doing so he shows that he now acknowledges the Phantom's existence, but vastly overrates his own power to defeat him. Christine does not want to play the role of the virgin being offered to the dragon, but is not yet strong enough to refuse Raoul or to resist the Phantom. Thus she remains the helpless ingenue, conscious of the battle raging in her psyche but powerless to stop it. At least she speaks up for herself, voicing a true feeling ("If you don't stop, I'll go mad!") and pleading with Raoul not to put her through "this ordeal by fire."[20] But the only way through the impasse *is* an ordeal by fire, and in her next encounter with the Phantom, this is exactly what happens.

Help Me Say Good-Bye: Grieving for the Father

For Christine, the only way out of her dilemma is to look deeper into her own psyche and to free herself from the chains of the father complex which have bound her until now. This she does in the next scene, as she flees to the cemetery where her father is buried. Standing at his grave she sings,

> Wishing you were somehow here again...
> Knowing we must say good-bye...

> Try to forgive... teach me to live...
> Give me the strength to try....
> Help me say good-bye.[21]

During this lament Christine is finally alone, away from the drama of the Opéra and the conflict between Raoul and the Phantom. Her solitude indicates that she has allowed herself to go into the graveyard of her buried memories and to uncover the origin of her inner struggle. What she finds there is her unresolved grief for the "one companion"[22] who died before she could fully integrate his gentleness and wisdom. By mourning for him and letting go of her dreams of reunion, Christine begins the process of assimilating his warmth and his creative spirit. Until now she has looked outside herself — to her father, Raoul, and the Phantom — for energy and strength. Now she realizes that she cannot live fully unless she finds these qualities within her own soul. But of course, such a deep complex does not give up so easily. Raoul and the Phantom follow Christine to the graveyard and redouble their efforts to win her over. As soon as she finishes her lament, the Phantom sings to her again in his Angel of Music voice and she is mesmerized. Raoul charges in on his white horse, the very image of a knight in shining armor, and proclaims, "[T]his thing ... is not your father!"[23] Now the two battle each other directly, like warriors fighting for the love of a fair damsel. To Christine's credit, she does not stand by helplessly but intervenes and pulls Raoul away. Her newly-won consciousness has not been enough to depotentiate the complex, but the balance of power now shifts as she sides with Raoul, becoming for a moment his Protector against the Phantom. In response, the Phantom declares war upon both of them and sets the stage for their final confrontation. In a woman's individuation, this moment of insight into the origin and influence of her unresolved father complex is a major turning point. But the insight itself is not enough: it must be followed up by finding her own voice and taking her own position *vis à vis* her inner conflict. Christine does this by aligning herself with Raoul and pulling him away from a battle that would surely kill him. Thus she backs up her insight with action and demonstrates that she has said good-bye to her father, distinguished him from the Phantom, and opened herself to a new relationship with her inner man and outer partner.

Past the Point of No Return: The Final Threshold

Christine's final encounter with her Angel of Music/Demon Lover begins during the performance of his opera. Raoul sets a trap to ensnare him, but (as usual) the Phantom outsmarts him and lays a trap of his own. Offstage, he kills the tenor singing the role of Don Juan and takes his place onstage as Christine's lover. His seductive "Past the Point of No Return" serenade recalls the opera's earlier love duets, but this time the lyrics and tango rhythm are blatantly erotic:

> When will the blood begin to race,
> The sleeping bud burst into bloom:
> When will the flames, at last, consume us...?[24]

Christine recognizes the Phantom's voice and pretends to yield to him—but then, showing that she, too, has integrated his trickster energy, calmly pulls his mask away and reveals his deformed face to the audience. In terms of individuation, we might say that the ego now possesses enough consciousness and strength to "unmask" the Demon Lover and to behold his true face. She no longer succumbs to his seductive voice because she sees behind his ruses and hears between the lines of his words. But she is not yet free of his power: to accomplish that, she must make one more descent into his underground labyrinth. As soon as he is unmasked, the Phantom sweeps his cloak around Christine and carries her down to his lair, this time (like Hades) against her will. And this time his song is not sweet and seductive but angry and bitter, as he voices the "black despair" in "the prison of [his] mind."[25] But Christine's voice has changed too, and she echoes the discordant tones of his own music to "address him fiercely." Then, staring straight into his face, she sings more tenderly,

> This haunted face holds no horror for me now...
> It's in your soul that the true distortion lies....[26]

Finally she sees him for what he is: a pathetic, lonely creature who has been feared and hated all his life and who has vented his hatred upon the world. This is the climax of the story, the moment when the Beast touches Beauty's heart and transforms her from a helpless victim into a strong and compassionate woman. It could transform the Phantom, too — but he does not let that happen yet. At this very moment Raoul appears, and the Phantom resumes his mocking tone and angry stance. Raoul pleads for Christine's freedom, but the Phantom responds by lassoing him about the neck and using him as bait to force Christine to choose between them: if she stays with him, he will free Raoul, but if she refuses, Raoul will die. In the face of this impossible choice, Christine finally gives voice to her hatred for the Phantom and acknowledges that she "gave [her] mind blindly." Then she finds the courage to act in an entirely new way. Approaching the Phantom slowly and resolutely, she sings,

> Pitiful creature of darkness...
> What sort of life have you known...?
> God give me courage to show you
> You are not alone...

...after which she embraces him and kisses him "long and full on the lips."[27] His spell broken, the Phantom releases Raoul and urges the young lovers to leave before the mob which is tracking him reaches his lair. They start to move away, but then Christine returns and gives the Phantom her ring. Placing it upon his finger, he finally voices his love for her — and this time it is real love, not the desire for mastery and possession. As she and Raoul exit, the Phantom wraps his cloak around himself one last time and disappears. When the mob enters his lair, nothing is left of him but his mask, resting silently upon his throne.

The final scene of the story takes place in the lower world, the realm of the unconscious. This is the only level on which the chains that bind Christine to her Angel of Music/Demon Lover complex can finally be loosed so that she can return to the upper world with a new connection to the Animus, her inner man, and to Raoul, her outer partner. When she acknowledges that she gave her mind to the Phantom, she admits that she participated in her own delusion. Then, for the first time, she allows herself to feel hatred. This is a major accomplishment for an innocent young woman who has been blind to her own Shadow. Her honesty about the dark side of her emotions enables her to feel genuine compassion as well, and frees the Phantom from the burden of hatred which he has carried alone. Then he, too, is able to feel compassion and to release her and Raoul from the choke-hold he has had upon them both.

By doing so, he sacrifices his power-drive and feels, perhaps for the first time in his life, the sadness and grief at the center of his soul.

He is not transformed from a Beast into a Prince, but is revealed as a wounded man who, despite his suffering, is capable of empathy for other human beings.

Raoul, too, is transformed by his descent into the unconscious. At the mercy of the Phantom, he experiences the limits of his heroic stance and realizes that it is not in his power to rescue Christine. He wants to sacrifice himself for her, but does not understand that she could not live with the knowledge that he had died for her. In fact, neither man can see beyond the all-or-nothing, either/or thinking at the center of the Phantom's forced choice. Only Christine, with the wisdom and courage gained by her ordeal by fire, is able to find the third way, the paradoxical solution to her own dilemma.

In the end, each member of the triangle sacrifices something to accomplish the story's resolution. Christine sacrifices her naiveté and her expectation that the men in her life will be there to take care of her. Raoul sacrifices his heroic posturing and admits that he cannot prevail against his shadowy rival. And the Phantom sacrifices his erotic fantasies of conquest and possession. All lose, and yet all win. Christine departs with Raoul and, according to the movie version of the story, marries him and becomes the mother of his children. The Phantom remains alone, but experiences love for the first time in his life. In Christine's inner world, the Angel of Music and the Demon Lover lose power but gain energy as she claims their gifts and their faults as dimensions of her own psyche. The result is a young woman who has heard the sound of her own voice and has begun to integrate her own Shadow and her own creative genius. The ring which she gives the Phantom is the symbol of her wholeness — and perhaps a promise of his as well.

But what of the Phantom? Does he really vanish, or does he only "go underground," to appear again at another time and in another place? Films are our modern-day fairy tales, and many fairy tales end ambiguously, with the mysterious disappearance of the wicked witch or evil villain. The Phantom vanishes and reappears many times in this story, implying that he will do so once again. The Angel of Music/ Demon Lover complex never really dies in a woman's psyche. But the next time he appears, she may be able to recognize him and to deal with him more consciously.

On the collective level, the "Phantom complex" can be interpreted as a natural development as women seek to find their own voices and places in the world of men. Young women are still brought up to hide their true feelings, muffle their true voices, look for Prince Charming to save them, and measure themselves by the standards of a patriarchal culture. These attitudes have changed radically since the publication of *The Phantom of the Opera* in 1911, and yet the dual figure of the protective Angel and the persecuting Demon is still a dominant presence in the psyches of women. It will continue to function as a Phantom until women like Christine acquire the courage to descend into its underground lair and to claim its dark energy and creative power as their own.

NOTES

1. Gaston Leroux, *The Phantom of the Opera* (New York: Perennial Library, 1988).

2. George Perry, *The Complete Phantom of the Opera* (New York: Henry Holt, 1988), 144.

3. *Ibid.*, 146.

4. *Ibid.*, 144.

5. *Ibid.*

6. *Ibid.*, 146.

7. M. Esther Harding, *The Way of All Women* (New York: Harper & Row, 1970), 37.

8. *Ibid.*, 36.

9. Marion Woodman, *Addiction to Perfection: The Still Unravished Bride* (Toronto: Inner City Books, 1982) and *The Pregnant Virgin: A Process of Psychological Transformation* (Toronto: Inner City Books, 1985).

10. Woodman, quoted in Donald Kalsched, *The Inner World of Trauma: Archetypal Defenses of the Personal Spirit* (London and New York: Routledge, 1996), 109.

11. Perry, 147.

12. *Ibid.*, 145.

13. *Ibid.*

14. *Ibid.*, 147.

15. *Ibid.*, 153.

16. *Ibid.*, 154.

17. C. G. Jung, *Two Essays on Analytical Psychology, Collected Works of C.G. Jung* (London: Routledge & Kegan Paul, 1966), Vol. 7, § 471-475.

18. Perry, 155.
19. *Ibid.*, 157.
20. *Ibid.*, 159.
21. *Ibid.*, 160.
22. *Ibid.*
23. *Ibid.*, 161.
24. *Ibid.*, 164.
25. *Ibid.*
26. *Ibid.*, 165.
27. *Ibid.*, 166.

Hitchcock's *Strangers on a Train* and Leconte's *Man on a Train*: Denying and Befriending the Shadow

JAMES PALMER

> It is said that each of us has a twin. Psychically we are all Geminis. Every person to whom we react with strong fear, desire, repulsion, or admiration is a twin of our own inner unacknowledged life. We have qualities, both positive and negative, that appear visibly in others but are invisible in us and to us. The challenge is to be on friendly terms with everything about ourselves.
> —David Richo, *Shadow Dance*

P rojected in darkness, the film image is a play of light and shadow that has proven to be a rich medium for delving into the world of archetypal images. The multiple screen adaptations of Robert Lewis Stevenson's *The Strange Case of Dr. Jekyll and Mr. Hyde* alone point to the attraction of film and the shadow archetype.[1] Although half a century separates Alfred Hitchcock's *Strangers on a Train* (1951) and Patrice Leconte's *Man on a Train* (2002), both films explore the

James Palmer, Ph. D., is Professor of Film Studies and a President's Teaching Scholar at the University of Colorado at Boulder. He has published numerous articles and co-authored *The Films of Joseph Losey*. Currently the Director of the Conference on World Affairs, he also teaches several interdisciplinary courses, including Jung, Film, and Literature.

psychological struggle of characters coming to terms with their "inner unacknowledged life."[2] In taking a psychological approach to these two films, I wish to avoid reductive interpretations that simplify or use the films as mere illustrations of Jungian archetypes. The close readings offered below are intended to explore the richness and complexity of archetypal imagery and patterns of human behavior embodied in both films. As Hitchcock said of the motifs and structure of *Strangers on a Train*, "Isn't it a fascinating design? One could study it forever."[3] Finally, while the shadow archetype will be the main focus of the paper, the transcendent function and the persona archetype receive considerable attention, particularly as they relate to the success or failure of characters to bring to consciousness, to acknowledge and integrate, their dark sides.

Exploring the denial of the shadow in Hitchcock's film inevitably involves the relationship between shadow and persona. In *On Jung*, Anthony Stevens offers an excellent summary of this relationship:

> [T]hese two aspects of the personality complement and counterbalance each other, the shadow compensating for the pretensions of the persona, the persona compensating for the antisocial propensities of the shadow. Should this compensatory relationship break down, it can result in the shallow, brittle, conformist kind of personality which is 'all persona', with its excessive concern for 'what people think', or, alternatively, it can result in the sort of criminal or psychopathic individual who has little time for social niceties or public opinion.[4]

Although Stevens surely did not have the plot and characters of Hitchcock's film in mind, his summary of the dynamics between shadow and persona resonates with *Strangers*. The psychopathic Bruno Anthony (Robert Walker) meets tennis player Guy Haines (Farley Granger) on the train and proposes that they exchange crimes, each committing a murder for the other. Bruno will kill Guy's estranged wife, Miriam (Laura Eliot), freeing Guy to marry the daughter of a senator. Guy, in turn, will rid Bruno of his domineering father. With an authoritarian father and a doting mother, Bruno is caught in a textbook Oedipal conflict. Although Guy neither accepts nor rejects Bruno's proposal, Bruno considers the conversation to be a pact between them. Bruno proceeds to stalk and strangle Guy's wife at a carnival, but Guy refuses to dispatch Bruno's father. Bruno then "shadows"

Guy, insisting that Guy fulfill their "agreement," and finally attempts to frame Guy for his wife's murder. Near the end of the film, Guy must become aggressive, win his tennis match quickly, and beat Bruno to the site of Miriam's murder. The climactic scene is a return to the carnival setting where Guy and Bruno battle each other on an out of control merry-go-round, a kind of whirling and finally disintegrating mandala, whose collapse kills Bruno. Guy survives the crash, saving a young boy on the merry-go-round, and successfully exonerates himself by preventing Bruno from planting evidence that would have incriminated Guy in his wife's murder.

The meeting of a socially ambitious tennis player and a psychopath makes for a fascinating dyad. A world of persona and shadow is signified immediately in the image that forms the background for the credits. The opening shot of *Strangers* is emblematic of its visual motifs and themes and its two worlds of light and dark. The foreground of the dark, cavernous train terminal contrasts with the archway in the background that frames the shining world of Washington, D.C., symbolized by the prominence of the Capitol dome in the distance. Washington's public monuments become associated with Guy's persona, his relationship to Ann Morton (Ruth Roman) and her senator father, and to Guy's own political ambitions.

In Jungian terms, Guy is clearly over-identified with his persona, while Bruno is as representative of the archetypal shadow as Mr. Hyde. For all of his flashy eccentricities, Bruno has a rather fragile and contradictory persona. He is the classic *puer aeternus*—thrown out of three colleges, a self-confessed drinker, gambler, and bum. Bruno is drawn to Guy's fame as a tennis player and socialite. As Bruno says, "People who do things are important. Me, I don't seem to do anything."[5] Is this a trickster's comment or candid self-assessment?

If Guy is a celebrity, Bruno nonetheless remains the compelling character. In interviewing Hitchcock, Francois Truffaut speculated that Bruno is the more attractive character and suggested that Hitchcock "preferred the villain." Hitchcock emphatically replied, "Of course, no doubt about it."[6] We might attribute Hitchcock's preference to Robert Walker's brilliant performance, and to Hitchcock's (and our) innate fascination with evil. Still, what Robert Johnson calls "the gold in the shadow"—e.g., humor, inventiveness, sexual energy, and spontaneity—also explains Bruno's appeal.[7] Guy's earnest, inhibited, passive, humorless demeanor reflects both what he has repressed and what makes his shadow an attractive, if disturbing, villain.

However flighty and unpredictable, Bruno holds considerable sway over Guy, whose lack of self-awareness and repressed shadow empowers Bruno. The edited cross-cutting and motif of "criss-crossed" paths and converging train tracks which bring them together suggest the inevitable, fated encounter of Guy and his long denied shadow. The relentless play on doubles and doubling opens the film, with references to doubles tennis, the crossed tennis rackets on Guy's cigarette lighter, bigamy (double marriages), and the pair of double scotches Bruno orders—scotches the two drink in one comic, synchronized move.

Invested in his persona as Guy is, his initial pleasure in being recognized by Bruno is short-lived. Bruno reads the society column as well as the sports page, and he mentions Guy's liaison with Senator Morton's daughter. Guy's comment, "You're quite a reader, Mr. Anthony," carries the obvious literal meaning, but Bruno is also a particularly incisive reader of Guy's character, motives, and desires. In a typically self-deprecating, insinuating way, Bruno says, "I'm not like you, Guy. You're lucky, you're smart. Marrying the boss's daughter, that's . . . that makes a nice shortcut to a career, doesn't it?" Not only does this comment precede and foreshadow Guy's later admission of political aspirations, but the comment is the shadow's hook, for Guy uncharacteristically leans defiantly towards Bruno, and his protest is simultaneously immediate and halting, aggressive and defensive: "Marrying the senator's daughter has nothing to do with . . . Can't a fellow look beyond a tennis net without being out for something?"

Interestingly, the senator's other daughter, Barbara (Patricia Hitchcock), acts as an uncensored voice of the unconscious, or what in polite society would remain unspoken. After Miriam's death, Barbara tells Guy and Ann, "Well, you two, nothing stands in your way. Now you can be married right away." She even pops back into the room briefly to say to the couple in her comic candor, "I still think it would be wonderful to have a man love you so much he'd kill for you."

Eyeglasses (sight and insight) and doubles are notable motifs throughout the film. Barbara wears glasses, which contributes to her resemblance to Guy's wife. Also like Miriam, she is a teller of unpleasant truths to Guy. Barbara is an incisive babbler who speaks her truth, but her outspokenness does not go unpunished. At the senator's party,

Bruno "pretends" to strangle an older woman (herself a double for Bruno's dotty mother); he focuses on Barbara's face and glasses and slips into a trance, nearly killing the older woman. As Barbara immediately tells Ann, "He looked at me. His hands were on her throat, and he was strangling me . . . He thought he was murdering me."

Doubles and "criss-crossing" proliferate in the film. In the initial train scene, when Bruno proposes his exchange of perfect, motiveless murders, he confirms his role as the shadow that expresses what the persona denies. As they part, Bruno asks Guy, "Now you think my theory's okay, Guy? You like it?" Guy's answer—"Sure, Bruno, sure," is a casual dismissal and refusal to take seriously this shadow encounter. Guy's careless condescension toward Bruno triggers all the trouble to follow, including Guy's further contact with and denial of his shadow.

If I assign too much guilt to Guy, Raymond Durgnat, in his spirited essay in defense of that character, ascribes too little responsibility. Commenting on the same scene above, Durgnat insists that "Guy rejects the offer, although, humouring a madman, he doesn't actually say no, and Bruno interprets a gesture with a drink as agreement, picking up Guy's forgotten lighter as a whimsical afterthought."[8] Guy's lighter, with its crossed tennis rackets and "A to G" inscription is crucial to the plot, since this is the incriminating object Bruno will try to plant at the murder scene. Although Bruno shrewdly infers the "Ann to Guy" initials, the lighter even more intimately connects the two men. While in Bruno's possession, "Anthony to Guy" more accurately decodes the meaning of the inscription and hints at Bruno's homoerotic motivations.[9]

The scene in Metcalf between Guy and the adulterous and pregnant Miriam, where she double-crosses him, takes his money, cancels the pending divorce, and threatens to come to Washington, leads to a brief physical struggle, broken up by the music store owner. Guy tells Miriam, "I don't want to see you or hear you again." These words closely parallel Guy's later denial of complicity in Bruno's murder of Miriam.

Guy calls Ann to report on his meeting with Miriam from the same train station phone booth that Bruno later uses to look up Miriam's address before he stalks and murders her. Over the increasing rumble of an onrushing train that parallels and reinforces the outburst of repressed psychic emotion, Guy says that he could break Miriam's neck. The train drowns out these words, and Guy shouts into the phone, "I said I could strangle her!" At this point, a dissolve of the close-up of the raging Guy is slowly replaced by Bruno's claw-like hands. This dissolve works as a transition between the station and the Anthony home where Bruno's mother has just finished manicuring his hands. Hands are Bruno's preferred weapon and are a frequent motif in the film, including the large lobster claws pictured earlier on his tie. In this instance Bruno's hands seem almost conjured by Guy's expressed homicidal urge to strangle Miriam.[10] Guy's persona, usually so formal and reserved, breaks down here. His instinctive outburst recalls T. S. Eliot's persona-ridden Prufrock when he suddenly connects with his repressed aggressive vitality: "I should have been a pair of ragged claws/Scuttling across the floors of silent seas." In this dissolve, Bruno's hands not only express Guy's primitive instincts, but they briefly appear to grip Guy's head and neck and point to Bruno's potential control and threat to Guy himself.

The quintessential shadow scene in *Strangers* comes early in the film and influences everything that follows. Guy returns by train to Washington, D.C. after meeting Miriam but failing to secure the divorce agreement. Bruno is waiting outside of Guy's Washington apartment with Miriam's broken glasses, proof that he has killed Guy's wife. The opening image of Guy arriving by taxi includes the lighted Capitol dome in the background, providing locale, but emblematic of laws and the world of light and order and of Guy's persona and political ambitions. A bell tower strikes three, giving us the time, but also warns of the impending, ominous meeting of Guy and Bruno.

As Guy walks up the steps to his apartment, the tilted camera angle conveys a world askew, unstable and out of balance. Opening his door, he hears the whisper of his name, but his look across the street reveals no one. The handling of sound here invokes the psychological, as if some inner voice or psychopomp announces a calling, an initiation. Guy places his luggage inside the door, leaving behind the accoutrements of his persona. He hears and sees Bruno's shadowy figure behind an iron gate calling his name for a second time. A low and tilted camera angle again catches Guy's fateful descent and crossing, and his puzzled, wide-eyed look conveys vulnerability.

Bruno, dressed in a dark suit in contrast to Guy's lighter suit, is shot, unlike Guy, behind the gate and grill work. His face mottled in shadows, Bruno presents Guy with Miriam's shattered glasses and describes her murder in detail. Guy's protestations of innocence are countered by Bruno's persuasive, if demonic, assertion of Guy's motive and complicity in the planned exchange of murders. When the characters take their stance on opposite sides of the iron fence, both appear trapped, though Bruno's statement, "You're the one who benefits, Guy, you're a free man now," is richly ironic as Guy is now seen through the bars. This effect is echoed as the phone rings in Guy's apartment, and the shot through the bars emphasizes Guy's alienation from his former life. Once the police car arrives, Guy steps behind the fence with Bruno. The camera views the police activities through the bars, and though the point of view cannot be ascribed to either Bruno or Guy, the shot briefly identifies Guy with his shadow. This point is reinforced by Guy's comment that works simultaneously as accusation and denial, "You've got me acting like a criminal. Why you crazy fool." While Bruno may well be psychotic, he is no fool, and Guy's attempt to label him so only contributes to his pattern of denial and underestimation of Bruno.

Once the police leave, Guy walks quickly toward his apartment. Bruno follows closely behind, still articulating his plans for Guy's murder of Bruno's father. Pursued by Bruno, Guy can no longer repress his own shadow impulses, which erupt in a highly significant but muttered line, "Stay away from me before I give you what you gave Miriam," again confirming Guy's homicidal impulses. Bruno, neither surprised nor intimidated by Guy's threat, offers an unintentionally comic excuse for Guy's eruption by noting "You're not yourself, Guy, you're tired." Volatile, desperate, and guilt-ridden, Guy reacts to Bruno's charges of complicity first by threats and then by suddenly reasserting his denial of the shadow. Seemingly dominating Bruno, Guy stands on the top steps leading to his apartment, turns on Bruno, and vehemently protests, "I don't know you, I never saw you before, I never want to see you again." With this denial of evil, which is also the rejection of self-knowledge and self-acceptance, Guy abandons Bruno on the steps and enters his apartment.

As a kind of coda to this remarkably rich verbal and visual scene, Guy immediately answers a phone call from Ann and begins his dissembling. What is so visually arresting in this shot are the objects that bracket Guy's phone conversation. As Guy is lying to Anne, denying that anything is wrong, he fondles Miriam's broken glasses in one hand. The table lamp that lights the room recalls the lighted Capitol dome that began the scene. Thus, evidence of murder, deceptive words, and a reminder of the Capitol dome, symbolizing Guy's persona and political ambitions, are visually linked in a single shot.

In a later scene, with the Jefferson Memorial as background, Guy will explicitly admit to the detective assigned to him that he won't become a tennis professional because, "I don't have to do that. When I'm through with tennis, I'm going into politics . . . I hope." Guy's troubled gaze then immediate fixes on Bruno, a small, dark, and foreboding figure outlined against the Jefferson Memorial.[11] Once Bruno kills Miriam, he becomes a hovering, intrusive presence in Guy's world. However much Guy would like to excise this repressed shadow from his life, Bruno increasingly closes the distance between them, moving from phone calls and notes to background appearances and finally to social gatherings at the tennis club and Senator Morton's party. At one point a frustrated Bruno even tells Guy, "You're spoiling everything. You're making me come out in the open."

Although other scenes warrant close analysis, particularly Miriam's murder, Senator Morton's party, and the return to the carnival setting and final pursuit of Bruno, the ultimate question concerns Guy's status as a static or dynamic character. Lesley Brill's balanced assessment of *Strangers* within the romance tradition is both sensible and persuasive:

> In the end, Guy gets where he needs to go. His second trip back to Metcalf wins him his freedom, a wife, and a future. The earlier images of failed or perverted journeys do not reverse the significance of the ending, but they complicate its sense of triumph.[12]

At the end of the film, Guy has saved the endangered boy, proved his own innocence, and answered the carnie man's question about who Bruno was. Guy's answer, "Bruno, Bruno Anthony, a very clever fellow," seems accurate but simplistic, and more a deflection of Guy's shadow projection onto his antagonist. If Guy refuses to acknowledge his shadow, he has, at least, come to respect its formidable power.

Projecting evil and trickery onto Bruno doesn't really relieve Guy of answering the film's final assertion. When the minister on the train repeats Bruno's first line, "Aren't you Guy Haines?", Guy and Ann walk away from the minister, leaving his question unanswered. This may indicate that Guy is now less wedded to his persona or more aware, as Brill suggests, of the world's ever present and unpredictable danger. Still, this comic coda with the minister leaves me wondering whether so dark a film can carry off so light and droll an ending, a conclusion that seems to reward Guy for the many denials of his darker side. This final turning away from the darkly clad minister only punctuates Guy's refusal to confront his full identity. The darkness of *Strangers on a Train* is all too visible and pervasive. Police, politicians, and academics have all been dipped in Hitchcock's acerbic, sardonic solution, and the droll and macabre dialog of Ann's sister, Barbara, is comical; nevertheless, the characters with the most incisive, perceptive understanding of Guy—Miriam and Bruno—are killed off; and the outspoken Barbara, Miriam's double, becomes traumatized as Bruno's surrogate murder victim.

For whatever reason, Guy's hellish journey, if it is his dark night of the soul, offers him little individuation. A partial answer for this lack of character complexity may be found in Hitchcock's comment to Truffaut about the casting of Farley Granger:

> But I must say that I wasn't too pleased with Farley Granger; he's a good actor, but I would have liked to see William Holden in the part because he's stronger. In this kind of story the stronger the hero, the more effective the situation.[13]

Guy seems more a static than dynamic character if we try to chart his self-knowledge, his personal growth. Is it really enough that Guy changes his defensive tennis tactics to a more aggressive style of play in order to win his match and thwart Bruno's plans? I think not. His hero's journey—separation, initiation, and descent into the underworld, a struggle with evil—seems incomplete because we are not sure what knowledge this compromised hero has gained on his return. We understand Bruno's relation to Guy, but does Guy? Bruno's murder of Miriam has freed Guy, and the cigarette lighter has exonerated him, but the film leaves us with that nagging question about Guy's self-knowledge and identity. While the film quite brilliantly charts Guy's persona and the alternating repression and eruptions of his shadow, the act of acknowledging and integrating the shadow is largely ignored.

Hitchcock's endings often raise as many questions as they answer. He teaches us to be suspicious of summaries and neat conclusions, thereby honoring the dictum of French director Robert Bresson about psychologizing film: "No psychology (of the kind which discovers only what it can explain)."[14] Almost ten years after *Strangers,* Hitchcock ends *Psycho* with a psychiatrist's plausible, pedantic, and unsatisfying explanation of Norman Bates's character and actions. In *Strangers,* Hitchcock leaves us to struggle with a happy ending and the uneasy awareness of Guy's limitations. How is the main character to answer the question that brackets the film—"Are you Guy Haines?" Suffice it to say that too much of Guy's unconscious remains unconscious—the shadow, indeed and in deed, has been denied.

* * * * *

Patrice Leconte's *Man on a Train* offers a fascinating contrast to Hitchcock's *Strangers on a Train.* The plotlines of the two films are quite dissimilar, though each film focuses intensively on the relationship between two characters who are at once opposites and doubles of one another. Both films are character studies developed within different genres. Hitchcock's film may be classified as a suspense thriller. To some extent, *Man on a Train* also depends on genre expectations, as the film is a skillful conflation of the Western, the gangster, the caper, and the "buddy" film.

As *Man on a Train* opens, Milan (Johnny Hallyday) is traveling by train to meet up with his fellow gangsters to rob a provincial bank. Reaching his destination, Milan strikes up an unlikely friendship with Manesquier (Jean Rochefort), a retired teacher, whose staid, unadventurous life is exemplified by his surroundings—the sleepy country town and ancestral house where he has always lived. Manesquier offers Milan a room, and the two characters' contrasting personalities and experiences come to represent a complementary and compensatory bond that leads to a deepening friendship. Saturday becomes the climactic day, as it marks Milan's planned bank robbery and Manesquier's "quick tune-up," his triple bypass surgery. To quote one of the gangsters, "Forever always ends on Saturday." As the plotline pointing to these two events converges, the crosscutting between bank and hospital provides a transcendental ending.

Leconte's title and certain motifs clearly allude to Hitchcock's *Strangers.* The criss-crossing train tracks near the beginning of both films suggest a fated crossing of paths by the main characters. Recalling all the doubling in *Strangers,* we come to understand that the "man" riding the train in Leconte's title applies equally to both central characters, one at the beginning and the other at the end of the film. Even the editing and fragmented presentation of Bruno and Guy that opens *Strangers* finds its complement in the introduction of fragmented body shots of the gangster on the train.

Still, such intertextuality is less important than the contrast between the films and the comprehensive view of the shadow archetype provided by a side-by-side analysis of both works. Rather than the denial of the shadow, Leconte focuses on a positive and transformative friendship of opposites between an older, extroverted, retired teacher and a middle-aged, introverted, and world-weary gangster. Both men have undeveloped, unlived sides to their personalities, the buried treasure in the unconscious that wants to be discovered. *Man on a Train* celebrates the opposition and integration that comes from holding the tension of opposites which, in the end, confirms what Jeffrey C. Miller describes as the transcendent function, "a phenomenon ubiquitous to human experience that implicates opposition/duality, liminality, descent, initiation, and transformation."[15]

Criss-crossing paths are crucial to both films, but what gets exchanged between the principal characters has vastly different implications in each film. The exchange of objects in *Strangers* begins with Guy leaving behind his "A to G" inscribed cigarette lighter with all of its multiple sexual implications and its role in Guy's guilt and innocence. What follows thereafter are Bruno's ominous and threatening "gifts" to Guy, which include Miriam's glasses, a Luger pistol, notes, and the key to Bruno's house. The exchanges between Manesquier and Milan are of a different kind and significance. Manesquier does give tangible gifts to Milan—slippers (a mark of domesticity), a book of poetry with the resonant "Pont Neuf" poem, and a house key, which becomes crucial to the ending. Certain things are also briefly appropriated—Milan's jacket and Manesquier's pipe and mentoring work, for instance. It is, however, the intangible gifts—the exchange of skills, attitudes, identities, mutual appreciation, opportunities to change, fantasies and reality checks, and finally, profound friendship—

which matter most. The list of what the two men learn from each other is long and complicated.

Music, for instance, is one of the gifts exchanged between the men that encompasses most of the intangibles listed above. Milan has little experience with music, though he once played the harmonica (the right instrument, says Manesquier, for a traveling man). Although the teacher talks of Beethoven, Chopin, and Schumann (the latter composer appealing to the teacher's "love of failure"), Manesquier is most closely associated with his playing of Schubert's Impromptu. Not Milan's kind of music, says Manesquier—"It's like me driving some sports convertible." The film undercuts Manesquier's judgment, as we later see Milan soaking in the bath and, eyes closed, clearly relishing the Schubert being played. More importantly, Milan himself is at the piano at the end of the film, playing the simple melodic line of Schubert's Impromptu. The complement to this musical trading for Manesquier is the "Western" guitar music on the sound track. Associated with Milan at the beginning of the film, the guitar underscores in every sense Manesquier's transition to the train at the end.

The exchanges between the men point to new perspectives and to steps toward individuation and wholeness. Though any one exchange may seem insignificant—Manesquier acquires a taste for cognac from Milan and through the teacher, Milan shows an interest in poetry—the gifts accumulate and resonate. On the terrace, the cautious Manesquier ponders his relationship to women and confesses that "I stopped living before I grew old." An exasperated Milan forces the teacher to see himself reflected in the window: "Know why women don't look at you? Because they're dazzled by you. Look at yourself. Look at all there is to see. It's all there." Milan's affirmation is much more than an acknowledgement of Manesquier's attractiveness or masculinity—it is a testament to wholeness, to "all there is to see."

Both Milan and Manesquier's lives are marked by routine and stagnation, and they both fear and desire change. They first meet in an apothecary, though neither man's malaise can be cured by medications. Psychologically, their respective personae, gangster and teacher, have worn thin, and both men seem trapped behind their masks. Their friendship will lead, paradoxically, to their deaths and to their psychic, holistic healing. The retired Manesquier lives in a boring, provincial town in an ancestral house unchanged since his mother's death fifteen years ago. He works jigsaw puzzles and plays the piano, though "playing the piano," he insists, "can be a dead bore." He admits to Milan that even the stars bore him, to which the generally hard-nosed, unromantic Milan responds, "Apparently we all have a star each."

When Manesquier invites Milan home, the teacher's gate and door are unlocked. Somewhat cryptically Manesquier declares that the keys are lost *and* he has spares. Only later do we learn that the teacher divides humanity into two categories—the planners who have two of everything (three in Manesquier's case), and the adventurers who take on life's risks. Significantly, Manesquier and his house are open to and ready for this stranger. This house represents so much of Manesquier's character and how and why his life seems stuck. Even his "heroic" ancestors, especially the one not needed at Austerliz who later accidentally blew off the side of his head, seem emblematic of the irony that undercuts Manesquier's Romantic impulses. This house is "*ancien*," kept precisely as Manesquier's mother left it. Although the teacher says he prefers Zen minimalism, the house is ornately decorated and crammed with mementos; he admits that "I mustn't like change either."

Stuck in this unchanging house, Manesquier is surprised to learn the rootless Milan likes the house precisely because "It's full of the past." Few images better represent the psyche than houses, and Milan soon resides in an upper room. As Jungian Joseph Henderson writes:

> Presumably, the investment of ego in a house is something that can help one at any time. People change and need to develop something in relation to their changing lives. A house expresses the continuity of the psyche or of the Self; the ego puts into it or takes from it what it needs. Finding a new room in a house often comes into dreams and in fantasies. Finding a new room would mean finding a new sense of self-containment.[16]

This insight has implications for both main characters. What traps Manesquier is the same house that represents fulfillment for Milan. The gangster will end the film ensconced in the house, just as Manesquier will replace Milan on the train.

Milan, the stranger and intruder with an Italian name, the gangster in a black leather jacket, arrives by train, and his appearance invokes the gangster genre, while his silent, solitary figure on the train platform, accompanied by the guitar music, is reminiscent of a Sergio Leone Western. Movie genres are a frequent subject of conversation in *Man on a Train*, with the gangster/caper genre part of the plot and the Western genre part of Manesquier's rich fantasy life. He even finds a photo of Milan sitting on a horse in an apparently Western setting, a French version of the "Marlboro Man." Later, Manesquier tells Milan, "I saw that photo of you in the West." Asked where it was taken, Milan indulges in a bit of storied fantasy himself by saying, "Nevada." Not wanting to expand on his fabrication or trigger the teacher's overactive imagination, Milan immediately cautions him, "Don't start." Worth noting is the guitar music and the sound of a moving train that underscore this exchange. When teacher and gangster spend their last moments together on Saturday morning, Milan confesses, "I lied about that photo. It wasn't in Nevada. It was taken in a circus. I was a stuntman for fourteen years." Preoccupied by his own thoughts, Manesquier hardly notes the confession, though it seems necessary and important in confirming the integrity and authenticity of their friendship.

Much of the film contrasts Manesquier's fantasies (often tied to his cinema-saturated life) with Milan's cool, even cynical, realism. Milan is not much of a talker, and the teacher admits he also wants to be more like Milan, "a silent onlooker." Manesquier takes on this role at the end of the film, silently looking at the landscape from the train window. In its most positive aspects, Manesquier's fantasy life is an example of active imagination, a dialog between the unconscious and the conscious that he has both with himself and with Milan; at its best, it leads to transformation and individuation. But active imagination has its dangers, and Milan's role is partly to temper the teacher's visions with a hard-earned realism.

After Manesquier shares with Milan an early fantasy where the teacher imagines walking into a bar, where all talk stops and the women, presumably impressed with Manesquier's strong masculine presence, check their own reflections, Milan, the realist, tells Manesquier that he has watched too many thrillers. To a large degree, cinema feeds Manesquier's fantasy life and simultaneously undercuts his doggedly held romantic views. His first kiss was at the cinema, but the romance is spoiled when the woman rams her tongue down his throat and hauls him out of the Roxy by his privates. His deflation and humiliation doesn't end there, because he tells Milan, "She dropped me for a sports club janitor's son." This episode is further reinforced when Manesquier, after his mother's death, takes a trip to Paris where, instead of finding romance, he encounters two days of rain and resorts to seeing eleven movies.

As in *Strangers*, Leconte's film explores the relationship between persona and shadow. Stuck with his house, his books, his piano, his gentle teacher's persona, Manesquier is desperate to try on other personae. Milan's room becomes the site of one of Manesquier's earliest fantasies. With Milan out of the house, Manesquier enters his room, tries on his leather jacket, looks in the mirror, impersonates Wyatt Earp, intimidates the Tombstone cowboys, and downs an imaginary shot of whiskey. This comic scene is undercut when Manesquier slips immediately out of this fantasy into his tired and retired persona as a teacher and asks the imagined students from his past to take out their exercise books and write. The culmination of this pattern occurs with Milan in the bistro. Jostled by a customer, Milan doesn't react because he knows he is outnumbered, and "one guy can't take two on, except in the movies." Manesquier decides to take on the toughs, only to confront a man who turns out to be a former student who quotes poetry to him. From Western saloons to French bistros, Manesquier's imaginative attempts to live the life of the tough guy adventurer are stymied by reality.

All of Manesquier's tough guy fantasies may relate inversely to his rather strong anima or feminine side. While playing Schubert on the piano, the teacher tells Milan, "Apart from needlepoint, I have all the skills of a well-bred early 20th-century young woman." The only woman character central to the film is Manesquier's mistress, Viviane (Isabelle Petit-Jacques). Her visit raises considerable sexual tension, jealousy, and conflict between herself and Milan. Milan wants, in Viviane's words, "to stir up shit," and drive the lovers apart. Wary of each other, both outsiders assume that they know the other's motives and activate the anima/animus archetypes. Interestingly, it is Milan who changes or recants by admitting to Manesquier, "I was wrong earlier—an old mistress must be a comfort." Although the line could be a putdown, Milan offers it as a genuine apology and an acknowledgement of the feminine. Clearly, the movement from the unconscious to the conscious involves the interaction of multiple archetypes, including persona, anima/animus, and shadow.

One of the poignant scenes that addresses the persona involves Manesquier's confrontation with his sister and his own death anxieties. She has come to help him pack and prepare for his hospitalization. Facing his triple bypass operation and possible death, Manesquier determines to break through his own and his sister's adult personae, because they have never said what they thought. He insists that she admit her husband, Fernand, is "a fat prick." When she refuses, he wonders aloud how "one day we struck a pose and turned into mummies." Before she leaves, the sister breaks through her persona of niceness to honestly admit her husband "is a fat prick." To mark the epiphany, brother and sister rush to embrace one another.

In the very next scene, Manesquier astonishes a barber by insisting on a new hairstyle, something "in-between 'fresh out of jail' and 'world-class soccer player'. " He also insists on no part in his hair—"no part" may point to no divisions, to more wholeness in his life. He will keep his mustache, but may try a goatee (and we recall Milan sports a goatee). Pleased with the results, Manesquier twice admires his reflection in the windows he passes. This amusing scene leaves us wondering if this makeover really is the beginning of a new persona.

Likewise, Milan is at home assuming much of the teacher's persona. Complete with pipe and a book, Milan welcomes the young boy whose tutoring session Manesquier forgot. The text is Balzac's *Eugenie Grandot* about a woman who waits, faithfully and futilely, for her lover. Milan suggests that the boy consider what the woman of today would do; photographs and the telephone, Milan intimates, would solve the woman's problem. Charming and ludicrous as these two scenes are, Manesquier and Milan are playfully and genuinely exploring their shadows, the undeveloped aspects of the unconscious. What is persona for one man is shadow for the other and vice versa.

Playing with the shadow and confronting the unconscious always carries risks and real dangers. Patrice Leconte is masterful in controlling the shifting tones of *Man on the Train*. The threat and reality of death hang over this film. Although not quite the allegorical figure of Ingmar Bergman's *The Seven Seal* (1956), Death appears as Manesquier's gardener, Mr. Gora. Returning home, the frightened teacher hears a strange scraping sound; from around the corner of the house comes the gardener, complete with scythe. Manesquier wonders aloud why he never expects to see the gardener, and Mr. Gora explains, "No one ever remembers the gardener." In the concluding shot from just behind the gardener aligns his scythe with Manesquier's departing figure. Though hardly subtle, the scene is rooted in realism and carries to perfection its Edward Gorey tone of comic foreboding. In trade for the gift of the slippers, Manesquier gets a pistol shooting lesson from Milan. We understand why the teacher asks if he can imagine shooting his gardener, in lieu of the tin can targets.

It is not by chance that *Man on a Train* mixes the Western and the gangster genres. As Jane Tompkins says of the Western,

> To go west, as far west as you can go, west of everything, is to die. Its aura of death, both parodied and insisted on in place names like Deadwood and Tombstone, is one of the genre's most essential features . . . . The ritualization of the moment of death that climaxes most Western novels and films hovers over the whole story and gives its typical scenes a faintly sacramental aura.[17]

Death is also the destiny of gangsters. The dialog of the gangster subplot in *Man on the Train* is replete with comments about aging and with ominous foreshadowings, pointing to the inevitability of Milan's death. When one gangster, Max, calls the bank they plan to rob "a piece of cake," Milan's succinct reply is, "You can choke on cake." All the meetings of the gangsters and the bank job itself are shot with an icy blue tonality. Despite his sense of foreboding, Milan seems fated to carry through with his plans. Manesquier offers Milan money to call off the bank job. Significantly, this is the one gift that Milan rejects.

What explains the fatalism surrounding the robbery, particularly the revelation of the SWAT team and the police set up? Perhaps Max, one of the gangsters to escape, has betrayed them to the police, but this is unclear. Manesquier's attempt to prevent the robbery by offering money to Milan must be weighed against his possible responsibility for the bloody shootout. Manesquier, meeting Milan as he is casing the bank, talks openly and carelessly of his fantasy—announcing "a hold-up" loudly enough to draw the attention of several bank clerks. His conventional movie script fantasy ends with him in the Bahamas, "casino, white linen suit, suntan . . ." If this is active imagination, it is played out at precisely the wrong time and place. For Milan, this fantasy turned reality leaves him gunned down in the street.

Man on a Train is not, finally, about a botched bank robbery or a fatal medical operation, nor is the ending rightly framed as life after death. The ending of the film is the culmination of the friendship, of the psychological change and exchange between Manesquier and Milan. "You'll be a new man tomorrow," Milan assures Manesquier, and the vow proves wrong about the success of the teacher's triple by-pass but prescient about the transformation to come. Preceded by a restrained but emotional leave-taking over a breakfast neither man can eat and where they thank each other for various gifts, complex parallel editing begins, linking the bank and the hospital. No amount of detailed analysis can capture a numinous experience, but Leconte's skill in uniting aesthetic form and psychological transformation makes a transcendent ending.

As both men start their final journeys, the guitar music is laid over the sound of the train, recalling the film's opening shots of Milan. Cold blue tones link the scenes of the gangsters and the hospital, as do moments where the doctors and the gangsters put on their different masks. Cross-cutting suggests that both operations go wrong simultaneously as Milan notes the marked money and the medical procedures fail. Milan, meeting his destiny by stepping in front of one of his fellow gangsters, is gunned down in the street, and at the hospital Manesquier's cardiac monitor flatlines.

Both men die, but the heart machine suddenly begins beeping again; in a series of cross-cutting shots, Manesquier and Milan open, close, and open their eyes, and the Schubert Impromptu is heard. A dissolve shows a stone wall, an empty street, and finally Milan and Manesquier face one another from opposite sides of the road. This liminal space anticipates boundaries to be crossed. Manesquier throws his house key to Milan, and the two men, suitcases in hand, pass each other crossing the street and walk in opposite directions. The importance of the moment is emphasized by the two separate shots of the crossing that are overlapped in time.[18] Schubert, the clack of the train, and the steady pulse of a heartbeat dominate the sound track. Shots of Manesquier in the operating room, then on the train platform, and Milan lying on the street and then in Manesquier's house convey their envisioned destinations. Finally, dark tunnel shots alternate with Milan playing the Schubert and Manesquier on the train as it emerges from the tunnel. The alternating tunnel shots suggest the transition, a kind of birthing as each man assumes the place of the other.

What, exactly, have we witnessed? Stanley Kauffmann posits that "Leconte provides two endings for his film, which are interwoven: one is sad, the other droll. We can choose."[19] Are we meant to choose from an equivocal, either/or ending? I think not. Unlike the hero's journey in *Strangers on a Train,* destiny here leads to individuation. Integration, wholeness, a befriending of shadow—all are realized through the operation of the transcendent function. Jeffrey Miller's account of liminality as the ground for the transcendent function helps us understand this ending:

> The liminal is the territory not only where both death and birth coexist but becomes an archetypal place of pure possibility that is the potential source of all sorts of original and new ideas. A space that can simultaneously hold opposites as polarized as death and birth where neither one nor the other prevails can, indeed, be the space of pure possibility.[20]

Fantasy and symbol, the numinous and the irrational, the tension and transfiguration of opposites are all at play in "the space of pure possibility." Milan is at the piano, Manesquier is journeying through the landscape, and *Man on a Train* has transported us to another realm.

NOTES

1. The three best known adaptations of Stevenson's novel include the 1921 silent film starring John Barrymore, Rouben Mamoulian's 1931 version with an Academy Award performance by Fredric March, and the 1941 version starring Spencer Tracy and Ingrid Bergman. For psychological complexity and cinematic style, the 1931 Mamoulian film is by far the superior adaptation.

2. Although French director Patrice Leconte has made over twenty films, his work has received little critical attention outside of occasional reviews. In addition to *Man on a Train,* Leconte's films released in this country include *Monsieur Hire* (1989), *The Hairdresser's Husband* (1990), *Ridicule* (1996), *The Girl on the Bridge* (1999), *The Widow of Saint-Pierre*

(2000), and most recently *Intimate Strangers* (2004). These films alone point to an impressive, if eclectic, body of work warranting serious study.

3. Francois Truffaut, *Hitchcock/Truffaut* (New York: Simon & Schuster, 1985), 195.

4. Anthony Stevens, *On Jung* (New Jersey: Princeton UP, 1999), 43.

5. All quotations from both films are taken directly from the sound tracks. In the case of *Man on a Train*, I have relied on the English subtitles.

6. Truffaut, 199.

7. Robert A. Johnson, *Owning Your Own Shadow* (San Francisco: HarperCollins, 1993), 8. Also see Robert Bly, *A Little Book on the Human Shadow* (San Francisco: Harper & Row, 1988).

8. Raymond Durgnat, *The Strange Case of Alfred Hitchcock* (Cambridge: The MIT Press, 1978), 217-218.

9. For a thorough discussion of homosexuality in *Strangers*, see Robert J. Corber, *In the Name of National Security* (Durham: Duke UP, 1993), 56-82.

10. Robin Wood, *Hitchcock's Films Revisited* (New York: Columbia UP, 1989). Wood makes this point about the dissolve, although he mistakenly refers to the transition as a cut (p. 88). Wood's commentary has influenced my own analysis, particularly his discussion of the light and dark symbolism throughout *Strangers*.

11. Widely remarked by critics, this long shot of Bruno and the famous shot of the head-turning tennis crowd all following the ball except for Bruno, whose gaze remains fixed on Guy, point to Hitchcock's cinematic style informing his content. Bruno's small, dark figure against the white background of the Jefferson Memorial conveys his threat to Guy's political ambitions. With these shots, Hitchcock also subverts a cinematic convention—long shots for context, close-ups for emphasis. Despite the long shots, our eye is directed, through contrast or lack of movement, to a very small, but particular spot within each image.

12. Lesley Brill, *The Hitchcock Romance* (New Jersey: Princeton UP), 83. Brill offers an astute, detailed analysis of the journey motif, the nether world of descents, and mythic allusions in *Strangers*. I am indebted to his analysis of the film, to his comprehensive study of Hitchcock's work, and to his willingness to read and comment on this essay.

13. Truffaut, *Hitchcock/Truffaut,* 199. Hitchcock's wish to cast Holden as a stronger Guy Haines is certainly understandable. William Holden, having just completed *Sunset Boulevard* (1950), arguably the best performance of his career as the conflicted and compromised Joe Gillis, would have created a much different and more brooding Guy Haines.

14. Robert Bresson, *Notes on Cinematography* (New York: Urizen Books, 1975), 39.

15. Jeffrey C. Miller, *The Transcendent Function* (Albany: State University of New York Press, 2004), 99.

16. Joseph L. Henderson, *Shadow and Self* (Wilmette: Chiron Productions, 1990), 82.

17. Jane Tompkins, *West of Everything* (New York: Oxford UP, 1992), 24-25.

18. This shot is also the signature image for the film, used in its advertising. On the cover of the DVD, this crossing image of the two men calls to mind a picture of Siamese twins.

19. Stanley Kauffmann, *The New Republic,* May 19, 2003, 27.

20. Jeffrey C. Miller, *The Transcendent Function,* 105.

WESTERNS AND GLOBAL IMPERIALISM

JOHN IZOD

The Western on screen constitutes a primary locus in which battle was joined for the collective white soul of the United States of America through much of the last century. This seems the key to the genre's formidable strengths and weaknesses.

Comparison with Brazilians' experience of collective identity sharpens this idea. Gambini argues that because Brazil lacks a myth of origin its people are ashamed of their remote past which they regard as a black hole. By their instead building an identity dating from the so-called 'Discovery' of 1500, the nation's history is based on the false premise that it began with the Portuguese Conquest. This has serious consequences for the structuring of the collective consciousness and, as an incidental effect, for the way Brazilians relate to the deep layers of the collective unconscious. Gambini argues, "Since we deny our ancestral origin, we distort it..." That has prevented Brazilians from developing a vibrant synthesis, both practical and spiritual, between European and Amerindian ways of being.[1]

John Izod is Professor of Screen Analysis and Head of the Department of Film and Media Studies at the University of Stirling in Scotland where he has taught since 1978. He has adapted Jungian methodology to the analysis of film and television in *The Films of Nicolas Roeg* (Macmillan, 1992), *Myth, Mind and the Screen: Understanding the Heroes of our Time* (Cambridge University Press, 2001), and *Working with the Audience?* (Routledge, forthcoming).

Gambini's rueful account of Brazilian cultural history resonates with the North American experience because significant features of their histories run parallel. Until the late twentieth century the Western furnished a myth of origin that was profoundly Euro-centered. It was a rewriting of history into legend that suited the white male perspective but had little to say to those women who were not willing to find their consciousness through the psyche of men. It did not address the experiences of Asian migrants; and (with rare, honourable exceptions) it had nothing whatsoever to say to the dispossessed original inhabitants of the continent. Yet as Gambini says, "All of mankind's great questions were worked on and solved by the indigenous peoples inhabiting the New World since pristine times," constituting a wisdom very distinct from that of the European incomers.[2] It was the stuff from which soul was made only to be destroyed by the invasion.[3] This also occurred with the near eradication of Native American culture in the USA.

If Western movies constitute a primary locus in which the struggle for the collective soul of the USA has been fought and that struggle implicates the characters on screen, how does it involve the deep psychology of the audience? Does the Western of the early twenty-first century differ from its predecessors in ways which reflect changes in the audience's circumstances and reveal psychological shifts associated with those societal changes?

Cultural Provenance

After the Western genre had (once again) been declared dead at the start of the twenty-first century, the release of some fine movies in 2003 indicated that it could still engage audiences — a reminder of how deep its roots run in collective emotions. Those roots sustain boldly drawn archetypal images that energize the Western's highly charged myths. Since we are discussing a genre that has grown a strong timber of resilient iconography, the archetypal images it deploys are both its established boughs and the nodal points from which new growth buds.

The Western has occupied the screen (albeit with several gaps) for one hundred years; but some of its sources are much older. The first western novel, James Fenimore Cooper's *The Pioneers,* an immediate success, was published in 1823. However, the literary heritage of two of the genre's thematic strands can be traced back to a seventeenth-

and eighteenth-century British vogue in odes that celebrated the idyll of the self-sufficient gentleman-farmer who had withdrawn from city life. Parallel to this sub-genre runs the pastoral tradition contemplating the shepherd's existence in the meadows—an imagined life that would be perfect but for human frailty and vice.

Libido and the Land

The pastoral idyll and the celebration of the self-sufficient farmer lie close to the themes of many great Western movies—none more so than *Shane* (1953). But the rural ideal gains its potency less from secular literary sources than the Bible. The commanding image underlying the idyll was a symbol vividly present in the minds of European immigrants even before their arrival as an ancient, religiously and mythically charged image cluster. So it resonated with meaning for those who moved to take up new land in the West. And it gave spiritual credence to that historic migration.[4]

Gambini notes that Portuguese men too had landed in Brazil with a Paradise fantasy in their heads—an enormous and very dangerous fantasy, which certainly included a vision of naked and willing women in a place where everything was permitted. There (as in North America) this dreamland was for the exclusive enjoyment of white men, never for the Indians.[5] The dominant ideology of the North American immigrants of the sixteenth and seventeenth centuries was Protestantism rather than the Catholic faith that dominated immigrant communities in Latin America. In the north, many of the newcomers came in family and community groups to settle and find new lives rather than to rape, pillage, and return to the motherland. Nevertheless, the dark whore is a recurring archetypal figure in the Western, juxtaposed to the pure, fair-haired woman.

The genre's robber barons may not send gold to Europe, but they surely do steal the land. In the North American states, the Paradise image cluster metamorphosed into a seductive notion that the new territories were the garden of the world which could be made into the new Eden by the labor of an honest people. In its metamorphosis, that idea's potency extended the biblical symbolism of the garden as the blessed place, a Paradise on earth, to include in the cluster the farm, the smallholding, the wilderness, nature, and even the desert. Looking at the image cluster from the perspective of analytical psychology, we can read it as an emerging symbol of an idealized, collective self. It was a sacred icon which took on its own distinctive warp from the political and cultural exigencies of the white North American experience. However, entry to this Eden was invariably represented as a matter for struggle because the land was always contested — both in actuality and mythologized memory.

I have written elsewhere about the displacement of libidinous energy in the Western myth in the nineteenth and twentieth centuries. Eros, which would ordinarily attach man to woman, drew the Western male to nature, such was the appeal of the pastoral ideal. This obsessive love leads him to invest the wilderness with feminine qualities. The resulting displacement makes for a dangerous, uroboric courtship of the Earth Mother. It inhibits the proper maturation of the Western hero's psyche and accounts for the often infantile nature of his relationships with white women. This quasi-incestuous love affair with nature was further troubled because the newcomers could not ignore the peoples already settled in the West who enjoyed a bond with the land that the immigrants could not share. So the white man found a dark-skinned rival whose presence intruded on his jealous love for the wilderness.[6]

That rivalry troubled the psycho-sexuality both of the whites themselves and their conception of Native Americans' nature. Since the new arrivals meant to possess the land by seizing it from its original inhabitants, they soon demonized the latter by intuitively making them the object of their collective shadow projection, as all peoples do with their enemies when they prepare to go to war. These racist shadow projections endured long after the end of the Indian wars and tainted the Western genre, where they remained a staple feature through much of the twentieth century. Furthermore, the impact of woman as anima was marginalized. She seldom functions as an archetypal image whose power can give a man insight into the contents of his unconscious and enrich his personality.

The splitting of the female image runs right through the genre until well into the third quarter of the twentieth century. The male hero cultivates his strength (the power of his will) in order to defend from what are in fact his own split-off desires, and the chaste, civilized, but rather bloodless woman represents the only type he can accept as a marriage partner. In marrying her, he defends the urbanizing culture that he despises but of which she is the steadfast representative. In short, we find that the white hero employs his highly focused conscious will ultimately to resist the seductions (both benign and evil) of the unconscious.[7]

The difficult endeavour to ensure that will should triumph also affected the representation of Native American peoples. Luigi Zoja observes that there is a cultural conflict here that goes right to the heart of ideologies embodied in the mainstream products of the American motion picture industry.

> The Hollywood hero strives for justice when his rights have been offended; the Indian Chief knows that life is the seat of drama, not of justice, and prepares himself in all tranquillity for the next blow of destiny... The Hollywood hero believes in the supreme power of will; the Indian Chief, like the tragic hero, believes that will counts for nothing... The Hollywood hero is ingenuous; the Indian Chief is wise.[8]

Zoja argues that America's need to listen to the voices of its native peoples is not only a historical necessity — it reflects a need of modern collective consciousness.[9] Gambini's account of Brazilian needs supports this position.

> Consciousness looks for its eternal other, the unconscious. Our ego searches for its other, an ego no longer identified with shadow and persona, but one striving to express the self. The quest for the other is always archetypal, and for [Brazilians] *this other is the Indian.*[10]

However, Brazilian access to the Indian as other is almost lost because of the destruction of native culture. The other is not integrated and has become a renegade in the psyche and in its own land.[11] Once again, the resemblance to the North American experience is marked. Historically the Western has overwhelmingly been racist. The notable exceptions to the general rule struggle against the tide so that examples of Westerns reflecting American Indian culture are to this day few and far between. Are the latter definitive of modern American culture as Zoja would anticipate? Or rather, is the Western still for many in the audience, as it predominantly was through the past century, a site of resistance to Native American culture — a site of resistance, perhaps to the needs of the unconscious? Ron Howard's *The Missing* (2003), discussed shortly will prove an interesting test case.

Landscape and Economic Power

Westerns frequently center on the ownership and use of land. I have referred to the genre's allegorical representation of territory insofar as it evokes readings that attend to sacred, psychological, and political matters. However, as an obsessional *topos*, the land also takes in economic issues. The Western seldom allows respect for characters who do not own property — one of the factors that denies heroic stature to townspeople (excepting only sheriffs and marshals). It is the usual ideological sub-text to driving Native Americans from their homelands, notwithstanding their symbiotic relation with nature and their prior claim to dwelling there. The loose derivation of many Western plots from the historical battles for land makes them fitting vehicles for allegorical reflections on the functioning of capital. Property will continue to be fought over on screen unless either the dominant capitalist ideology of the USA or the demography of its peoples should change out of all recognition.

Just as literary pastoral was once written for the educated, few of whom would actually have been working the land, so commercial factors always ensured that Western movies found the bulk of their audience not with cowboys but among town dwellers. In 1953, *Shane's* smallholders had their urban equivalent in the young families who were using their postwar affluence to become home owners. *Shane* associated love of family and the cherished garden smallholding with redemption, while linking greed with damnation — an allegorical frame which readily mapped onto the new suburban values of the time. Although *Shane's* newly settled small farmers have legal rights to their property, they are threatened by the rancher who tries to drive them off the land in order to secure ownership of the entire territory. Ryker (Emile Meyer) reckons that they are stealing his land. His monstrous greed has the characteristic of irresponsible corporate capital — seizing property and taking profit without regard for the small man. Such action would have been strong in folk memory for many in the USA twenty years after the great depression of the 1930s. Projected fear of the bankers who held liens on so many recently purchased suburban homes may also have vested in Ryker's demonic figure. The audience is clearly positioned to see that the management of capital has to be altered to accommodate the interests of 'smallholders.'

In 1985, Warner Bros released Clint Eastwood's *Pale Rider*, modelled on *Shane*. Coy LaHood (Richard Dysart) represents corporate greed. The owner of a mining outfit, he lacks Ryker's excuse, his Lear-like quality, the bygone glory of a man out of his time. LaHood's operation uses hydraulic mining techniques which threaten the living of small-claim miners in the valley below and rape the environment. Although the state legislature is discussing moves to outlaw this invasive technique, the only effect on LaHood is to make him drive his men harder to extract every ounce of gold the land holds before the law stops him. Eastwood's take on corporate culture in the mid-1980s is gloomy in the extreme. The film plainly shows that ecological irresponsibility is sacrilege. But it goes further by suggesting that human agency alone is not strong enough to curb the appetites of corporate capital: it requires apocalyptic power embodied in the Preacher (Eastwood) to destroy LaHood's enterprise.

Open Range

Open Range (Kevin Costner, USA, 2003), a slow-moving film that rewards the audience with its restraint, dignity, and grace, picks up the same theme. Here an Irish immigrant, Denton Baxter (Michael Gambon), is the ranch owner. He has purchased the town of Harmonville and the land for miles around, for good measure buying the Law too. Like Ryker in *Shane* and LaHood in *Pale Rider*, he rides roughshod over laws that give rights to the less powerful. Despite the fact that free grazing was lawful in 1882, Baxter has his men slaughter cowboys whom threats do not scare off his land. Representing capital running riot with addictive greed, nothing about this pustulous creature attains to tragic dignity.

Baxter deliberately starts a conflict with Boss Spearman (Robert Duvall) and Charley Waite (Kevin Costner), drovers who are moving their cattle across his territory. Like most conflicts with rancher barons, warfare helps trigger in Boss and Charley an individuation process resembling that which many screen cowboys have undergone since the psychological Western evolved in the mid-1950s. Fostered by interaction with other characters and plot events, it brings about in the heroes an individuation having two related aspects. Firstly, it opens the individual to a deeper (often astonished) understanding of himself. And secondly, it reveals to him that he is 'individual' in the antique sense of 'indivisible'— that he is more alike to than different from his fellows. Indeed, the tension between the claims of the individual and those of the collective can often be seen in the Western. It resonates loudly in times of nationally felt disturbance, as when mass paranoia is aroused (formerly directed at Communists, lately against terrorists) or war is waged (whether armed or psychological). How a Western resolves tensions between the claims of the individual and those of the collective reflects the ethos of its era.

The Western is good at limning spiky ego-centered differences between characters that at first make the members of a team hostile to each other. As the action proceeds, various exigencies (usually the overwhelming opposition of an enemy) show them that they have much in common at the level of emotions and their semi-conscious desires, fears, loves, and loathings. Of course, the resultant bonding linked only the male victors in twentieth-century Westerns, a narrative outcome that legitimized a psychologically imbalanced regime lacking full-blooded integration of the feminine. It produced a dynamic prepared to counterbalance either war or paranoia only by force and will — the psychological forte of the genre through the last century.

Open Range refreshes this familiar pattern. Contrary to the established norm, Boss and Charley seem at first to be closely attuned in temperament. But as the crisis with Baxter develops, crucial underlying differences in their psychological orientation emerge, rooted in their dissimilar experiences of life. These differences are eventually subsumed into profound harmony when they share their readiness to die, and later (after they survive Baxter's villainous posse) when Charley learns from the older man how to live. They participate in a process of individuation which deepens their consciousness of self and connects them to their fellow beings. The process accords sweetly with Jung's thoughts about the opening out to scrutiny of complexes that had previously been unconscious.

There is, nonetheless, a paradox in the Western's economics. It shows in the condemnation of large corporations and preference for the small-to-medium sized enterprise. However, many members of the audience will work for or deal with large organizations in both the capital market and the publicly funded sector. Such organizations have

size and influence which make it easy to stereotype them as impersonal
exploiters — the opening stance of the films I have discussed. The
question to ask is how the genre resolves the existence of these capital
empires.

Open Range is a revealing case in point. Boss and Charley win
their war, but decide to leave the range and return to Harmonville
once their herd has been driven to market. Boss will take over the
town bar and Charley will marry Sue Barlow (Annette Bening), the
town doctor's capable sister. Both are venturing on enterprises on a
small, human scale which the audience can easily identify as plausible
containers for psychological investment and development. Significantly,
however, the film does not specify what will happen to Baxter's vast
acres. In this it is typical of Westerns that end in defeat for the baron
of capital but gloss over its economic consequences, focussing instead
on the victory of the 'small' people. It is not hard to see why a utopian
solution appropriate to the thrust of the genre (namely that these vast
landholdings should be broken up and sold off in small parcels) would
be implausible. If the outcome of the fictional events were to accord
with America's economic history, it would require that great ranches
be bought up by an even larger corporation. But such a resolution
would fatally damage the economic individualism to which the Western
myth is tied. When the genre invokes economic issues, it remains
pastoral in being founded on escapist nostalgia.

In other aspects, however, the Western does connect purposefully
with societal reality. It changes to reflect current perceptions of the
family. *Open Range* and *The Missing* are early twenty-first century
Westerns that discarded none of the genre's traditional concern with
power, but changed their female characters' access to it. They thereby
not only reflected shifts in American society but also moved toward
establishing a better balance for the genre as between anima and animus
images. Sue Barlow in *Open Range* and Maggie Gilkeson (Cate
Blanchett) in *The Missing* have substantial roles as lead women which
require them neither to be self-effacing nor adept at trickery. Both of
them have full, active lives and address men as their rightful equals.

In addition to running her brother's household, Sue practices as a
nurse and looks after the drovers' casualties. She treats mind as well as
body, encouraging the men to talk about themselves. Her inner strength
is formidable. A typical Western heroine would urge her man to avoid

killing, and might back away from him if he used his gun. Sue, although the compassionate voice of reason, knows that a time comes when compromise is impossible and fighting is justified.[12] She eases Charley's mental torments by showing him that he is a good man at heart and that what he has done as a killer does not bar him from her love.[13] When Charley finally realizes that he is not unfit to marry Sue, we can see that each is completed by the other — an ordinary enough resolution to many genres, but not the Western. Establishment of the family unit implies shared individuation such that in *Open Range* the victors' bonding includes women and parenting. In developing the genre's timeworn pattern, the film concludes by legitimizing a psychologically balanced group that flourishes only because the feminine has been fully integrated.

Emancipation in the Western?

Two factors make *The Missing*'s Maggie Gilkeson significant in the genre's development. Firstly, she presents a further extension of the role of women in the Western. Secondly, the way that she and the Native American characters are presented invites the question whether in psychoanalytical terms women are taking on a healing role which in the history of the genre it has been so difficult for American Indian characters to fulfil. Are women protagonists, such as Maggie in *The Missing* and Sue in *Open Range* (Native Americans having for the most part been refused this role by filmmakers and audiences alike), now acting as psychopompi for white male heroes and putting them in touch with the unconscious — a connection resisted by screen cowboys for a century? Are Western women healing the split in the Western hero's psyche?

Maggie cooks and cares for her daughters and her lover, runs a farm, and heals the sick. She is a formidable woman with a strong sense of purpose who, since her father walked out and her mother died, carries the unconscious for her family. The consequences of abandonment hurt so deeply that she has to keep rage on a tight leash. Nevertheless she has the courage to make her father feel the heavy burden he unthinkingly dumped on her. She confronts him so forcefully as to make him taste the complexes that govern her personality. So doing, she provides him, no less than the Western genre itself what is for it a rare insight into a woman's psyche.

Comparison of Maggie Gilkeson with some of her recent screen ancestors sketches the evolution of women's roles. In 1988 David Jacobs and Robert Porter created a television series *Paradise* (Lorimar Television). It featured several significant role changes that reflected progressive American society of the 1980s rather than the 1880s. These included the young widow Amelia Lawson (Sigrid Thornton) who manages the bank. Her sardonic tongue militates against any sexual attraction for the gunfighter hero. She abhors Ethan's profession, but helps him out of compassion for the four children who have been bequeathed to an inadequate father in an alien environment. An influential figure in the community, Mrs. Lawson represents a clean break from patriarchal domination.

In *Pale Rider* Eastwood substitutes a pubescent girl, Megan Wheeler (Sydney Penny), for the boy in *Shane*. Her moral education does not concern killing (still men's work) but the nature of love. Megan and her mother will be the carriers of an insight into the ways that the secular and the sacred are linked through the forms of love. In *Shane*, as in *Pale Rider* and many other Westerns, mystical questions lie behind moral issues. The domestic moral crux centers on a spiritual crisis for the women, who become confused by unexpected passion. Like Marion Starrett in *Shane*, Megan's mother Sarah Wheeler (Carrie Snodgrass) has domesticated feelings for Hull Barret (Michael Moriarty), the decent and mundane man with whom she lives. But like Marion with Shane, she feels an attraction of a different order to the Preacher. The issue for Sarah is whether she should marry Hull and forego the religious intensity of passion she would experience with the Preacher. The night before he rides out to destroy LaHood's operation, the Preacher does take Sarah as his lover. Spirit touches body and momentarily animus and anima connect. Sarah's encounter with the sacred power he embodies settles her yearning heart. Speaking of herself as having been confused, she now recognizes that her passion for a numinous figure who encompasses the twin extremes of love and vengeance must be of a different order than a devoted bond between ordinary people. The knowledge frees her to accept Hull's proposal.

Eastwood's next Western, *Unforgiven* (1992), provides an indication of the kind of change that endowing female characters with greater power could induce in the male hero. The wife of Will Munny (Eastwood) has died before the story begins, leaving him to scrabble a living as a pig farmer and bring up their two children. Her legacy has been the moral code with which she rescued him from the drunken abandonment of a professional killer's existence and by which he tries to live. Although the thought of murder now revolts Munny, the reputation gained in his former life attracts a would-be gunslinger with a proposition. Munny's grinding poverty tempts him to go after the bounty on one last killing. Throughout what proves to be a ghastly venture into wholesale slaughter, his divergence from the path approved by his wife triggers hellish visions of men he has murdered, traumatizing him. When the whole gruesome business is done, he returns to his children. Rumor reports that he moved to San Francisco and made a living as a storekeeper. It seems safe to assume that the force of his wife's teachings has endured and her authority over his moral and spiritual life, though tested to the ultimate degree, is firmly restored at the end.

Thus alterations in the roles of women this distinctive not only affected their screen relationships with men but were beginning to show consequences for the roles that male protagonists played and the nature of the Western male psyche. The anima-animus balance in the genre was indeed being recast.

The Missing: *Complex Allegory for a New Era*

As mentioned, Native Americans in Westerns bore the projection of White America's fear and hatred of its enemies through most of the twentieth century. The theme is re-examined for the twenty-first century in Ron Howard's *The Missing* (2003). Lieutenant Ducharme (Val Kilmer), a white Southerner who commands a company of soldiers, laments that whites are consorting with Indians and there is no longer any telling who is who. But while he has observed the surface change, like all bigots he has no understanding of what racial mixing means for society as a whole, let alone for his own conduct. He makes this beef only moments after summarily ordering his troopers to execute a man without trial. Because 'Indian' and 'guilty' are conjoined terms in Ducharme's dictionary, he has taken it as proven that the long-haired man found in the house of a murdered white family is an Indian who has killed them. But Ducharme's deductions about Samuel Jones (Tommy Lee Jones) are wrong on both counts. Here is one of many reflections in *The Missing* of the politically complex

American society watching the movie. The New Mexico on screen comprises bigots from every community cast in the old mold intermingled with people who have learned to live in harmony with other races.

Samuel is Maggie's father, a complex figure, no less edgy than his conflicted daughter. This 'sorrowful mystic' left his family twenty years earlier and opted to live with the Navajo and Apache, adopting their culture and costume.[14] As a consequence he suffers the contempt of bigots of all races for embracing a mixed culture. He comes back to Maggie for treatment of a torn ligament. But although she sees he wants to rejoin the family, Maggie cannot forgive the years of loss and angrily insists he move on when she has treated him. He rides into town to dull with whisky the pain of this rejection, and is thrown into jail as a drunk.

As Sandford says, Samuel knows how to walk the line between the two worlds;[15] but his ability to open up to the collective unconscious keeps him restless. The poetic wisdom that comes from being drawn by the spirit world has endowed him with some shamanic powers but no domestic virtues: he has been the passing lover of several women, and a lousy father. His absconding has left deep traumas in the family, particularly in Maggie who blames him for the death from exhaustion of her mother. Maggie heads a dysfunctional family in which the anima-animus relationship is radically altered from older Western norms. Although physically strong, like her mother before her, Maggie is psychologically drained. She is a wounded healer like Asklepios, simultaneously tough and vulnerable. But whereas the healer of Greek mythology responded empathically to the psychological needs of others, Maggie's animus problems choke that ability in her. Samuel will attempt to cure the injured spirit, she deals only with physical ailments.

The generations in the family mirror each other in that the fathers of Maggie's two daughters are long gone. Lilly (Evan Rachel Wood) is an angry teenager desperate to escape her mother's hard-grafting life and racially contemptuous of her grandfather. Young Dot (Jenna Boyd) exhibits an equable temperament, suffers blows bravely, accepts her fate and gets on with life. Exhilarated by the fantasy that she might be Indian, she has inherited the best qualities of both Maggie and Samuel and, in her easy relations with her grandfather, repairs the anima-animus relation.

Maggie and her hired hand Brake (Aaron Eckhart) are lovers. She entrusts the girls to his care for a winter's day recreation in town. Maggie has no time for such fripperies and stays back to tend her cattle. But when her family fails to return before dark, she watches through the night in deepening apprehension until one of the horses returns riderless before dawn. She tracks through the deadwood of winter forests and finds Brake's corpse suspended gruesomely from a branch, trussed in a cowhide bag. Lilly has been kidnapped and Dot left by the attackers as witness.

Maddened by grief, terror, and loathing, Maggie gallops to town to get the sheriff's help. Projecting raging hatred onto her father, she believes he has ambushed her family in revenge for being driven off the ranch. But she soon discovers that the sheriff has gaoled him for drunkenness before the killings occurred. This law officer, from within the familiar pale of white paranoia, assumes the attackers to be Apache; but he refuses to pursue the killers despite their being not far off, insisting his duties confine him to the town.

When Samuel is released, he rides back to the ranch, having read the raiders' tracks. They are travelling south to the Mexican border — not north as the sheriff believes. Maggie accepts that he is the only person who can help her, and when Dot refuses to be left safely with neighbors, the three start the search for Lilly. Whereas Ethan Edwards in *The Searchers* circled for five years, Samuel leads his party rapidly after the raiders: he understands their *modus operandi* and purposes.

The raiding party differs from what Maggie (and the audience) expects, comprising a mixed group of bandits, the greater number Apache but some whites. The core group are renegade soldiers, with a few captured civilians. Greed motivates these deserters. David Thomson mistakenly alleges that their leader, in every other way a vile character, rapes the captive girls they kidnap.[16] On the contrary, Chidin (Eric Schweig) forbids his men to touch them because they are to be sold into prostitution and will bring a better price as virgins.

This makes for a distinctive variant on the countless Westerns which allude to conflicts with Indians as though two racially homogeneous forces opposed one other. Here, rank and file soldiers resemble the raiding party in being thieving riffraff, equally motivated by greed. Instead of protecting property, they openly defy Lt. Ducharme's orders and loot the goods of a murdered farming family. Ducharme resembles the sheriff in fatuity. His troop stumbles upon the family when they are closing in on the kidnappers. However, the company is on another mission and, although his men disobey him at will, Ducharme insists on following orders, refusing to detour and pursue the local villains. Meanwhile the force actually ordered to track the raiders has been inaccurately briefed and is heading in the wrong direction. We witness an army focused on the wrong target, a society the several parts of which are in dispute with each other over what should be done, and self-interest governing everyone. It makes an interesting microcosm for the confused North American military and political strategies post-September 11th, 2001, Afghanistan, 2002, and the second Iraq War, 2003-4.

Let's follow the politico-military allegory further. During Maggie's dawn search for her family, as she forces her horse forward through creaking forests, the animal's terror is felt by Maggie and communicated to the audience. She finds a flayed cow, the corpse of her Latino hired hand and, hanging from a tree, a heavy bag made from the beast's bloody hide. It turns to reveal Brake's grotesquely trussed body. The raiders, striking stark fear in their victims and insulting them in death, act like terrorists. Unlike his men, their leader Chidin is a *brujo* or witch, motivated less by greed than hatred. He possesses supernatural powers and uses them to maim and kill, being able to do so even at a distance.

The Missing presents Chidin as commanding mystical power in the contest of evil against good. Like the avenging preacher in *Pale Rider*, he is a *mana personality*.

> Mana... pertains to the extraordinary and compelling supernatural power which emanates from certain individuals... [It] can attract or repel, wreak destruction or heal, confronting the ego with a supraordinate force... This is the quasi-divine power which adheres to the magician, mediator, priest, doctor, trickster, saint or holy fool — to anyone who partakes of the spirit world sufficiently to conduct or radiate its energy.[17]

Mana figures are important because they enable a person to project power at a time when that is a necessary step in confronting the ego with the nature of the inner self.[18] In *Pale Rider*, Sarah's encounter with the Preacher does indeed empower her to realise her true nature. Chidin threatens Maggie with death, but her fight for life has psychologically fortifying consequences. Her struggle comes when the witch uses a few strands of her hair to make a fetish, exerting malign power through it. In the contest which ensues for Maggie's life and soul, her father uses his shamanic powers; but unable to match his opponent's strength he seeks help from Chiricahua friends. They assist him counter the fetish, gather healing herbs, and perform tribal rituals while Dot reads from the Scriptures. Co-operation between the two traditions — Christian and Native American beliefs, European medicine and tribal healing — is essential to their hard-won victory over Chidin's evil. Though she is not fully aware of what has happened, the contest for Maggie's soul has enriched her psyche in other ways. She can now distinguish her father's weaknesses from the evil mana by which she has been attacked. Her relationship to her animus begins to ease and her racism to dissolve.

The rescuers twice fight the raiding party at terrible cost to both sides. But before the final battle, father and daughter reconcile, Maggie recognizing that she would have had no chance of recovering Lilly had it not been for her father. The battle itself takes place by night above a rocky canyon worthy of an Anthony Mann Western such as *Winchester 73*; but in a reversal of the device that Mann applied to several James Stewart roles, here the good hold the high ground. Just as hellish shadows in dreams and myths often force their way up from below and out of the unconscious into consciousness, so Chidin, most evil of bandits, worms his way irresistibly upwards under fire from Samuel and Maggie. When the *brujo* attacks Maggie (the shadow animus making a murderous foray under cover of the dark), Samuel (in his role as redeemed, positive animus) comes to her aid and wrestles with the witch at the cliff edge. The ferocity of the battle banishes the men's sense of place, time, and circumstance, and they fall locked together to their deaths. Good and evil, despite the occasional dominance of one or the other in their endless strife, are, in the long perspective, in balance. Such a reading is supported by the fact that two of Chidin's villains escape the final slaughter. So too does a fine young Chiricahua ally of the rescuers. Forces from either side survive to fight another war.

The battle frees Maggie to return home with her daughters. In the personal domain of the hero, the psychological map of what has occurred is extraordinary for the Western genre. We first meet Maggie when her animus is uncertainly projected onto her lover Brake; but the deeply repressed image of her father indicates an unresolved animus problem (confirmed by hints that she has had a number of lovers). When the father surfaces, intense tribulation immediately overwhelms her. A truly evil male shadow is unlocked in Chidin, not only an anti-father but to her a racially nightmarish figure who destroys her chosen animus by killing Brake. This activation of her archetypal shadow and the conflict that follows allow Maggie eventually to discharge the negative energies that had vivified her repressed parental and racist animus. With all these men dead, her animus has been internalized and at least partly integrated, an indication reinforced by the sweet presence of Honesco in the otherwise all-female group of survivors.

Maggie will head her own family, perhaps taking under her wing the teenagers whose families have been slaughtered by Chidin. Heading the family: that is rare for a woman in a Western, yet another indication how the new assertiveness of women in western society has altered their psychological typing and their functions in the genre. Once again we see how the rebalancing of gender roles in the Western (and behind them, of anima and animus) connects with the displacement of evil. The vitality of Chidin as a mana personality is significant in this respect since, according to Samuels, *et al.*, "as an ideal and incorruptible image [it] is essential to the process of initiation after which one has a renewed sense of individuality."[19]

Since film is a public medium it is appropriate to look beyond the domain of the personal to interpret the myth-charged imagery which the mana personality generates for the collective sphere. Although it may be hard to see Chidin as an "ideal and incorruptible image," he does have the purity of undiluted evil. As such, he fits the early twenty-first century American mold of the 'terrorist' leader such as Osama bin Laden. After September 2001, the latter was not generally perceived as a cold-blooded, quasi-military strategist with political goals — an idea which might plausibly have been generated by reflection on the objectives behind the massacres he allegedly masterminded. Rather, the Bush Administration fostered an image of a man demonically driven by insane hatred of all things American and good. Our fictional villain can thus be read as an allegorical representation of the guerrilla leader.

In the UK the idea was much discussed after September 11, 2001 that the events of that terrible day were a wake-up call dragging the USA into a world (a sphere both of politics and the imagination) from which it had successfully isolated itself. That insulation from the grim horrors of organized guerrilla conflict had since the late 1960s been all too apparent seen from Europe. The resuscitation of IRA activity and the surfacing of various groups deploying terror (such as the Red Army Faction in West Germany and ETA in Spain) familiarized Europeans with this dire, extra-democratic side of politics; but most North Americans were impossibly innocent of these horrors, as 9/11 finally taught. Now in the wake of those fearful events and the national trauma they delivered, it seems sensible to ask whether there was something anguishingly painful happening in the collective American psyche for which Osama bin Laden and (in the allegorical world within *The Missing*, Chidin) was a dark and powerful agent.

The abhorrent nature of the murderous events of 9/11 cannot be mistaken; but it was not a necessary consequence of those horrors that Evil incarnate must be perceived as lying behind them. No such personified demon animated collective responses in Britain to atrocities carried out by the IRA or its Protestant counterparts despite the rage, despair, and grief that those attacks caused. The issue is particularly relevant to the Western because the genre habitually addresses America's leadership culture. As the world's dominant empire, the USA was through most of the twentieth century controlled by a profoundly masculine culture of Logos-centered power. In the movie genre, the endless contests for the land (Indian wars, the Civil War, range wars) are not sufficiently explained by the much mythologized history of the West. For the conflicts continued to rage on screen more than a hundred years after the frontier closed. As we have seen, read in terms of the expansion of the interests of capital, these conflicts revealed a split between ranchers and smallholders. On the surface, the latter win, but the cattle barons, whatever their personal fates, never suffer the break up of their vast properties. Change the focal plane, and it is possible to read these fictional contests over land as allegories for the massive expansion of American political influence. The small guys — American domestic concerns — seem to win; but, interpreted in this register, the monstrous, greedy figure who buys up and oppresses the West can be associated with global US imperialist expansion, never completely exterminated. Now the genre has summoned a demon in the menacing presence of Chidin, an archetypal figure which offers itself as the monster's shadow.

Jungians do not need reminding that archetypal images enter the public domain when needed to correct an imbalance in the psychological disposition of large numbers of people. Nor that when archetypal images are given undue supremacy and reified they convert to their contrary in order to balance the psyche. Thus, psychologically speaking, an absolute 'Father in Heaven' must call forth the devil.[20] Conservative America of this era has its 'Father in Heaven' assuring it that America is always right, is the greatest nation on earth (George W. Bush), and has God on its side. There is little room for doubt that bin Laden's image is the devil; but the question that cannot yet be answered is whether it (or future displaced substitutes) will have the potential to act as a corrective to a long-standing imbalance in dominant ideology.

The political and psychological climate in which *The Missing* was released makes the conjunction between the emergence of Chidin (the potent negative mana personality) and empowerment of Maggie (acceptance of feminist values in the Western) particularly interesting. This is the more significant in that Samuel is unable to defeat Chidin without the help of Maggie and the Chiricahua. The latter are fine warriors but also gentle and sensitive friends. In short, this contest with evil calls for the deployment of both 'male' and 'female' values, linking Logos power to Eros kindness and cherishing. My allegorical reading of *The Missing* as referencing the collective psychological consequences of American involvement in the Middle East implies that the deployment of Logos alone (imperialist policies backed by overwhelming but badly targeted military force), far from suppressing or obliterating the demon, has instead summoned him. The film can be read further as implying that a combination of Logos authority with active Eros (which at the very least entails an effort at understanding and appreciating others' values) might have a better chance of deflating this enraged presence.

NOTES

1. Roberto Gambini, "The challenge of backwardness," in *Post-Jungians Today: Key Papers in Contemporary Analytical Psychology*, ed. Ann Casement (London: Routledge, 1998), 150.

2. *Ibid.*

3. *Ibid.*, 150-1.

4. Henry Nash Smith, *Virgin Land: The American West as Symbol and Myth* (London: Harvard University Press, 1970), 123-32.

5. Gambini, 156-8.

6. John Izod, *Myth, Mind and the Screen: Understanding the Heroes of our Time* (Cambridge: Cambridge University Press, 2001), 40-1.

7. *Ibid.*, 41-2.

8. Luiga Zoja, "Analysis and tragedy," in *Post-Jungians Today: Key Papers in Contemporary Analytical Psychology*, ed. Ann Casement (London: Routledge, 1998), 42.

9. *Ibid.*

10. Gambini, 153.

11. *Ibid.*, 153-4.

12. Philip French, "*Open Range*," *The Observer*, 2004. Downloaded 30/3/04 from http://www.guardian.co.uk.

13. Jim Kitses, "Forgiven," *Sight and Sound*, 14, 4 (April) 27, 2004.

14. Ty Burr, "Howard's western is 'Missing' something,'"*Boston Globe* 26 November 2003, downloaded 26 March 2004 from http://www.rottentomatoes.com.

15. James Sandford, "The Missing," *Kalamazoo Gazette*, 2003. Downloaded 30 March 2004 from http://www.rottentomatoes.com.

16. David Thomson, "The last frontier," *Sight and Sound*, 14, 2 (February) 14, 2004.

17. Andrew Samuels, Bani Shorter, and Fred Plaut, *A Critical Dictionary of Jungian Analysis* (London: Routledge & Kegan Paul, 1986), 89.

18. *Ibid.*, 89-90.

19. *Ibid.*, 90.

20. Carl Gustav Jung, (1935), "The Relations Between the Ego and the Unconscious," *Two Essays on Analytical Psychology, The Collected Works*, Vol. 7, 2nd ed. (London: Routledge & Kegan Paul [1966],) § 395.

Transformations in the Mythic Construct of the Hero: The Manchurian Candidate from 1964 to 2004

Jane Alexander Stewart

Recasting *The Manchurian Candidate,* 1962, into a Gulf War context revivifies our terror of mechanized mind control with twenty-first century state-of-the-art brain implants — but it also revamps Freud's Oedipal complex and C.G. Jung's negative mother complex with a heart over mind message. 'Mother' has long been associated with emotional memory and it is no secret that a man's destiny depends on the peace he makes with both. But to believe mother love holds a dark underbelly of deceit and danger more deadly than a foreign enemy is old mythology brewed in a patriarchal pot. *The Manchurian Candidate*, 2004, puts forward a contra-patriarchal image of masculinity in the role of hero, challenging the negative mother complex itself as a misbegotten source of power.

Perhaps catching a private corporation in the act of nearly taking over the American government for its own greedy purposes in the 2004

Jane Alexander Stewart is a clinical psychologist in Los Angeles, California, who weaves psychology, mythology, and popular culture together in reviews of films that have been published in academic journals and newsletters, reprinted in two book anthologies, and appear currently on the ezine, www.NewtopiaMagazine.net, and on her website,wwwcinemashrink.com.

reprise of *The Manchurian Candidate* would be reflection enough of a basic twenty-first century fear of capitalistic control. But the 2004 film goes beyond grandiose corporate machinations to where the real control of the future lies. In the psyche. The film's close examination of the fight for individual freedom to think, to care about others, and to question any system attempting to control people's minds proves to be about much more than money. If memory can be erased, laid down artificially, and made to 'feel' as real as the truth, any dark deed is possible. If it can't, what could possibly prevent it? What might protect truth? Where might hope reside?

Mind control is not new to the movies, not new to life. But *The Manchurian Candidate*, 2004, presents a surprising postulate for retaining humanity in a society increasingly dominated by technology you don't want to miss. Unlike the original in 1962, no outside re-programmer need be brought in! There is an antidote lying within the hearts of men, creating a capability to fight back against brainwashing and strong enough to restore healthy mental functioning. It may stay dormant during indoctrinations, but ultimately it's capable of resisting the invasive technology of artificial encoding. To release the antidote, however, some fear-based patriarchal mythology about the emotional susceptibility of a man to his mother's selfish motives must be given up.

Historically, societies dominated by patriarchy have feared the relationship between mother and son, developing a mythology that casts it in a dark light, denigrating mother love. The standard analytic interpretation of Oedipus is that mother-son love has a dangerous underbelly. A son enamored of his mother leads him to kill his father and claim his mother for his own. A mother, enamored of her son, colludes in the son's emotional dependence and keeps him under her control against the father, in service to her own purposes. This conspiratorial mythology not only distrusts and distorts the love between mother and son from early on in a boy's life, it provides justification for a father's authoritarian control. In effect, a father's egoistic fears of losing power to his son are blamed on reasons buried in the unconscious. Such Oedipal interpretations ignore the fact— especially in ancient times — that a woman's well-being and desire to better herself as well as her safety was dependent upon her men. In a society dominated by patriarchy, a woman does well to align herself well with powerful men — including her sons.

Sadly, C.G. Jung gave this patriarchal distortion of mother-son love a name that stuck; he identified it as a 'negative mother complex' inherently innate to the human psyche and, like Freud, slid past cultural influences. He says,

> On the negative side, the mother archetype may connote what devours, seduces, and poisons; it is terrifying and inescapable like fate. I have expressed the ambivalence of [maternal attributes] in the phrase 'the loving and terrible mother.' (emphasis mine)

Those words, 'inescapable like fate' places Jung in a framework before women had a presence of their own in the public world and femininity was defined by men, seen through their eyes and bound by their expectations. It also dates him in a world before men of radically different ethnicity, financial means, and class were thrown into wars where they would become close buddies, arousing an unprecedented felt connection between men (and women) of wide ranging diversity across the boundaries of nations and continents. It dates him before an instant invisible net of cyberspace existed around the globe, creating a web of international access, intrigue and knowledge far more powerful than radio or TV. These modern times challenge the soul of mankind to preserve a capacity for human caring against greater odds than have ever been known before. And *The Manchurian Candidate*, 2004, lends an image to how this may come about.

In both versions of *The Manchurian Candidate*, the mother's capacity to manipulate her son's love is co-opted by patriarchal entities — in the first by a foreign country and in the second by an international corporation. The mother yields to patriarchal forces — first without, and then with her knowledge. Given patriarchal reasoning, the use of the mother's ill-gotten power over her son for the father's goals is fair game. Patriarchal desire for control of the emotionally charged relationship between a mother and her son drives the drama in both films. In the 1962 version, *The Manchurian Candidate* turned a mother's influence over her beloved son into a hypnotic spell of compliance that could be triggered by a playing card, the red queen. She rendered her son an assassin to kill the nominated presidential candidate of the United States, elevating her husband to presidential pawn for a foreign power. *The Manchurian Candidate*, 2004, turns the son of an ambitious female senator into a war hero. Military brainwashing lays the ground for mother and son to become a presidential combo of shills in service to corporate greed. The son comes home from war programmed to fall victim to his mother's determination to make him president as well as to kill on command from her — or from a mysterious 'them'. In the revamped version, a mother powerful enough to manipulate an entire political campaign fronts a corporate takeover of the U.S. government. And a brainwashing system strong enough to dupe a complete squad, including its Commander, spins the son into a cultural war hero in front of an entire world.

The 2004 mother differs from 1962 when a mother's influence on her weak child-man son elevates her weak husband to power, not knowing that she's selling out her son to get in solid with the foreign power that takes over. In the second, a mother's political ambition lifts her techno-implanted son's path of societal entitlement toward the presidency, promoting them as a dynamic duo, and allowing them to work as partners for worldwide corporate greed. The central change in role of the son over a span of forty years, 1962 to 2004, from the end of one generation to the beginning of another, is from presidential assassin to presidential partner, from deadly sycophant to deadly consort, to a mother who knowingly sells out her son to gain power in society. In both films, the mother-son relationship gets co-opted for the evil purposes of patriarchal greed. In *The Manchurian Candidate* 1962, the personal mother acts separate and alone from her son. In 2004, she acts within the archetypal relationship, and the negative mother-son complex itself becomes the source of danger and destruction. And, the construct of the complex, symbolically speaking, gets to become the rightful target for a deadly bullet. *The Manchurian Candidate*, 2004, like a cultural dream, seems to reflect a shift in mythology.

In both films, the son's older Commander plays the hero, uncovering the scheme of mind control. However, in the first version, the Commander (Frank Sinatra) single-handedly breaks the code of control triggered by the red queen of hearts (with its obvious mother symbolism) and frees the son from his mother's clutches. In the second, the Commander (Denzel Washington) appears preoccupied with images of a recurring nightmare that have haunted him since the war. He's in a low-level public relations position, giving speeches for the army to Boy Scout troops and living in his apartment as if contained in a cell. No friends, no social life, no change in routine. Years pass. He believes his nightmares contain a key to a confusing web of lies being spun around him by the military. But the meaning of his nightmare seems impenetrable until a soldier from his squad shows up at a talk he's giving and shows him a sheaf of papers, revealing that he too continuously dreams the same nightmare. The soldier's scrawls are the same images that come in the night to the Commander. Spurred by the possibility that his nightmare represents the remnants of a shared, rather than private, trauma of war, the Commander's ruminative obsession turns into a search for truth. He sees one of his previous soldiers on TV, running for president, and wonders if he too is having these nightmares. Eventually, meetings with fellow soldiers set off flashback memories to a week during the war when the whole squad was secreted away for a sci-fi, medically inspired military indoctrination. He's part of a group.

As the story progresses, *The Manchurian Candidate*, 2004, heads into less traditional mythological territory of the hero than presented in *The Manchurian Candidate*, 1962. The men's collective memory, in effect, kept a reality intact on an unconscious level that couldn't be erased by artificial mind control. An instinctive emotional bond felt between ordinary men, under the worst of circumstances, proved strong enough to counteract the machinations of evil men. Men who draw upon a felt connection with one another prevent the misuse of love between mother and son for dark purposes. They are stronger, not weaker, for believing in a feeling of caring for one another that won't be pushed aside by aspersions cast against their manhood by the military. The second film breaks away from the archetype of a singular hero, standing alone and on his own. The 2004 film characterizes the Commander as a hero woven into a bonded identification with the men who served with him. He's a man embedded in an identity of camaraderie, one who's an integral part of a group and prompted to action by empathy. And he connects to other men through a dream — not through logic or sport. When this Commander discovers that his nightmare is being dreamt by others in his squad, his personal quest for the truth begins. He's frightened, believing that the dream signifies something major being covered up. And little does he know.

Both versions of *The Manchurian Candidate* exploit the concept of a psychoanalytically based 'negative mother complex' to intensify the meaning of "Enemy", as if war were less dangerous than a man's relationship with his mother! When an outside enemy with weapons of mass destruction is construed as less dangerous than one developed in our own heads, it's time to examine the truth of what's inherent and what's learned. The film assumes audiences will infer the patriarchal origin of 'negative mother complex' as purely innate. The use of an innate maternal trigger for a technological brain implant lends it greater evil, implying a cold dispassion for mankind laid deeply — inevitably — in a son's psyche, not simply his brain. The complex gets put conveniently in service to an ideal of ultimate patriarchal dominance, influencing a mother to "devour" her own son to further a private corporation's greed, power, and control. This is a good moment to remember that a complex is not a person, not a real — living and breathing — mother. It is made up of emotional memories distilled into our most intimate habits of feeling to which we cling for survival. We will resist giving up what we require in love, how we style our bodies, what we feel to be a homecoming, the fears to which we have become accustomed. This is all a mother memory ruling a man's life, a continuity of patterns we have lived with for so long that we become them. The personal mother is not the archetype. The archetype lives, influenced and shaped by cultural circumstance.

Both films make it clear: the mother's need for power in a male dominated society drives her willingness to use her son as a pawn in a much larger game. What might be overlooked, however, is that a son taken over by a mother's scheme to succeed in a man's world can also be used to drive him into an ambition not his own, align him with a greed not his own, and deprive him of freedom of choice — keeping him neatly in the service of a commercially driven patriarchy. For a young man to break away and think clearly, he must debunk the whole notion of the devouring mother as an inevitable underbelly of intimacy between a mother-son. A son's freedom to grow up, mature, and develop as a man independent of patriarchal programming remains in jeopardy as long as the underpinnings of the 'negative mother complex' go unrecognized for what they are — induced by society.

How to rid one's psyche and culture of the control by a 'negative mother complex' is where the two films depart.

In *The Manchurian Candidate*, 1962, the cure for brainwashing lies in a superior intelligence — still military, male, and patriarchal in origin — that breaks the code binding son to mother. And the death of the mother. The resolution of the first version requires only the son's riddance of the physical mother — and the idiot stepfather. In the 1962 film, the son breaks away from the spell of the Red Queen at the end by killing his scheming, incestuous mother and her puppet husband (his stepfather) instead of the programmed target, the next president of the United States. That old mythology required revenge, an adolescent, Oedipal anger rising up in a cold heat to slice the umbilical cord and free not only himself but also his country from all mothers who would bargain their sons' souls to secure their own place with a patriarch. That son, played by Laurence Harvey as a whining child-man, conveyed the image of mother as the instigator of infantilization in her son. A mythology of heroes who broke away from the mother — symbolically killing her as his only way to free himself — idealized men who stood alone and relied upon individual acts of heroism to prevail.

In *The Manchurian Candidate*, 2004, the cure lies dormant in a man's basic make-up — in his natural ability to form emotional, empathic connections with the man next to him. The antidote to brainwashing begins in a feeling of camaraderie aroused between soldiers who fought together day in, day out, in a war. Together, they form a multi-faceted chorus not so easily silenced as a single voice. This grand, captivating portrayal of a heroic bond of empathy between men offers an alternative to the mythology of Freud's famed Oedipal complex and Jung's monomythic hero, the exceptional man symbolized by Odysseus. Alfred Adler, the third originator of psychoanalysis along with Freud and Jung, considered the 'feeling of intimate belonging to the full spectrum of humanity' to be a dominant motive of life, as basic as Freud's sexual drive or Jung's urge toward meaning. The twenty-first century may be Adler's turn to shine. 'Intimate belonging' urges men to connect emotionally in *The Manchurian Candidate*, 2004, forming an immunity to a masterful scheme to invade the human psyche with actual mechanical implants.

Then, as illuminated in the film's stunningly symbolic ending, a man's transformation from shill to free spirit lies in a riddance of the whole concept of a negative mother complex, a full death of the incestuous complex superimposed on the mother-son relationship, planned and directed by a son empowered by his found feeling for other men. The implication? Possibly that young men who know a different truth about their emotional natures can rid the culture of the negative mother complex, identified for the patriarchal concoction it is. *The Manchurian Candidate*, 2004, dramatizes — as the theatrical dramas of ancient Greek reflected fresh and timely cultural sentiment — an alternative base of emotional strength for men and a timely answer to an old problem of competition between fathers and sons.

In 1962, *The Manchurian Candidate* begins with a scene in a bar, a rowdy sexualized interaction between soldiers and foreign women. An uptight Captain enters, putting a damper on the fun with a stern call for his men to report for duty. By contrast, *The Manchurian Candidate*, 2004, opens with a group of young soldiers sitting in the back of a humvee, playing cards and laughing shoulder-to-shoulder while Kuwaiti oil fields burn in the background. They're strangers thrown together in a strange country by the Gulf War in 1991, harking not only from different parts of the United States but also from different ethnic backgrounds. Here they are. Friends, like alloys forged into steel under fire, doing what they can to lighten a dark night while waiting for the call that will put their lives on the line. The music on a boom box echoes ethnic diversity in songs from reggae to rock to rap. The camera pans their faces, bridging a dozen differences while the rhythms in the background blur their boundaries and many biases. Here, in a foreign land under fire, they're all the same man, tense beneath the skin and scared, but comfortable enough to be friendly toward their Captain who, separated from them by rank and class, dampens their fun with his condescending, cold call-to-action attitude. One of the men jokes that the Captain needs a friend and a hug. Everyone laughs. Little do they know how right they are.

Captain Raymond Prentiss Shaw (Liev Schrieiber) stands apart from his men and his commanding officer, Major Bennett Ezekiel Marco (Denzel Washington). Shaw appears socially awkward and distracted by a private irritation. A few minutes after ordering his men into battle, he's seen fulfilling the role of war hero. Ostensibly, he saves all but two of his men's lives, earning the prestigious Congressional Medal of Honor. This sets the stage for his mother's ambition. The second film veers from the original, propelling Shaw (rather than his boorish step-father) as the man of choice in his mother's determination to project one of her own men onto a fast track through the U.S. Senate straight to a nomination for Vice President. His mother, Eleanor

Prentiss (Meryl Streep) is a Senator with a reputation for getting her way. She single-handedly engineers a small coup among her colleagues to make sure her son gets the nomination. In the professional hands of Meryl Streep, the image of Eleanor Prentiss rises to the symbolic resonance of an archetype, conjuring up C.G. Jung's negative mother complex with the artistry of William Shakespeare creating Lady Macbeth. She will push her son to greatness, leaving blood on the carpet if she must.

Twelve years after the war, as Prentiss Shaw's star is rising in the presidential race, retired Major Ben Marco continues to suffer from a recurrent nightmare from the Gulf War. Embedded in his psyche, disturbing images have resisted treatment by drugs, psychotherapy, and time. He lives within his dream; his apartment and his choices are still identified with the strictures of war. He also finds himself tormented by a freakish repetition of obsessive behaviors that won't let go, making him feel more robot than man. Another soldier from the Kuwait battle seeks Ben out to show him a notebook full of the identical insomniac dream images and writings. Marco wrestles with a growing internal pressure to dig up the root of his nightmare. He begins to contact and confront Shaw, insisting Shaw shares the nightmare from their days as soldiers together in Kuwait – insisting the dreams cannot be ignored.

Shaw can't imagine he's part of a nightmare even more disastrous than the love-hate relationship he experiences with his smothering, controlling mother. However, as actual events unfold, he realizes his mother not only has an uncanny control of him but also has — true to an old mythology — aligned herself with a power-mongering corporation determined to use him in a dastardly plan to take over the U. S. government. Unable to lift herself to the political heights of grandeur enjoyed by her father, hindered as she is by being of the female gender, she uses her 'motherly' talents to secure her ambitions through her son. *The Manchurian Candidate* in 1962, which redirected the assassin son's aim at the last moment to kill his mother and his stepfather instead of the designated target, the next president, was a sufficient break in mind control programming to startle expectations at the time. It represented an act of freeing sons from the emotional torment and constraint of a suffocating mother complex. But it didn't kill the real enemy; it didn't kill the belief in the distortion of a mother-son relationship purported to exist within the collective psyche that binds a son pathologically to his mother. In that version, a son has only one choice — to rid himself and society of the mother as if it were she and not the distortion that was the problem.

The Ben Marco of the early film represented the conscious side of a man and helped the son who was a good man held captive by incestuous, crippling memories. The analytic Marco unveiled Shaw's emotionally based mother complex. As a buddy – a friend dedicated to truth – he could step forward and compete with the mother, even break her grip. But the extension of a man's friendship to another man was transitory, not transformative. Feelings made a man suspect of being feminine and, by faulty deduction, associated with weakness, so Ben approached the problem intellectually, using mysticism to defeat hypnosis.

The mythology of heroes in 1962 had not yet begun to include hero as common man, an ensemble hero of everyday who wasn't a man of destiny from an elite family. It's worth noting the evolution that takes place in *The Manchurian Candidate*, 2004, where Alfred Adler's concept of an legitimate, emotional but not sexualized sense of 'intimate belonging' between men shows up as an interesting, deep, and powerfully connective tissue that can withstand the pressure of mind control and open a new door. It steps away from the legacy of an inevitable, inescapable aberrant mother complex by shifting away from the familiar hero's journey as the only journey, the only source of heroism. Many are now walking the hero's path, made an integral part of popular culture by Joseph Campbell's book, *The Hero with a Thousand Faces* and George Lucas's epic franchise, *Star Wars*. That questions its elitist hold on the only way to prevail against evil. Men — and women — from all walks of life, levels of society, and gender identifications evolve toward a consciousness that contributes to and insists upon good for mankind.

Taken as companion pieces, the old and new *Manchurian Candidate* films can be seen as a dramatization of differences between the old singular type of hero and a new type of hero whose identity is multiple, ordinary, and coincidental with a team of men. His conflict is their conflict. He draws his strength from an invisible, instinctive, and emotional bond with them — not an inanimate cosmos. His power comes not from some abstract, mystical place in outer space but from within his own feelings, manifested and held in place by a dream. A dream! This ineffable, imagined, and felt bond existing between men proves more real and more central to their survival than a rule of law. When the lone man on the battlefield proves vulnerable, easily implanted and manipulated with state of the art triggers to kill, the heroic image of superstar loses its luster. *The Manchurian Candidate, 2004,* finds its tale of an attempted double invasion into a country and a man's psyche defeated by an ethereal air of energetic, intense, and empathic exchanges between men who believe more strongly in the truth of their own nightmares than the spin of outside authorities. Heroism emerges from the flimsy stuff of a collective dream to penetrate the conspiracy and unseat the enemy. And it engenders hope. It's a vision of heroism based in natural psychological resources, possessed by every baby born — feelings and dreams.

In the 2004 version of *The Manchurian Candidate,* a heroism synonymous with a bond felt between men offers an alternative to the single-minded heroism of one man. It opens up and ushers in new prospects for balancing good and evil in a technology-driven world. The mythic and psychological message of this latest version of *The Manchurian Candidate* is different than the first, promoting a felt connection between men that can act as a strength as well as a guide to truth and new options when faced with artificial intelligence. It's not enough to kill the wicked symbol of 'mother' to alter narrow-minded patriarchal goals. No, what must be shot straight through is the whole 'negative mother' complex.

The final act of the son in *The Manchurian Candidate,* 2004, represents a reckoning, a redemptive act that frees him, his commander, the men who fought with him — and the audience — to move on. He instigates the death of his fear-based, disabling enmeshment with his mother not by suicide, as if it were contained within him, or even homicide, as if it were contained in his mother. He steps together with her in an embrace, letting a single bullet from Marco kill them both simultaneously, demonstrating the clarity of his intent to do away with what exists between them. Symbolically, the pathological distortion of the dynamic between mother and son is eliminated by a new hero. The son's insight makes possible the emergence of a new archetype of heroism, one that honors the veracity of a masculine bonding and awards all sons their rightful legacy of feelings. With the death of the distorted complex, the film suggests that a fresh mythology can begin to rise in which men can identify masculinity with empathy as well as a healthy emotional bonding with each other — and their mothers. At the end of the new version, Ben Marco returns to the scene of the crime on a deserted isle where minds were warped and futures ruined. He slips a group photo of his men, along with a single Congressional Medal of Honor, into the sea. It's a ritual of return, referencing the symbolism of reclamation and renewal. But it also signifies a transformation in the type of leadership that can now mean 'hero', one of a man belonging to a matrix and not a complex. The men with their medal return to the source of life on earth — an inclusive, elusive fluidity that sustains a natural flow between human beings and repeatedly withstands evil.

Patriarchal mythology, based upon and creased with values supporting iron-fisted domination of one order of human beings over another, must yield its complexes. When the son, programmed as an assassin, wakes up in *The Manchurian Candidate*, 2004, and discovers links of destruction in his own psyche reaching from personal mother to corporate father, he throws light into a cultural construct of developmental psychology in need of change. His self-instigated release from the artificially implanted nightmare of a twisted mother-son dynamic symbolically 'kills' the archetype that destroyed his chance to become an independent young man. The hopeful mythic thread of "Resonance, Return, and Renewal" shows a way out in *The Manchurian Candidate*, 2004. Empathy forms an abiding bridge between men, liberating acts of independent thinking even when individual choice seems to have been programmed into oblivion.

***The Manchurian Candidate*, 2004, was directed by Jonathan Demme, written by Daniel Pyne and Dean Georgaris, with writing credit to Richard Condon (novel) and George Axelrod (1962 screenplay).Performances by Denzel Washington, Meryl Streep, Liev Schreiber, Jon Voight, and Kimberly Elise.

The Manchurian Candidate, 1962, was directed by John Frankenheimer, written by George Axelrod (screenplay), and with writing credit to Richard Condon (novel). Perfomances by Frank Sinatra, Laurence Harvey, Janet Leigh, Angela Lansbury, James Gregory, and John McGiver.

BOOK REVIEWS

SUSAN ROWLAND. *Jung as a Writer.* New York: Routledge, 2005.

REVIEWED BY GINETTE PARIS

S usan Rowland writes a fascinating literary analysis of Jungian theory as a "literature." She brilliantly demonstrates the extent to which Jung, like every other depth psychologist, built his theory around his personal myth. In doing so, she manages the *tour de force* of reaching two opposite goals: an uncompromising critique of Jung, as well as a passionate defense of his work as literature. It is a stunning example of the "holding of opposites." It is unclear whether she is fully aware of how radical her critique is. Scathing! I happen to appreciate the intelligence of it, but the "orthodoxy" may interpret her critique as more of a demolition than *hommage*.

As if reading a detective story, I was hooked by her exploration of the relationship between Jung and his spooky cousin. Ms. S.W. appears in Jung's doctoral dissertation as a patient. She seems to have defined for Jung "the spectral landscape" in which so much of his later psychology resides, especially his vision of the anima.

Ginette Paris is core Faculty in the Mythological Studies Program of Pacifica Graduate Institute in Santa Barbara, California. She is also a member of the board of the *Center for the Study of Depth Psychology,* also in Santa Barbara.

Paraphrasing Jung, Rowland concludes, "Invoked or not invoked, gender is the specter haunting the dialectical inception of Jung's psychology." She argues with brilliance that

> Jung's entire psychology is a negotiation with the specter of the unconscious as that which defies rational meaning. At the same time the persistent association of the feminine with the *occult* is a poignant demonstration of its haunting power in his imagination.

In other words, Jung's concept of the anima as *occult* and *irrational* is modeled on his attraction/repulsion to this young woman from his past, a ghost, a specter, somebody neither dead nor alive. "His psychology becomes spectral because his inner being is spectral." The word *occult*, in Jung's works, translates as *unscientific*, but also as *intellectually and socially inferior*. It creates a strange dialectic where, on the one side, stands the ignorant but intuitive and imaginative cousin, and on the other side stands the rational doctor capable of analyzing such neurotic delusions with a superior authority. Such a notion of the anima leads to an inevitable slippage into gender definitions, coloring all of Jung's discussion concerning gender identities.

Rowland is probably the sharpest critic of Jung's problem with gender identities. She began exploring this issue in *Jung: A Feminist Revision*. (Cambridge: Polity Press, 2002) Once again, she balances her critique, showing how Jung contradicts his own misogyny, because his theory of individuation suggests that a solid gender identity is never a given; it is part of the process of individuation.

At the end of Rowland's analysis of *Jung as a Writer*, one is at peace with the idea that Jung's work belongs to literature and cultural studies. The value of her analysis lies in the manner in which she is able to show that such a discourse may also be "of the future" as it bridges psyche and culture.

> It would be facile to call [Jung's] *On the Nature of Psyche* a conventional novel of science-fiction because that would belie the way it deconstructs the deep cultural division between science and art. I would rather call it science-aesthetics, or perhaps, more pedantically: speculative science-aesthetics. (99)

I applaud the intelligence and the sentiment.

BOOK REVIEWS

THOMAS SINGER AND SAMUEL L. KIMBLES. (Eds.) *The Cultural Complex: Comtemporary Jungian Perspectives on Psyche and Society.* Hove and New York: Brunner-Routledge, 2004.

REVIEWED BY DAVID TACEY

The term 'cultural complex' is new, but I am not sure if the idea is new. Jung wrote a great deal about archetypes in nations: Wotan in Nazi Germany, the *senex* or old man in Switzerland, eternal youth in America, and so on. His attempts to invent a 'national psychology' of the Aryans and the Jews is by now notorious, and plays a huge role in the international exclusion and demonization of Jungian psychology. Jung argued in 1933 that to find "differences between Germanic and Jewish psychology ... implies no depreciation of Semitic psychology", but his detractors and Freudian antagonists did not agree. Jung chose the worst possible time in history to develop his theory of national types and differences, and it is due to this lack of synchronicity with the

David Tacey, Ph.D., is Associate Professor of Critical Enquiry and Reader in Psychoanalytic Studies at La Trobe University, Melbourne, Australia. His research interests are analytical psychology, philosophy, religion, and cultural studies. He has published seven books and eighty journal articles on these topics, and his most recent book is *The Spirituality Revolution* (New York: Routledge, 2004).

world, and to Jung's own naiveté regarding political matters, that Jungians have shut down on this aspect of his work.

Thomas Singer and Samuel Kimbles have lifted the lid on this Pandora's box. The time is right to reconsider nations, places, countries, continents in light of their archetypal constellations and psychological complexes. However, I do question the claim of Singer and Kimbles that their project is new. I would say: recovered from years of suppression, yes, but not new. Although Jungians worldwide have agreed to stay quiet on the 'national differences' theme, there have always been major figures like Joseph Henderson who have argued for more cultural exploration in Jungian analysis. Similarly, in different ways, James Hillman and Andrew Samuels have long argued that Jungian analysis must not confine itself to the individual and the private, but must become engaged more directly with world, politics, society, ecology, economics.

There is a sense of excitement to this volume of essays which is positively infectious. Jungian analysts set themselves the task of exploring 'problems' called Mexico, Brazil, Australia, Japan, Africa, the United States, psychoanalytic culture, Western Europe. The windows of the clinical room have been opened to the outside world, and everyone relishes the fresh air. This is wonderful in itself, and I warmly welcome this volume and look forward to more in this tradition. But I have to admit that the sight of Jungians 'discovering' culture can be a little embarrassing. Some of these chapters attempt massive leaps of interpretation with very little groundwork preparation or academic material. The volume is uneven, with some weak chapters caught up in the temporary inflation of taking on the world.

To fully grasp 'cultures', we need more than anecdotal evidence gleaned from clients or personal leaps of intuitive insight 'applied' to the world. We need to know a lot of history, geography, economics, literature, and social enquiry — and not just know them, but also internalize them. It is good when introverts discover there is an outside world, but let us not forget that a rigorous bunch of disciplines called the social sciences and humanities have already noticed the outside world, and have been interpreting it for many decades. I don't think the Jungian flash of personal insight is any substitute for hard study, wide reading, and legitimate engagement in sociology, history, literature, philosophy, and cultural studies.

While I am being critical, let me add that a book of this nature ought really be addressed to the wider culture. It is the culture itself that requires knowledge of its complexes, and yet the persistent feeling I gained from this work was that it was Jungians talking to other Jungians. This is a conundrum in which many of us battle on a daily basis, myself included. Our field has specialist knowledge, and so it requires specialist language. But when we seek to communicate with the world and to convey important insights, we are still speaking within a bubble of jargon and specialized terms, so that the world cannot hear what we are saying. It sees our lips moving, our evident animation, but it cannot hear what we are saying. We cannot blame the culture for not listening if we are not speaking a language it can follow.

The fact that 'culture' has to be rediscovered or reinserted in Jungian thought from time to time is a cause of real concern. According to Jung's theory, we can never know the deep unconscious directly, only indirectly through culture. Similarly, in the theory of archetypes, we cannot know the archetype in itself but only through 'archetypal images' found in art, religion, literature, dream, and social environment. There is, in classical Jungian theory, no direct apprehension of the unconscious or its archetypes. The archetype itself is empty, without content, only a predisposition. As Thomas Kirsch writes in this volume: "It is rare that one sees an archetypal experience without it being embedded in historical or cultural patterns" (185). When most people speak of 'archetypes' they are really speaking about archetypal images, without knowing it. The image is phenomenological, and as such is deeply embedded in cultural experience.

What is the problem, then? The problem is that the Jungian tradition forgets the theory of indirection and cultural relativity, and carries on 'as if' direct knowledge of the archetypes is possible. In other words, culture falls out of sight, into the unconscious, and we imagine we are dealing directly with Platonic forms or archetypal absolutes, with the 'things' in themselves. Then there is only a short step to the appropriation of Jungian ideas by the New Age: gods and goddesses on display, eternal objects of the mind, always available and always 'usable' by the ego in need of guidance and direction. The New Age misreading of Jung is actually incipient in the tradition, to the extent that it forgets its ideas are embedded in historical and social processes, and not metaphysical. Jungian thought is forever forgetting the relativity of its ideas, thus antagonizing the social scientists who find its explanations portentous, unreal, inflated.

The reminders of Henderson, Samuels, Hillman, and others are actually calls out of the clouds and into earthliness and humility. The fact that we have to discover and then rediscover a 'cultural unconscious', a 'cultural complex', a 'cultural attitude' is a sign that the field is failing to combat its own *hubris*, its flight into metaphysics. As Jung said, any contact with the archetypal is inevitably inflating, and I think we should attempt to counter this with the grounding experience that immersion in social and historical context can give. Jungian thought is a phenomenological science that forgets what it is, and then thinks it is metaphysics. As I have suggested, this irritates its critics even more, who take delight in knocking it off from its high perch.

I especially enjoyed the chapter on Australian complexes by Craig San Roque. His study on Alice Springs, my own home town, spoke directly to me and evoked enormous emotion. In his powerful narrative of psychic dissolution and atrophy of instinct in central Australia, one could almost see the cultural complex rising from the land itself, as a spirit of the place. Only, this spirit is no vivifying force or elevating pneuma; it is a veritable demon who lures people to destruction. When the spirit is not nurtured, it does not die, but turns into a monster. Through lack of attention to human fairness, racial equality, and social justice, through wilful ignorance to questions of meaning, purpose, and spirit, the 'soul' of Australia has become dulled, zombie-like, self-destructive. It no longer serves a purpose in the whole, and seems intent on subverting the whole and bringing the human enterprise to collapse and ruin.

All in this country share this complex, but it tends to be carried and held by black Australians. White Australians are so busy and frenetic, they rarely glimpse the appalling abyss that is now the dead heart, or empty center, of the nation. Unless, of course, white Australians happen to slip and fall, to be disrupted in their routines of busyness and avoidance. Then they sink into depths of depression and despair that claim victims on a daily basis. Australia has one of the highest rates of suicide and depression in the world, and yet its conscious narrative is that it is a Lucky Country, where all are adequately served, and where everyone enjoys the benefits of democracy and freedom. But freedom from what, and freedom for what? When we fall out of the persona, and into the soul, the world down under is not as good as we imagine.

San Roque traces the processes of decay, dissolution, and despair in the psychic life of indigenous Australians. Yet as he points out, the plight has really gone beyond despair. We are possessed of a destructive complex of enormous proportions that has lulled many of us into the belief that destruction is good, okay, inevitable. It seems to come with its own soporific, its own dose of anaesthetics. As Henry Lawson said, there are elements of the soul that are "past caring." Aboriginal Australians appear to offer little in the way of defense against this psychic vortex. Suicide is rife, so is drug addiction, chroming, petrol and glue sniffing, violence, alcoholism, and personality disorders. White Australians throw some money at these problems, but naturally they do not go away.

The insidious feature is that the complex belongs to the whole culture, yet only one race of people is fully and totally suffering from it. The race which is least defended against the psyche, which has fewer material possessions to serve as diversions and digressions, is the one that receives the full and lethal force of an activated cultural complex. This takes us back again to the problem of 'race' — to the problem that opened, and closed, Jung's investigations into questions of national difference. I certainly hope that the search for cultural complexes is not a novelty or passing phase, and that this work will not remain a side issue to Jungian studies. The next step is to understand that all complexes are cultural, or enculturated, just as all archetypes are historically and socially conditioned. The gods make us, but we remake the gods in our own image.

BOOK REVIEWS

LUCY HUSKINSON. *Nietzsche and Jung: The Whole Self in the Union of Opposites.* Hove and New York: Brunner-Routledge, 2004.

REVIEWED BY PAUL BISHOP

Nietzsche and Jung stand like two giant mountains on the vast terrain of the history of modern philosophical and psychological thought. Various commentators have attempted the climb, with varying degrees of success, and some perhaps have never returned, but the most recent intellectual explorer to have scaled these heights is Lucy Huskinson in her study of the concept of the self in these two thinkers. The self, the whole self, and nothing but the self? Far from operating with a simplistic notion of the self as a product of the union of opposites, an archetypal synthesis which simply shoots into being from a psychic nowhere, Huskinson begins her study with a crucial differentiation: she argues that, for Nietzsche, the whole self is a matter of "creation," whereas for Jung, it is a matter of "discovery" (pp. 3-4). The consequences for Jung, it emerges, are fatal, and this distinction forms the basis of her

Paul Bishop teaches German language and literature at the University of Glasgow. He is the author of various books and articles on the intellectual affinities of C.G. Jung with the German tradition, including *The Dionysian Self* (1995), *Synchronicity and Intellectual Intuition* (2000), and *Jung's 'Answer to Job': A Commentary* (2002).

Nietzschean critique of Jung. Now, the notion of the opposites is an ancient one, and polaristic thought was a key feature of eighteenth-century thought, the immediate philosophical context out of which Nietzsche, and later Jung, emerged. The recently departed Derrida has shown us, however, that the classic oppositions of traditional metaphysics are subverted by the "logic of the supplement," as Nietzsche realized when he wrote "light and dark, bitter and sweet are attached to each other and interlocked at any given moment like wrestlers of whom sometimes the one, sometimes the other is on top" (cited p. 11). Jung's observation that "the conscious mind is on top, the shadow underneath, and just as high always longs for low and hot for cold, so all consciousness [...] seeks its unconscious opposite" (cited pp. 35-36) offers a similar insight, albeit with an emphasis on its existential implications. Having surveyed the concept of the opposites in Nietzsche and Jung (via some fascinating excurses on alchemy and on Levinas), Huskinson presents Jung's critique of Nietzsche, largely, although not exclusively, as that emerged in his seminar from 1934 to 1939 on *Thus Spake Zarathustra*. Yet, for Huskinson, Jung's diagnosis of Nietzsche is in fact his self-diagnosis (pp. 133, 139), and she draws on Jung's admission of his fear of identifying with Nietzsche's madness, his significant omissions in his *Zarathustra* seminars, and the fact he had used previous case-studies, such as Miss Miller, to analyze himself, to argue that the *Zarathustra* seminars "harbour hidden psychological truths about Jung" — specifically, that the face of Nietzsche, as it is reflected in the mirror of those seminars, is nothing less than "a rough and imperfect reflection of Jung's" (pp. 133, 143). This argument, which is more than "merely speculative" (p. 143), amounts to a series of powerful charges against Jung: Nietzsche's model of the self is not one-sided and neurotic, but Jung's misrepresentation of it is; Jung's diagnosis of Nietzsche's "pathological personality" is a consequence of his own mental imbalance; "Jung is mentally ill according to his own insights" (p. 150), she claims. Moreover, from a Nietzschean perspective, the Jungian self fails to unite the opposites satisfactorily, for it does so in an external symbolic element (p. 151); his preoccupation with form cannot accommodate the freedom and creativity that chaos initiates and the *Übermensch* demands; and so, ultimately, Jung is concerned with Being over Becoming (p. 157). This is a severe judgment, although the evidence adduced by Huskinson is impressive. Admiration does not preclude criticism, however, and I wonder if Huskinson is not at times a bit too hard on poor old Jung. It is certainly true that a major difference between the two men is that, whereas Nietzsche locates the vital principle in the body, Jung refers to it as *Geist* (p. 111). Yet Jung's insistence on *feeling* and *sensation*, as well as thinking and intuition, secures the bodily nature of the Self in his psychology, and his typology emphasizes the interaction of the psychological functions, not just within the individual, but between the different types as embodied in individuals. So for all that he liked to cite St Augustine (*Noli foras ire, in interiore homine habitat veritas*), Jung may have also shared the scepticism of Goethe, a positive figure for both Nietzsche and Jung alike (pp. 34, 97, 164), that the injunction of the Delphic oracle to *know thyself* was "a deception practised by a secret order of priests," for "human beings know themselves only insofar as they know the world."

This study deserves the highest commendation, providing the definitive treatment of the question of the union of the opposites and the constellation of the whole self in Nietzsche and Jung, a task that is probably second in difficulty only to the union of opposites in life itself. Huskinson has planted her flag on these two giant mountains, and made a successful return to base camp. Let us hope she will make further forays into the intellectual history of analytical psychology in the future.

BOOK REVIEWS

DAVID ROSEN & JOEL WEISHAUS. *The Healing Spirit of Haiku,*with illustrations by Arthur Okamura. North Atlantic Books, 2004.

REVIEWED BY SUSAN ROWLAND

In *Spring 71*, the Orpheus edition, Robert Romanyshyn describes Orpheus as the kind of poet that Plato did not banish from the Polis.[1] Descended from the shaman, Orpheus is the mythological figure in depth psychology who holds the tension between the heady beauty of Apollo and the bodily frenzy of Dionysus. His poetry is a painful process of anamnesis, a return from forgetting, and in his fateful decision to turn to look at Euridice, so losing her, is the choice that converts our fate into our vocation. As a figure for the mutuality of poetry and philosophy in the song of the soul, Orpheus needs to be liberated from the consulting room and into the world. *The Healing Spirit of Haiku* is one of his works.

A truly inspired book, *The Healing Spirit of Haiku* is a collection of poems and prose that work as a conversation between the authors

Susan Rowland is current Chair of the International Association for Jungian Studies and author of *Jung as a Writer* (Routledge, 2005). She is Reader in English and Jungian Studies at the University of Greenwich, UK, and has published two other books on Jung and gender and literary theory.

over several years. Crucially both David Rosen and Joel Weishaus are longstanding friends and fellow poets whose involvement with haiku and Japanese culture has deep and sometimes very personal roots. For them, making haiku poetry is like Jungian active imagination in which an archetypal image blooms into a verse. Such psychic descent into the depths and return, choosing to *look back* in the conscious shaping that poetry also requires — such a process is an alchemy of the soul that mediates archetypal possession into the vocation of the poet. While not citing Orpheus, Rosen and Weishaus are Orphic poets of healing. For as Weishaus explains in the preface, healing originates in the notion of becoming whole and is shamanistic in its ethos. As poetry drawing on depths and wounds, "[c]ompounded of wholeness (healing) and emptiness (non-being/being), every haiku is a prescription for a larger life" (p. 5).

There are many paths into an-other world and one of the strengths of this book is its psychic journeys into other cultures. Where making the link to Jung may be important for western readers, the book begins in, and never strays from the richness of the cultural origin of haiku. Rosen explains that haiku evolved as a series of linked short poems as a sort of conversation between fellow poets and friends, the form of *The Healing Spirit of Haiku* itself. Generally considered to consist of seventeen syllables in a 5-7-5 sequence, haiku can vary in length while remaining attached to articulating something beyond ego consciousness. Significantly, the dialogue intrinsic to haiku is one that embraces nature. Often linked to one of the four seasons, haiku structures a healing relationship with nature and other people as a web in which the personal ego is displaced. Rosen describes traditional haiku as, "characterized by egolessness, aloneness, acceptance, universality, humor, silence, awakening, compassion and death" (p. 1). What is particularly remarkable about Rosen and Weishaus's book, and gives it its potency for healing in the reader, is the delicate lightness of its dialogical quality between nature and human, the non-human in the human, between cultures (notably Japan, Italy, and the United States), between two longstanding friends, between these authors and their ghosts of parents, the deep encounters of family and beloveds, between dreams.

The seed of this potent form is in the book's origins in a series of synchronistic meetings in Japan and the US. It is important that Rosen first contemplated the book as a collaboration with a Japanese haiku poet, and that subsequently it evolved in dialogue with Weishaus as the two friends found their mutual pursuit of poetry turning round to pursue them into a joint project.

This review can go no further without mentioning the third in the book's creative relationships. Arthur Okamura's illustrations structure another stage in the alchemical work of transformation. Typically a chapter is announced by a thematic heading such as 'being alone' or 'setting birds free'. It consists of short sections of autobiographical prose by each writer accompanied by a haiku. Then comes the print with the text of one haiku attached. Such is the intensity of the collaboration that the dialogue of visual and verbal image seems to offer another instance of the transcendent function incarnating something out of a mystery. I think it is indicative that the image *repeats* the poems both by giving the text again and by its translation of it into another medium. There is a ritual quality to this structure, which encodes a repetition with transformation, even as it itself repeats throughout the book.

Of course as well as a tight circular form, *The Healing Spirit of Haiku* has an exploratory, outward going direction. The early chapters focus on the authors' immersion in Japanese culture, thereby performing a double function of introducing the reader to the philosophical resonance of haiku as they enter the work. With haiku a practice linked to the non-ego psyche, there is a huge cultural barrier between the western ego that has been built up by centuries of discursive strengthening and the basis of the Japanese mind. Weishaus points out that such long conditioning may constitute an insuperable barrier to the 'other' (p. 33).

Yet the recognition of something insoluble can itself be the stimulus to entering the mysteries of the psyche. To return to Orpheus for a moment, his visit to the underworld failed to entirely pierce the barrier, it failed to reverse the death of Euridice. On the other hand, Orpheus did visit another world and returned as the shaman, with the song of the earth. Likewise, David Rosen records a death of part of himself in Japan: "[b]eing alone also shows its dark side when part of my ego died" (p. 32). Such a loss does draw him closer to the egoless goal of the haiku poet. Indeed the next few chapters record a kind of initiation for both men. In the following, 'Learning to Bow,' both reflect on the physical necessity for westerners to bow down to fit into Japanese houses. The mundane recognition is a bodily action that becomes a rite, once one recognizes the spiritual requirement to bow, to lower oneself before the mystery of the other.

In the very next chapter, 'Wise Old Women,' both men record the spiritual strengthening bestowed by friendship with women who could offer guidance, if only indirectly. After the encounter with the feminine guide comes a liberation of the spirit through 'Walking in the Countryside' that leads on to the important 'Making Peace with One's Father.' Here the work of the soul reaches out to the blood ties of the kinship group and, particularly to how these are wrought raw by historical events. A note at the back of the book records that David's Rosen's father was traumatized by the war with Japan. So it is entirely in keeping with the powerful ritual quality of *The Healing Spirit of Haiku* that a stage in psychic transformation is reached when it is possible for him to pray for peace for his father's soul. And in the chapter where Rosen joins a collective Buddhist ritual in Japan, Weishaus describes making a solitary journey to the mountains near Albuquerque to light a stick of incense for his parent.

Then from the personal dead the book moves to an even more enveloping encounter with death in the total extinguishing of life caused by nuclear bombs dropped on Japan. Again, Rosen visits Hiroshima while Weishaus meditates on the ravaged American landscape of the nuclear tests. They both come together in the next section, 'Seeing the Mountain,' in response to the Japanese heights that are simultaneously physical, psychological, and spiritual. They move out of the lowlands of death while remaining conscious of how the mountains are rooted in them. So in the following, 'Basho's Journey,' on the life of the great haiku poet, there is a sense that the poets have achieved initiation into the panorama of Japanese haiku, rather than an over-simple adoption of its ethos. Indeed it is *because* of the profound exploration of cultural difference, including its darkest aspects, that the poets have plumbed such depths of unknowing in themselves. In so doing they have taken the reader on a personal, cultural, philosophical, and spiritual pilgrimage that continues throughout the book.

The main other foreign place of the book is Italy and suggestively, its coming is heralded by a chapter on the feminine side of the male psyche. Chapters on Italian themes resonate with feminine images, from the Catholic (mother) Church continuation of the Coliseum's rite of blood sacrifice to the goatherd who learns to call all cities Cecilia, to the androgyny of St. Francis. Structurally, St Francis answers Basho as a western practitioner of spirit and the poetry of nature. The European pilgrimage functions as a near 'other' to the United States. It is possible to read the Italian motifs of landscape in Texas, a comparison not so directly attempted with Japan, where its fundamental *otherness* is stressed. In large terms I think the book enters Japan and the culture of the haiku as a rite of separation, a movement *away* from the habits and defenses of western ego-consciousness. Italy, on the other hand, performs for this book an anima role for American culture. Once the ego has been de-centered by initiation into Japan (with all its ancestral and historical pain), it can open itself to a more delicate weaving of differences and resemblances between the classical and Christian architecture of both the European and American soul. For what echoes in the later section of the book is the re-negotiation of origins both personal (with a chapter on mothers), and cultural, in images both common and radically different on both continents.

One chapter is headed by a date that has become so much more: 'September 11th 2001.' For an event that has so moved the collective psyche, so that we do not know its progeny, Rosen and Weishaus helpfully offer the simplest of perspectives. Both powerfully provide one of haiku's most valuable qualities: compassion. Rosen concentrates on the immediate victims, Weishaus on the ethical imperative to bring also the suffering world into the embrace. This chapter perhaps most starkly prompts the reader to continue the soul's journey. *The Healing Spirit of Haiku* is poetry at its most shamanistic and a philosophy carved on the psyche. It will delight, inspire comfort, and stimulate in equal measure.

NOTES

1. Robert Romanyshyn, "'Anyway why did it have to be the death of the Poet?': The Orphic Roots of Jung's Psychology," *Spring 71, Orpheus*, Fall 2004, 55-87.

BOOK REVIEWS

JOSEPH COPPIN AND ELIZABETH NELSON. *The Art of Inquiry: A Depth Psychological Approach.* Putnam, CT: Spring Publications, 2005.

THOMAS MOORE. *Dark Nights of the Soul: A Guide to Finding Your Way Through Life's Ordeals.* New York: Gotham Books, 2004.

REVIEWED BY DENNIS PATRICK SLATTERY

I began reading *The Art of Inquiry* as I was finishing a manuscript for publication. Recently I completed reading it as I began to lay out a track for another work. In both instances, from beginning to end, I have been encouraged and enlightened by this rich and imaginative text that revives what for many remains the stiff corpse lying in the domain of one's study—the research project, its *rigor mortis* the literature review.

In such a thick and insightful work, the collaborators, Joseph Coppin and Elizabeth Nelson base their archetypal approach to research on the provocative archetype of the child, an image which

---

Dennis Patrick Slattery is a member of the core faculty in mythological studies at Pacifica Graduate Institute. His books include *The Wounded Body: Remembering the Markings of Flesh* (2000) and *Just Below the Water Line: Selected Poems* (2004) as well as over 250 articles, reviews, and cultural essays in journals, newspapers, magazines, and collections.

sustains their research from beginning to end. Research is both a very active psychological verb as well as an attitude of being, a being present to what is possible and inchoate in the child. Their Table of Contents reveals the range of this pursuit: "Inquiry and the Care of the Soul"; "Historical Contexts of Psychological Inquiry"; "Philosophical Commitments of Depth Psychology"; "The Moves of Psychological Inquiry"; "Applying the Moves of Psychological Inquiry': and "Honoring the Spirit of Play."

Their research guides are primarily, but not exclusively, the gathered insights of C.G. Jung, Sigmund Freud, and James Hillman, all of whom in their methodology and in their grasp of forces both conscious and unconscious, advance and deepen the method and the myth of research, a process of revisioning that does not so much repeat what is known as repair what has not been fully understood. At one point the authors offer this lyric observation: "From the depth psychological perspective, knowledge is always partial—it would be hubris to think otherwise—and the unfolding of knowledge is a thing of wonder, not contempt" (43). The figure of Oedipus Rex haunts these lines, as he does the entire text of research, as much because of the parallel to his own life's awakening as to the fact that his discoveries as he relentlessly researches his own history, evokes wonder, if not suffering. Research, the authors imply, is just that mythic in the freight of its method.

The important impetus of this rare book that asks us to reimagine not only what the act of research is but to meditate on the nature of knowledge itself, combines laws of physics with phenomenology and depth psychology, as in this observation: "one's approach to a subject affects what can be seen and learned...so that from moment to moment people operate from *within* a given perspective" (45). One's "posture" is directly intimate with one's position on a subject. To become conscious of this angle of vision is, for both authors, quintessentially important because it reveals both what one grasps and what gaps occlude understanding—at least for the moment. In fact, as they state directly, "depth psychology is a *psychology of the gap*" (90). Such an insight makes me wonder that what has been traditionally seen as "poor scholarship," when one has gaps or holes in one's argument, may be the most psychologically fertile space for the researching psyche.

I found as well the subtext of the work to be no less intriguing and illuminating: the tenets of psyche's own being that the writers list and discuss (48-88). The discussion of these tenets, as for example, "The Psyche is Fluid and Protean" (63) and "The Psyche is Symptomatic" (68) becomes, for the initiate to depth psychology, a short course on the essential belief system of this disciplined way of opening the research model to psychic realities often overlooked in the process.

This meditation on the act of research as a psychological, and even an embodied act of knowing, moves fluidly between theory and praxis, as for example chapter 4: "The Moves of Psychological Inquiry" and chapter 5: "Applying the Moves of Psychological Inquiry." Chapter 4 was most intriguing and my favorite in the book, because of what it revealed about psyche's intentional motion. My sense is that it is the heart of the book, its sustaining core, around which all other chapters revolve. A tenet of psyche's nature is that it is fundamentally ontological and that status must be granted her; following on this is that psyche is "a creative partner" so that in her workings one does best initially in research by "developing and maintaining a good attitude toward the work…taking a position, following a lead, drawing a line, establishing a boundary" (103). Such openness within limits allows psyche to move, to spiral back, to pause, to revel in a refrain, to reconstruct in the service of creating meaning through discovery.

To become conscious of one's questions, to pay attention to hunches and intuitive impulses, to find fresh language rather than lapsing into the lethargy of tired and worn out words to convey meaning—these are some of the hallmarks that this new angle on research promotes. Like psyche herself, the study is syncretistic, ranging between the creative work of the physicist David Bohm to the philosophical tenets of Hegel, to the dissertation process of one of the authors. Guiding the work's ending, as it did in the beginning, is the figure of the archetypal child who "reminds people that 'life is a flux, a flowing into the future, not a stoppage or a backwash'" (162-63). Why should research not be laced with wonder? the authors implicitly ask. Answering that question motivates much of the book's direction.

Finally, the authors revision the term "depth," that overworked knee-jerk term in depth psychology, to great advantage. They suggest it is not just "vertical," but also horizontal, as in "depth of field" (178), in order to take in what is immediate, mediate, and remote. I end with a few selfish suggestions on what else I would have enjoyed seeing these gifted researchers work into the book: 1. Inviting the researcher to add a few voices that disagree with his/her thesis, and to work these voices psychologically in the spirit of cooperative resistance; 2. to develop further the section on language and on how our words carry psyche into the world; and 3. a fuller development of the place of committee members in the pilgrimage of the researcher.

The above suggestions do not diminish in the least the quality of this study. I congratulate the authors then not just for amplifying what depth can include, but for animating what research can be, a psychological journey into new terrain.

Dark Nights of the Soul: A Guide to Finding Your Way Through Life's Ordeals

Thomas Moore's book is destined to be another national best-seller, perhaps not with the same intensity of *Care of the Soul*, a *New York Times* success story, but with its own life and character. It does not repeat the discoveries of his earlier book, but it does shift the motion of psyche as it seeks depth, emptiness, as well as a form of dehydration from the dry heat of darkness. The title is taken from the 16th century Spanish mystic, poet, and theologian, St. John of the Cross (1542-1591).

St. John writes in his classic text that as the soul moves toward God in love "it first feels dryness and emptiness and then begins to be cured in suffering through purgation of all desire." Aridity and abandonment, John of the Cross continues, mark "the soul's openness to conversing with God."[1]

As a modern mystic and archetypal psychologist, poet and musician, Moore sets his compass from the seas of St. John's insights and translates into modern psychological language the spiritual discoveries of the Spanish mystic. Divided into three sweeping realms—"Passages," "Disturbances," and "Developments"—*Dark Nights* begins to sketch out a theological or spiritual psychology wherein the imagination, like Dante Alighieri's pilgrim/poet of the *Commedia* initiates a pilgrimage from the fruitful darkness of *"la selva oscura,"* (3) to a condition of interrelated parts. Rather than solution-driven, this book is more a gentle and persuasive guide whose intention is to shift our attitude toward our common experiences so that we can perceive them in a different light or, perhaps, a more transparent darkness.

His questions set the rudder of the book: How might conditions like melancholy and despair and emptiness and feelings of ennui not be stigmatized as abnormal and then jettisoned in favor of some vague notion of normalcy? Rather, what conditions of the soul are served as it moves towards insight, deepening in awareness, in a fuller consciousness "that calls for a spiritual response, not a therapeutic one?" (xix). The alternative to such questing, he suggests later, is "a mediocre life" (313).

One of the controlling metaphors of the text is the "night sea journey," which is a figure "for our own dark nights" wherein we become "trapped in a mood or by circumstances that force us to sit and wait for liberation" (5).

He uses this and other examples as foundational in order to reveal how metaphors lead us to meanings about our own darkness. That darkness, however, need not be a negative state from which we try desperately to escape to the light, but a place in which "to incubate in the belly of the whale" (53), to prepare oneself for a birthing that cannot yet be articulated.

In his study, Moore is quick to caution that psychological language "is heroic and sentimental" (10) which often prohibits a "deepening of imagination" (11). The words, the sentences we choose to use should, he believes, "reflect some intelligence about life" (10). Therapeutic language, with its inherent limitations, may actually suffocate a fuller sense of discovery rather than encourage it. By contrast, poetic language, which values the figural quality of our life's contents and actions, a form of "sea language that keeps you in the waters of life" (11), actually increases the intimacy we can experience in reflecting on the more disturbing conditions we discover in ourselves.

He suggests a life full of ritual rather than laden with diagnoses; such a shift can evoke the imagination's responses and treat with respect the original and unique contours of our darkness. Rather than be deadened by a life of passivity so prevalent in today's American culture, Moore suggests that we shake loose from lethargy in order "to search for a living story that is yours and is crucial to health" (47). His method, he states much later, is "the way of homeopathy as opposed to allopathy. The first move is to flow with, while the latter is to fight against" (218). Offering attention to the narrative that is the flow of one's life rather than a symptom of it may yield a fresh, crispier and incisive vision of one's being. To make this shift touches upon a spiritual impulse in the soul that is less comfortable with dry dogmatic assertions, and more engaged by the dryness of soul that enriches the darkness that shrouds our lives.

If psychology and therapy move happily towards the sun, light, warmth, enlightenment, rational fixes, cures, and solutions, then Moore's method is counter current because it is more moon-like, lunar, dark, shadowy, invisible, opaque, open-ended, whale-bellied (94). Desired is another kind of imagination, one that does not insist that all darkness be dissipated or dried in the heat of light, but that darkening itself is a method, a mythic way of being present to the soul's melancholy, its irony, its paradoxes, and its ripening contradictions. His book reveals how to respect and even become a bit more comfortable in the muddle of the journey of our lives.

Lingering, waiting, being patient, abdicating control, accepting being stuck, inviting stillness, and even meditation, not goal-driven, living within suffering—these are all therapeutics of soul and spirit that, nurtured, reveal soul's voice that may otherwise be muted, its wisdom missed. To move in darkness, Moore believes, is soul's motion within paradox, for it is both a place of concealment and uncertainty as well as the realm of revelation.

Darkness has its own wisdom; silence has its own voice. His meditations reveal a sure and uncertain guide into the nether regions that therapy often wants to annihilate; yet to do so, Moore believes, is to shred into ruins perhaps the most fertile ground of soul-making and soul-caring.

As I finish writing this double review and peruse my notes from both texts, I begin to see for the first time how much they are cousins in attitude and temperament. My final suggestion is that these two excellent texts should be read simultaneously as a dual optics of soul's research into the darkness of her deepest wisdom.

NOTES

1. John of the Cross, *The Collected Works of St. John of the Cross,* trans. Kieran Kavanaugh and Otilio Rodriguez (Washington, D.C. ICS Publications, 1979), 74, 77.

Celluloid Heroes
& Mechanical Dragons

— Film as the Mythology of Electronic Society

John David Ebert

What do *Star Wars*
and *Lord of the Rings* tell
us of our mythic past and our
attitude to modern technology?

No one before Ebert has attempted to read the entire sweep
of contemporary cinematic productions... with respect to the levels of
mythical consciousness they represent.
William Doty, PhD, Mythic Passages

Available from Cybereditions.com or Amazon

The New Orleans Jungian Seminar

The Bolligen Stone, Photo by David H. Rosen, M.D.

An Approved Training Center of the Inter-Regional Society of Jungian Analysts

For information on
curriculum and faculty go to:

www.jungneworleans.org
and click on: Training

or phone:

504/866-0208

Foundation for Mythological Studies (FMS)

www.mythology.org

Mythologies are containers of heritage, threads that connect us to the cultural ancestors. A reawakened interest in this collective storehouse encourages us to detect commonalities and avoid fundamentalisms. The study of characters in archetypal dramas mirrors human foibles, illuminates shadowy corners of the psyche, and ignites the imagination.

By providing a sense of place for mythologists and depth psychologists, FMS hopes to build a community that utilizes the revolving abundance of talent and knowledge to further our studies and expand our ideas about mythology and archetypal psychology.

FMS Workshops are designed by and for scholars who wish to engage myth and depth psychology in creative and informative ways. Our goals are to provide affordable workshops and conferences that cover a variety of specialized topics geared toward the continuing growth and education of the participants, create a global networking database, provide access to rare works in related fields, provide stimulating articles and publications, news and events, and cutting edge research.

Become a Member of FMS and receive your monthly e-newsletter: a compilation of information, news, events, and opportunities in the fields of mythology and depth psychology. Receive discounts to *Spring Journal* and all FMS events. Tap into a global network of mythologists, depth psychologists and scholars in related fields; take advantage of opportunities to develop your professional career by becoming a Presenter at FMS events; keep abreast of news and research in the field, calls for papers, and upcoming workshops and conferences around the world.

For Membership and Event information: www.mythology.org

California 501c(3) organization.

New from Spring Journal Books

Maureen Murdock & Patricia Reis

FATHERS' DAUGHTERS:
Breaking the Ties That Bind

Author: Maureen Murdock
ISBN 1-882670-31-0
Price $20.00

Through myth, fairy tale, case studies, and
Jungian psychology, best-selling author
Maureen Murdock explores the unique
relationship between a "father's daughter" and
her father, its rewards and pitfalls, and how this
idealized relationship affects the mother-
daughter bond. This rich and thoughtful
analysis examines Beauty and the Beast,
Donkeyskin, The Wizard of Oz, King Lear, and
The Handless Maiden to empower the father's
daughter to untangle the ties that bind her to
her father and redeem a female vision that is
truly powerful and nurturing.

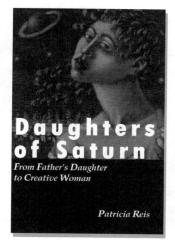

DAUGHTERS OF SATURN:
From Father's Daughter to
Creative Woman

Author: Patricia Reis
ISBN 1-882670-32-9
Price $23.95

Patricia Reis examines the father daughter
relationship with a particular focus on the
father's effect on a woman's creative life. Using
the charter myth of Saturn, the archetypal
devouring and melancholic father, she gives us a
map starting with a journey out of the Belly of
the Father. Matching the mythological
Daughters of Saturn - Hestia, Demeter, Hera,
and Aphrodite - with four women writers -
Emily Dickinson, H.D., Sylvia Plath, and Anais
Nin - she documents women's resistances and
rebellions, struggles, and strategies. Exploring
contemporary women's dreams and stories she
marks out the trails that lead to "The
Wildzone," a place that has existence for creative
women outside the realm of the fathers: a
woman-centered ground of creative authority.

New from Spring Journal Books

Studies in Archetypal Psychology Series
Series Editor: Greg Mogenson

DIALECTICS & ANALYTICAL PSYCHOLOGY
The El Capitan Canyon Seminar
Wolfgang Giegerich ◆ David L. Miller ◆ Greg Mogenson
Price: $20.00 (USD) ◆ ISBN 1-882670-92-2 ◆ 136 pages

What is dialectical thinking and why do we need it in psychology? Conceived to meet "the call for more" that followed the publication of Jungian analyst Wolfgang Giegerich's landmark book, *The Soul's Logical Life*, this volume serves as the most accessible introduction to Giegerich's provocative approach to psychology. It is a valuable resource for students of fairy tale, myth, and depth psychology and includes a complete bibliography of Giegerich's writings in all languages.

RAIDS ON THE UNTHINKABLE:
Freudian *and* Jungian Psychoanalyses
Paul Kugler
Price: $20.00 (USD) ◆ ISBN 1-882670-91-4 ◆ 160 pages

Paul Kugler critically rethinks the pivotal concepts of psychoanalysis and, in the process, makes evident what the theoretical differences between Freud and Jung have to offer contemporary depth psychology. Through a constructive 'dialogue' between Freudian and Jungian psychoanalysis, Kugler demonstrates that such a project is not only theoretically possible, but clinically valuable.

NORTHERN GNOSIS
Thor, Baldr, and the Volsungs in the Thought of Freud and Jung
Greg Mogenson
Price: $20.00 (USD) ◆ ISBN 1-882670-90-6 ◆ 140 pages

This imaginative and scholarly work uses stories from Norse mythology to understand major concepts from Freud and Jung. Jung's theory of the archetype is seen as a variant of Thor's encounters with the giants. Freud's death instinct is envisioned as a variant of Baldr's death, and the relations of Freud, Jung and Sabina Speilrein are reflected in the saga of the Volsungs.

To order, please visit our online store at
www.springjournalandbooks.com or call *504.524.5117*

Spring Journal

Archetypal Psychology ◆ Mythology ◆ Jungian Psychology

Spring Journal is the oldest Jungian psychology journal in the world.

Published twice a year, each issue is organized around a theme and offers articles and book reviews in the areas of archetypal psychology, mythology, and Jungian psychology.

Future Issues of Spring Journal

ALCHEMY (Spring 2006) *Interview with Thomas Moore, and articles by Wolfgang Giegerich, Stan Marlan, Beverley Zabriskie, David L. Miller, Murray Stein, Ron Schenk, Veronica Goodchild, and more!*

PSYCHE and NATURE (Fall 2006)

PHILOSOPHY and PSYCHOLOGY (Spring 2007)
Guest Editors: Edward Casey and David L. Miller.

To subscribe, please visit our online store at *www.springjournalandbooks.com,* call *504.524.5117,* or fill out the order form below:

- - ✄ - ✄ - -

Subscribe to Spring Journal and Save!

Published twice a year, a one-year subscription costs $32.00, and a two-year subscription is just $58.00. Postage within the continental U.S. is free. Please add the following postage for international orders: International Surface: $5.00 International Airmail: $15.00

Name: _____ City: _____

Address: _____ State/Zip/Country: _____

_____ Telephone: _____

_____ Email: _____

Check Enclosed*☐ Visa/MC/Amex ☐ Card Number: _____

Expiration Date: _____

* Checks should be made payable to Spring Journal, Inc. and
sent to Spring Journal, 627 Ursulines Street, #7, New Orleans, LA 70116